don't
family secrets

edited by
Donna McCart Sharkey
and Arleen Paré

DEMETER

don't tell
family secrets

Edited by Donna McCart Sharkey and Arleen Paré

Copyright © 2022 Demeter Press

Individual copyright to their work is retained by the authors. All rights reserved. No part of this book may be reproduced or transmitted in any form by any means without permission in writing from the publisher.

Demeter Press
PO Box 197
Coe Hill, Ontario
Canada
K0L 1P0
Tel: 289-383-0134
Email: info@demeterpress.org
Website: www.demeterpress.org

Demeter Press logo based on the sculpture "Demeter" by Maria-Luise Bodirsky www.keramik-atelier.bodirsky.de

Printed and Bound in Canada

Cover artwork and design: Peter Paré
Typesetting: Michelle Pirovich
Proof reading: Jena Woodhouse

Library and Archives Canada Cataloguing in Publication
Title: Don't tell : family secrets / [edited by] Donna McCart Sharkey and Arleen Paré.
Other titles: Don't tell (Demeter Press) | Do not tell
Names: Sharkey, Donna, editor. | Paré, Arleen, 1946- editor.
Description: Prose and poetry. | Includes bibliographical references and index.
Identifiers: Canadiana 20220443831 | ISBN 9781772584240 (softcover)
Subjects: LCSH: Family secrets—Literary collections. | LCSH: Families—Literary collections.
Classification: LCC PN6071.F2 D66 2023 | DDC 808.8/03525—dc23

 The publisher gratefully acknowledges the support of the Government of Canada

Acknowledgments

Many thanks to the women and men who wrote and so revealed—for some the first time—their personal family stories and secrets for this anthology.

A heartfelt thank you to Andrea O'Reilly, the indomitable, energetic, and insightful publisher of Demeter Press, who provided invaluable support for this book. With much appreciation to you, Andrea.

An awesome thanks to Peter Paré for his brilliant design of the cover of this book. Thanks also to friends Maureen, Chris, Mary, Fatos, Brenda, Andrew, and Tim, who enthusiastically encouraged this project when it was just an idea.

Many thanks and not-so-secret appreciation to both our families: Chris Fox, Peter Paré, Jesse Paré, Susan Rae, Soudeh Mosavi, Jack and Max and Ella, and to Renata Sharkey, George Leras, baby Silvio, and in memory of Alessandra Sharkey.

Contents

Introduction. Don't Tell: Family Secrets
Donna McCart Sharkey and Arleen Paré
13

1. Movies: The Secret Sin
Ralph Friesen
15

2. Man with Cucumbers
Myrna Kostash
21

3. The Front Door
Jane Munro
31

4. What You Didn't Tell
Elizabeth Templeman
33

5. My Mother's Madness
JoAnn McCaig
37

6. We Had One, Too
Maureen Hynes
45

7. The Lost Epistles of Margie
John Barton
49

8. Grief
Frances Rooney
55

9. Understanding My Face
Michelle Poirier Brown
59

10. Paired Secrets
Ann Davis
71

11. May Her Memory
Nancy Issenman
77

12. Roses
Jessie Carson
81

13. "We Should Talk about This Later"
Sharon Anne Cook
87

14. I Should Have Known (A Found Correspondence)
Blaine Marchand
95

15. Frozen Air
Linda Briskin
99

16. Shangri-La
Donna McCart Sharkey
105

17. Sabbath
Wendy Donowa
107

CONTENTS

18. Drawing Out Shadows
Caroline Purchase
109

19. Umbilical Noose
David Pimm
119

20. May 31, 1934: My Grandmother Writes to My Grandfather
Maureen Scott Harris
123

21. Fireflies
Soriya Turner
125

22. Just a Story
Deborah Yaffe
131

23. Mysterious Death on the Family Homestead
Renee Duddridge
135

24. Spectral Stories
Lenore Maybaum
141

25. Uncle Fred's Secret
Ruby Swanson
147

26. The Road Leads to Crosby Beach
Amanda Hale
155

27. Pistol Packing Momma
Phyllis Shuell
163

28. Cover Story
Betsy Warland
165

29. Twelve Red Letters
Jean Crozier
171

30. I Found a Picture of My Great-Aunt
Heather Ramsay
181

31. Bingo and Black Ice
George K. Ilsley
191

32. Shattered
Helen Gowans
201

33. In This Adaptation
Judy LeBlanc
203

34. Would You Trade This Family?
Kae Solomon
213

35. Stiff Upper Lip
Kate Eckland
217

36. Secrets Breed Questions
Carole Harmon
225

37. The Boyfriend
Liana Cusmano
233

CONTENTS

38. A Real Doozie
Pat Buckna
235

39. The Real Truth
Susan Braley
245

40. The Doll
Laurel M. Ross
247

41. Fractal
Adrienne Gruber
249

42. The Ribbon Tree
Shelley A. Leedahl
253

43. life examined through frames
Joan Conway
261

44. My Three Fathers
Patricia Preston
263

45. What's New, Wild Child?
Joy Thierry Llewellyn
269

46. Děda
Claire Sicherman
271

47. Little Bird
Cornelia Hoogland
277

48. A True Story
Anonymous
281

49. Family Still Life
Kathleen Vance
289

50. Wilted Valentine/Green Shame
Christine Smart
293

51. If It Weren't for You Kids
Leslee Silverman
295

52. A Risk Worth Concealing
Christine K. Anzur
299

53. The State of Our Father
Ingrid Rose
305

54. Family Secrets
Susan Scruton
315

55. Eulogy
Jim Nason
319

56. Shame
Barbara Barry
323

57. Knothole
Laurel Sproule
327

CONTENTS

58. Bottle Dump
Yaana Dancer
335

59. Went West
Cynthia Woodman Kerkham
339

60. Kingdom Hall
Leesa Hanna
345

61. The Curse of Sin City
Sarah Williams
355

Notes on Contributors
363

Introduction

Don't Tell: Family Secrets

Donna McCart Sharkey and Arleen Paré

After a friend related to us a family secret she had recently learned, we asked other friends whether their families hold secrets. We heard intriguing stories, and we found that women, particularly mothers, are most frequently the holders of a family's history. And they are most often the gatekeepers of their family's secrets—the person who might or not pass on a secret, sometimes through generations. In this intimate world where secrets are held, she may be cajoled by her own mother to stay silent or prodded by a child, suspicious that something or someone has been hidden away.

Whereas some of the secrets explored by authors in this book have pulled apart a family, others have kept a family intact. Some of the authors searched to find who they really are or who their true ancestors were.

Other secrets surround questions of an uncle's whereabouts, a suicide, a murder, an affair, jealousy, a cruel father, an institutionalized aunt, a criminal nephew, religious fervour that cast out a family member, as well as a relative estranged for unknown reasons.

Stories in this anthology span the world wars and the Great Depression and include tales about immigrating under unusual circumstances, living in an oppressive orphanage, hiding mental illness, as well as children running away to find a better way of life.

Some secrets were found in old official documents, letters, private journals, as well as in a framed sepia photograph. Some of the secrets are now resolved; others remain.

These secrets reflect the norms of place and time, and as time shifts, what families feel necessary to keep hidden also changes. Yet past family secrets can have a way of brushing up against current times, of still influencing and forming people's lives today.

1.

Movies: The Secret Sin

Ralph Friesen

I grew up in Steinbach, Manitoba—an almost exclusively Mennonite community then, in the 1940s and 1950s. My father was the pastor of the largest church in town and had a reputation to protect. From my point of view as his youngest child, he was remote and upright. And that was pretty much my idea of him until, many years later, my mother gave me a box full of the diaries he had kept before I was born. I opened the first booklet, beginning January 1, 1930, and found this entry:

"Went to Wpg yesterday and am staying at A. D. Friesens', 26 Maralbo Ave., St. Vital. Saw *The Virginian*, a good talkie." *The Virginian*! He went to a movie?! Going to movies was a sin. Our church said so, on the grounds that movies were "worldly," meaning they stirred unhealthy, fleshly appetites. But I was pleased at my discovery, which revealed a new dimension of my father, one I had never suspected. He was human. Like me, he had sinned. I did not think of him as hypocritical, but I was surprised at the silence he had maintained about his own youthful experience. Here was another part of himself that he had hidden.

In May 1930, while working in Winnipeg for a ten-day period, Dad went on a movie-watching spree, seeing at least five: *On with the Show*, *Show Boat*, *Montana Moon*, *The Gold Diggers of Broadway*, and an unnamed picture at the Roxy on Henderson Highway. He seemed to have an affinity for musicals, show tunes, and dancing girls. Sometimes he went with a male friend; often he went alone.

On with the Show has a thin storyline about a dance troupe in danger of going broke, but most of the movie consists of masses of dancers onstage—women as flappers or nymphs or ballerinas, men in tuxedos and top hats. A few Black actors appear, including Ethel Waters, who sings a mournful solo about her absent man. At one point, astonishingly, fox hunters riding real horses bound across the stage. In *The Gold Diggers of Broadway*, the format is similar, with tap-dancing performances, including George Raft doing a number so blazingly fast that you'd think it had been sped up on film. Dancers do cartwheels and backflips. The male actors are commanding or foolish, whereas the females are fetching and flirtatious. All of this could not even have been imagined in Dad's village childhood. Movies gave him a glimpse into the sinful world in all its entertaining splendour.

A few times, he went with his non-Mennonite friend, Henry Coote, to see the "he-man" melodramas *Frozen Justice* and *Dr. F.* They also saw a western starring Hoot Gibson and a rerun of the Jack Sharkey–Max Schmeling world heavyweight boxing championship match, won by Schmeling on a foul.

The following year, Dad was back in Steinbach, but he made a few visits to Winnipeg, including one in January, when he stayed with the Doerksen family. He took their daughter Helen to two movies. One of these was *Anybody's War*, starring comedians George Moran and Charles Mack, who were known for their vaudeville acts, in blackface. Earlier that day, Dad and his cousin Ed Friesen had already been to a movie at the magnificent Metropolitan Theatre—*Morocco*, a romance starring a tuxedo-wearing Marlene Dietrich and Gary Cooper as a womanizing legionnaire. Dad's assessment, "a very good picture," was borne out by the film's nomination for Oscars in four categories, including best director.

Dad also saw Charlie Chaplin's silent classic romance, *City Lights*, bringing his total of Hollywood movies, as noted in the diary, to eleven. This was at a time when he was facing the stark necessity of making a living but perhaps that was precisely the reality he wanted to escape. At the same time, he sidestepped, or ignored, another reality: The movies glorified the body, told stories of passion and lust and betrayal, made light of serious matters, glamourized smoking and alcohol and sex, and represented everything that a good Mennonite was to avoid.

After finding out about Dad's movie going, I thought of my own experience (much earlier in life than his) and wondered about my siblings' stories. I had already taken notes when listening to my eldest brother, Alvin, reminiscing, so I had that. I emailed my brother

Norman and talked to my remaining siblings, Don and Mary Ann, on the phone.

We grew up knowing that movies were strictly off limits, except for educational films we might be shown at school on special occasions. Even then, the teacher would block out taboo images, such as kissing scenes. Yet all of us, individually, were drawn by the dark magical appeal of movie theatres. We all sneaked off to the movies, knowing our parents disapproved.

As a fourteen-year-old, Norman went on an all-expenses-paid trip to Minneapolis that the *Winnipeg Free Press* put on as an incentive for its carriers, and for the first time ever, he went to see a real movie in an actual theatre. He told me about his experience:

> It was a western, and one of the heroes had to bite on a stick while whiskey was poured on his gunshot wound, and the bullet was extracted using little finesse with a knife. I was truly impressed by the huge screen and vivid colour. After that first icebreaker, I went to a couple of other movies. I only admitted to seeing one movie when Dad asked about it after I got home. I gave him the impression I had very little choice because we were all scheduled to go there as a group activity. That was stretching it. In my argument for the defence, I queried him on whether he had ever seen a movie ... and he admitted that he had gone to movies as a youth.

Norman did not share the news of this astonishing paternal confession at the time, so I grew up ignorant of it. In this story, Norman tells a lie. But Dad had lied, too, by telling us nothing about his own movie-going career while forbidding us this pleasure. He had a dilemma to be sure: If he had told us that he'd once gone to movies, we might have interpreted that as permission for ourselves.

Alvin had had a similar experience some years earlier. He was also a newspaper carrier and had recruited a sufficient number of new subscribers to the *Free Press* to win a two-day trip to Winnipeg in March 1947. His friend Stan Reimer also qualified. They stayed at the Marlborough Hotel and went on a tour of the airport with the rest of their group. But Al and Stan also went to a downtown cinema and saw a murder mystery. Al was scared—but hooked. The next day, he went to another one, a western. When he got home, he said nothing about it to our parents but started to go to the newly opened Playhouse Theatre in Steinbach. It was important to avoid detection. He would approach on the side of Main Street opposite to the theatre, look all around to see that the coast was clear, and then make a frantic dash to get in unseen. Inside, his heart pounding, he sat in the back row, trying to be invisible.

Donald also sneaked into the Playhouse as a teenager, using the same other-side-of-the-street approach as his brother. He did not have a clear conscience, and his enjoyment of the films was undermined by fear: "What if the Lord should come?" Then he would be found in a sinful place and in danger of losing his soul in the judgment to follow.

Mary Ann, naively, did not cross the street, and once as a teenager on the way to the Playhouse to meet her friends, she ran into Mrs. P. D. Reimer in front of our church. Mrs. Reimer wanted to know if she was coming to the revival meeting that evening. Mary Ann made some excuse and continued on to the theatre. Not surprisingly, Dad found out about this. He sat her down for a serious talk. She tried to argue that the movies she had seen were good ones, so there was no harm in it. Dad said: "If someone looks in the garbage can for food, they might find something they can eat, but it still comes from a garbage can." She had no answer for that.

The Playhouse had opened in 1941 despite protests from citizens, including Dad, who recorded this encounter: "The theatre manager came to see me in forenoon to talk 'friendly,' but I gave him to understand that we strictly didn't want the theatre in this town." That owner, a man named Frank Tarnopolsky—so, a Ukrainian, not a Mennonite—was found asphyxiated in his vehicle on a cold Sunday evening in January 1944, the car windows turned up, the garage doors locked. The new owner, a liberal-minded Mennonite, gamely carried on for a few more years. Then he sold the business to yet another man who also faced continued pressure from townspeople to shut down the theatre. This owner finally caved in and had the whole building moved ten miles down the Number 12 Highway to our neighbouring French village of Ste. Anne in 1956, leaving Steinbach without a theatre.

As for me, when I was around twelve, I accompanied my parents to Winnipeg, where Dad had some business to do. Probably Mom wanted to do some shopping. I told them they could drop me at the museum, and then I would meet them at the Eaton statue in a couple of hours.

When they had driven off, I made my uncertain way down Portage Avenue in the direction of Main Street, looking for a movie theatre. I'd never been to one before, but I knew they were somewhere downtown.

I spotted a place called the Rialto—exotic name with the promise of adventure—and crossed the busy street. The marquee read: *Beneath the 12-Mile Reef.* A poster showed a diver in a deadly conflict with a giant octopus, with a shark lurking nearby. I walked up to the ticket vendor, a woman wearing vivid red lipstick, and stood there, uncertain of what to do next. "Yeah, whaddaya want, kid?" she said, in a bored voice. "I want to see the film," I said. "So give me the money for the ticket," she replied. Blushing, I dug into my pockets and set my quarters down on the counter. I proceeded hesitantly into the high-ceilinged dark chamber, the theatre itself, where I found a seat and was immediately taken up into the technicolour world displayed on the immense—as it was to me then—screen. I had come in after the movie had begun, but that didn't matter; what mattered was, I was in a real theatre for the first time in my life. I took no notice of how seedy and dilapidated it was or that the movie had first been released a few years before. When the diver's air supply was cut off, I could hardly breathe myself. When the American girl kissed the handsome Greek, I imagined her lips on mine. For an hour, I succeeded in blotting out the nagging of my conscience. Part of my excitement arose from the very fact that I was sinning, and no one was stopping me. Then the titles came on, and I hurried out, blinking in the late afternoon light and hightailing my way to Eaton's, nervously rehearsing lines I would tell my parents if they should ask about my time at the museum. They did ask, as our car rolled along the highway in the direction of Steinbach. Having been to the museum before, I described an exhibit or two, and that seemed to satisfy them. I did not like lying and the uneasy feeling that went with it—but this was a price I was willing to pay for the experience I'd had.

At least, I think that's how it went. Would the Rialto really have been playing a three- or four-year-old movie? Also, did a strange man come and sit in the seat beside me and put his hand on my knee? I seem to remember that and jumping up and moving to another row of seats. Would my parents have been so trusting, or casual, as to leave me to my own devices in the big city when I was only twelve? It appears so.

The movies were lies, too, in a way—merely *ütjedochte Jeschichte*, thought-up stories. Mennonites had long condemned the productions of the imagination as not true. Good Christians were meant to keep to the script—the Scripture, that is—and even there, to skip over the wilder stories such as Lot's daughters getting him drunk and having sex with him. We were to keep our feet on the ground, in the barnyard, or, in our case, the machine shop yard. Giving free rein to the imagination could only result in mischief at best and evil at worst. Human minds and hearts were the devil's playground.

But in our household, we had free access to adventure novels, which Dad stocked in the bookstore he opened in 1949. Somehow comic books, large stacks of them, also found their way into my brothers' bedroom. Vernon and Norman also brought in *Mad* magazine, which they must have discovered somewhere at a newsstand in Winnipeg, as such "trash," as the *Mad* writers happily called their own work, would not likely have been for sale in Steinbach. We only half-understood the satire and anarchic humour of the writers, most of whom were from New York, but we loved it. Thus we absorbed urban culture and Yiddish vocabulary (our favourite word was "furshlugginer," meaning old or junky), mystifying our parents. In general, the sway of community and church rules was weakening, and our parents were helpless to stop this change. As time went by, the necessity for secret keeping receded. But it never went away.

2.

Man with Cucumbers

Myrna Kostash

The photo has fallen out of my mother's album, which lies on my lap. On the back in the lower right corner, my mother has written: "Mum's brother Nick, Lethbridge, 1934." I turn the photo over to look again at Uncle Nick.

The black and white photograph, such as taken by a Brownie box camera, shows a man, perhaps forty years old, with the sun- and wind-burned face of a farmer; a thick hank of dark hair falls across his forehead. He wears a workman's denim bib and coveralls and kneels on one knee in the middle of a flat ploughed field, perhaps recently harvested. The edge of the field is the horizon, and it cuts dramatically at an angle to the sky. The man, who looks straight into the camera with a bit of a smile, holds an armful of cucumbers.

I haven't the slightest idea who he is. I ask my cousins on my mother's side: Who was this Nick, our Baba's brother, uncle to our mothers? They haven't a clue either—although one vaguely remembers a story about a "fratricide" in the family—nor has my sister. No one remembers a photograph. Yet I am looking at him in a field in Lethbridge, appearing every inch the immigrant homesteader, who was purposely excised from the family story—or was it by sheer carelessness?

Now Baba and Mum and Aunty Anne are gone, and I am on my own to crack this case.

Blessing the gods of the Internet, and post-Soviet Ukrainian technological catch-up, I scanned the photo and emailed it to my second cousin, Petro Kosovan, who lives in Zabolotiv, western Ukraine. It is now our generation born after the Second World War that is the eldest and holds the treasure trove of family stories and perhaps even secrets. Nick is a great-uncle to us both.

What Second-Cousin Petro Kosovan Knows

In Ukrainian, Petro replied: "This [photo] is Mykola, 'Nick,' one of seven children including four brothers, your Baba's siblings. At the time of the 1917 Revolution, he was an activist and participated in meetings. Then he went to Canada (where his sisters, Sophie and your Baba, already lived) and there he again took up revolutionary activity. He was arrested and deported back to Ukraine. Myrna, I don't know anything more exact, but this is what I remember from my father's conversations. If I learn anything more, I'll write you." December 23, 2012.

(He never did.)

I wrote back: "Nothing about what then happened to him?"

"Nothing I recall."

(This was to become a theme.)

A young man from a western Ukrainian village near the Romanian border somehow becomes radicalized by a Bolshevik revolution miles and borders away in Czarist Russia. But, wait, if he is going "to meetings," there must have been a Bolshevizing organization near his village, Dzhuriv. Years pass. He leaves for Canada, perhaps invited by his sisters. A photo is taken in which he seems to be a man of the land (those cucumbers). Instead, he resumes "revolutionary activity" in Lethbridge! Where did he find it? Unsurprisingly, he is arrested and deported. End of story. How could such a fantastical tale have slipped out of the family yarns told in Canada?

I had once been shown how to glean clues from Soviet-era gazetteers, and out of curiosity, I had looked up the entry for Dzhuriv, Baba's and Dido's home village. Bingo! Dzhuriv had incubated an active centre of the (illegal) Communist Party West Ukraine in the 1920s and Nick's brother, "Yu. Kosovan," had been a member. Perhaps he invited Nick to the meetings. The next mention of political activity—in Dzhuriv village delegates are sent to the People's Elections of West Ukraine (1939–1941)—covers a period when Nick may already have been arrested and deported from Canada. He's not mentioned as a delegate. Next comes the fascist occupation (1941–1944), but again Nick is not mentioned.

Next the internet, prodded by search words, tosses up a long narrative full of incident about a Yuri Vyrostok who "tells the story of his immigration to Canada and first experiences in a new country." His story had first been told in the socialist *The Ukrainian Canadian* magazine. Socialist: This was promising.

In his story, Vyrostok had moved on, from Lethbridge and organizing radical Ukrainian coal miners, to Fernie, BC. "New forces came and went," he recalled, "depending on available jobs and where one could get them." Vyrostok found work in Fernie. His story went on.

Sometime in the 1920s a group of men sit around a campfire in the Crow's Nest Pass and reminisce. They are Galician immigrants, labourers from Sniatyn district in (now) western Ukraine, from Zabolotiv and Illintsi, and they break stones all day long that will be hauled to the coke ovens in Hosmer, BC. They reminisce about "how our peasants once rebelled in the neighbouring villages, initiated by those in Illintsi." There had been peasant strikes.

I put the question to //www.encyclopediaofukraine.com: What is a peasant strike?

Inspired by the Irish Land War of the mid-1890s, wave upon wave of work stoppages broke over landlords' estates in Galicia—four hundred villages in eastern Galicia alone in 1900 and 1902. The paltry wages, physical abuse, as well as constraints on access to forests and pastures pushed the tenant farmers and labourers beyond endurance. They occupied the land they worked, fought off strike breakers, and brought the wrath of soldiers down upon their heads. Ukrainian Radicals and Ukrainian Social Democrats—parties that were already planting branches in Canada—supported them.

Was Nick already dreaming? Perhaps he had heard these stories too, as a lad in one of those four hundred Galician villages. Did his father, employed hauling casks of beer from village tavern to village tavern, join the strikes? No such story has come down to us. Had he read the newspaper, *Hromads'kyi Holos* (*Community Voice*), or one like it? There he would learn that, failing all else in the way of revolution in Galicia, "a free community of our countrymen will arise in Canada."

His sisters, Palahna and Sophie, made the journey to Canada in 1911. It would take Nick another twenty years to join Sophie, and by then, he had been radicalized by village socialist intellectuals, the ones with the newspapers and pamphlets in their satchels, who wrote that property was theft.

I am left to imagine or construct how Nick managed entry into Canada with such a background and how once settled after a fashion in Lethbridge with Sophie and her husband he found circles of "revolutionary activity," which, inevitably, this being the Depression years, led to his arrest and deportation. But what had he done?

Nick in Lethbridge

Nothing for it but to read indexes in books in the local history section of the Edmonton Public Library and do a lot of internet searching. This is how I decide that Nick Kosovan arrived in Lethbridge in the middle of the brutal Depression, a working man seeking his fortune when municipal budgets could ill afford public works and services, let alone relief for the unemployed. By late 1929, Lethbridge City Council had met in emergency session to consider how to meet the escalating demands for relief. An emboldened Ku Klux Klan of Canada was protesting the employment of "Orientals" and Slavs when red-blooded white men themselves had become public charges. Perhaps Nick briefly found grunt work in the mines in Diamond City, Shaughnessy, or Taber.

I look again at the photograph. Nick has arrived in Lethbridge, is living with sister Sophie and her husband, and this is their land where he kneels with his armful of cucumbers, and behind him the cabbage patch, and on the far horizon stooks of hay. Let's say he then goes to the beet fields, one of the lucky immigrants to get a job.

The search engine has taken me straight to the indispensable work of two labour historians—John Herd Thompson and Allen Seager—to their article in the journal *Labour/Le Travail* in 1978, "Workers, Growers and Monopolists: The 'Labour Problem' on the Alberta Beet Sugar Industry During the 1930s."

They reproduce an undated pamphlet, its title handwritten in block letters: "FASCIST MOB ATTEMTS [sic] TO TERRORIZE BEET WORKERS." I elaborate a formula: Radical workers + antifascists + depths of misery = Uncle Nick

The pamphlet opens with a flourish: "We Beet Workers of Southern Alberta, after being driven to a starvation level through cut after cut in the price of our labor, have organized, as the only means of resisting further depths of misery, and regaining some measure of a decent standard of living."

Planting, thinning, weeding, and hand-harvesting sugar beets: "Most farm hands would do almost anything else before they would accept beet work." But immigrants from the nonpreferred nationalities would accept it, from east, central and southern Europe (e.g., Ukrainians, Czechs, and Italians), and beet farmers were being pressed to hire them. The unthinkable alternative was the "little yellow fellows" now excluded from even this menial labour.

Except for seeding, there was nothing mechanized about it, and beet workers crawled on their knees along the rows of plantings to do it: 115 hours of their hand labour to work an acre of beets, ten times what an acre of wheat required. Nevertheless, until the Depression cancelled any expectation of a living wage, beetworkers could earn at least two hundred dollars a month and were provided a habitable house and a garden plot.

It was downhill from there, as the glut of urban jobless women and men and the new immigrants all competed for the same scraps of contract labour, ever decreasing its value: Beetworkers saw their contract rate slide from twenty-one dollars an acre to seventeen dollars despite steady productivity. Perhaps inspired by Communist union action in the coal fields, the beetworkers organized as the Beet Workers' Industrial Union (BWIU), persuaded Peter Meronik—a black-listed Ukrainian coal miner now eking out his living as a music teacher—to be their president and issued their demand for the 1935 growing season: a twenty-dollar-per-acre cash contract and all contracts had to be signed in the presence of a field committee elected by the workers. And they stuck to their guns. Inevitably, the Beet Growers' Association yelled "Communism!" and appealed to the provincial government to protect them from the Reds. Despite his inability to speak English (I assume), all Nick needed to join the "Reds" was to witness blunt violence visited upon the weak (and unorganized) by the local strongmen, just as he may have seen done in the peasant land strikes in Galicia.

I see him rolling up his sleeves. He's a big guy.

May 4, 1935: *Worker* newspaper reports evictions and vandalism in sugar beet country. Supported by the Industrial Union, many hundreds of beetworkers, having refused to sign contracts, were tramping around the countryside encouraging (maybe even intimidating) other workers to join their strike. Premier William Aberhart himself received accounts from a Taber grower that unruly "Roumanians, Bulgarians, Slaves [sic]" were harassing and interfering with scabs trying to get to work on the fields. Then, *Worker* reports, "fascist gangs of 150" retaliated, "made up of storekeepers, school teachers, preachers, elevator men, reactionary, exploiting farmers, and two RCMP men."

The BWIU's own pamphlet described how the mob had ransacked the shacks of the workers' families while its members were at a meeting. The gang seized their property—meagre enough furnishings and personal effects as well as suitcases and bedding—and then having legalized this act of housebreaking and theft "by obtaining the assistance of two members of the RCMP," they duly dumped everything in the road.

This might have been the moment of Nick's story that second-cousin Petro's little narrative remembers: his arrest and deportation.

The Fear

In 1931, Canada deported seven thousand immigrants, among them the loathed and feared labour organizers of the left. By spring 1931, seeing their opportunity to decontaminate their communities of communist elements, over seventy city councils in Canada had sent resolutions to the federal government to demand increased deportations, as the cost of relief was now beyond their means, not to mention the cost of police operations launched against the unemployed who had a habit of marching around town squares, shouting revolutionary slogans—or at least shouts for bread.

In August 1931, the Communist Party of Canada was declared an illegal organization under section 98 of the Criminal Code. Now the only evidence that was needed for political deportation was proof that the immigrant—even when a naturalized citizen—was a member of a communist organization. By 1934, 94 per cent of applications for naturalization were refused.

Kicked off the beet fields, unemployable, and lined up with the others for relief, Nick was about to be deported. Between 1930 and 1935, some twenty-eight thousand immigrants were deported from Canada for having become a public charge. Or had he been among those accused of seditious conspiracy or of vagrancy? Was he plodding around the suffering countryside and pamphleteering among his low-born countrymen who seethed with resentment with every weed they yanked out of the stubborn clods of Canadian earth?

If they were deported to Poland (eastern Galicia), they may have survived whatever prosecution the Polish authorities meted out. But Nick simply vanished.

Why Doesn't Petro Know More? Why Don't I?

Baba and Dido in Canada were ardent Soviet sympathizers: Why hadn't they told and retold a family legend of Nick Kosovan, working-class hero booted out of Canada by the stooges of capital?

Of course they hadn't; they were frightened. Let Party leaders and union organizers take the risks and consequences of defying law and order. Baba and Dido, with their tenuous claim to Canada's rights and privileges, would keep their heads down. Celebrate a Bolshevik agitator on the family tree? Naturalization would not have protected them. Protest a deportation of a relative? Shame and stigma. Red scares rolled through Canadian society on a regular basis, an emotional reality my grandparents never outlived. Even I had bad dreams as a child of being pursued in the alley behind our house by men in long, black coats: *Russians*. In Dido's bad dreams, they were being run to ground by the RCMP.

There Are Other Photographs

Beginning in the 1960s, over the years, we received many, many photos of Kosovan relatives in Soviet Ukraine, an entire gallery of them posed stiffly and unsmiling in studios, as they grew up and grew old, and another generation arrived in front of modern cameras, on school trips as well as at weddings and reunions. These, too, I had inherited at my mother's death, and they were overly familiar to me: Baba, Mum and Aunty Anne had pored over them and set them aside from the square envelopes in which they had been sent. The Canadian address with its Latin letters had been inscribed by unsure hands. I go back now to this stash of Ukrainian photographs and lo! and behold! There is a photo of Nick, which is to say of Nikolai/Mykola Kosovan, in a studio with four other adults and one child.

Two young men in suits stand behind two women in embroidered blouses and kerchiefs; between them is the patriarch, a white-haired, white-mustachioed elder in a sheepskin vest, his white pants tucked into knee-high boots. A girl dressed in her own embroidered blouse and jacket stands on a stool between her mother and (I am guessing) her grandfather. She is in no obvious relationship with either of the young men. This is a postcard-style photo on which my mother has written: "My uncles, my aunts, my cousin and my grandfather."

I have no recollection of seeing this photograph before, much less of having its subjects identified. As far as I was aware, my mother had no relatives except the handful accumulated in Canada. But here they are, close kin in a picture from the Old Country. She writes: "Uncle Nick visited us in Canada and returned some ten years later."

Returned? Not Deported, Not Disappeared?

Stuck to the back of the postcard photo is a yellow Post-it note in my own hand, although I have no recollection of writing it. "Nikolai," I have written in Cyrillic, meaning the young man with a mustache and the same shock of lank, dark hair across his forehead as the man with the cucumbers in a field in Lethbridge. Here he looks some ten years younger, so the 1920s. I have written: Yuri Kosovan, Nikolai's brother; Nastunia, Nikolai's wife; Maria, his daughter; Pavlusia, Yuri's wife. And also the patriarch Petro, my mother's grandfather and my great-grandfather—he who rolled beer casks off his wagon into the village pubs.

On the back of another photo, some thirty years later, Baba has written a semi-literate explanation: "Brother Nikolai's daughter Maria and children, Marika and Mykola." Maria sits in an embroidered blouse and kerchief, her skinny legs in heavy shoes, frowning, as is Marika. Is she a widow? In a good hand (the fruit of a Soviet education), Maria has written in Ukrainian: "This is me and my children, Kolya [Mykola] and Marusia [Marika]. Kolya is in eighth class and Marusia in fourth. But Kolya has Dido Kosovan's character." This would be the radical Nikolai/Mykola/Nick. "It seems [illegible] drops of tears." And indeed it does seem that Kolya is on the verge of tears.

Now I am haunted by the possibility that, on my visit to Dzhuriv in 1984, and my presentation to all the relatives, I may have met Maria but had no questions. Would she not have had stories about her father, however absent or exiled or deceased? Wouldn't Petro have heard them? Why hasn't he told me more?

It seems, though, that all along, I have known more myself.

In 1984, on my visit to the Kosovan ancestral village, Dzhuriv, second-cousin Pavlina transcribed into a small notebook the names and relationships of everyone I had met, namely the children of my Baba's siblings—which is to say my mother's cousins, and their children, my second cousins: a plethora of Marias, Petros and Marusias, of Elenas and Paraskas and Olyas. Pavlina has included their (then-Soviet) occupations: accountant in a sugar factory, trucker for a juice-extraction factory, tradeswoman in a factory, bus driver, locksmith in a furniture factory, and shop assistant. They worked at the heart of the collectivized Soviet economy, having putatively won the class struggle that Nick had failed utterly to advance in Lethbridge. His and my Soviet Ukrainian relatives were proletarians, skilled labourers with a secondary education, who may be said to have made the equivalent progress through their society as Baba's progeny had made in Canada—an education, steady work, social benefits, and healthy children.

In 1988, I met Pavlina again, this time in Kyiv, in Ukraine of the perestroika (rebuilding) years, and now able to speak intelligibly in Ukrainian, I flesh out Baba's siblings and their kin with Pavlina's voluble help, one more time. So I hear again of Baba's father, Petro, and her mother (my great-grandmother: I have one!), Paraska, who died young, leaving seven children. Of how two of them, Baba and Sophie, got away to Canada. The other two daughters, Maria and Elena, continued to live in the village. Brother Yuri was killed by nationalist bandits in 1945. Brother Stefan and his wife, Dotsia, lived high above the village in the woods.

And brother Nikolai/Mykola/Nick? He lived eight years in Canada and then returned to Dzhuriv. No deportation, then? No revolutionary aspirations? End of story.

Months later, however, in the middle of this research, I excitedly emailed Petro again. I wrote him with new information I had completely forgotten from thirty years earlier. Although I have no recollection of writing this, alongside the notes from 1988, but in different ink, I have added: "Nikolai hanged himself."

Petro: "I know nothing of this."

He's not talking. Nobody's talking.

So now I have done the talking, here in Canada, about Uncle Nick, the radical from Dzhuriv, with his armful of cucumbers, outside agitator in Lethbridge, arrestee, deportee, suicide swinging from a rope in the village barn, vanished from recall—whom I am not supposed to know.

3.

The Front Door

Jane Munro

Ranjan and I were in Park Royal, a mall on the North Shore. I suggested it would be a good time for him to meet my parents and see the house I had grown up in. I called my mother on a pay phone: She said okay, so we drove up.

My father met us—by blocking the front door.

I could not believe it and tried to push in past him.

His big, muscular body stopped me from entering the home where my friends and I were always welcome. My home.

But not when I was with my Indian lover.

Stunned, I went home—to my house. It was summer; my children were there, in the kitchen. They heard me in the dining room on the phone, shouting at their grandfather. Tearing a strip off him. When had my children ever heard me like this? I did not care. I was furious with my mother, too. How could she concede to this?

Neither I nor my children would enter their house until they invited Ranjan to visit, I told them. They could see their grandchildren at my house, but Ranjan might be there, too.

November came, and they had not relented. So I wrote to them. Did they want a Christmas when their daughter and grandchildren did not enter their house? Wasn't it time to invite Ranjan and me for tea?

Finally, my mother called: Could we come Sunday afternoon?

My father was sitting at the coffee table in the living room with a leather-bound volume of the *Encyclopedia Britannica*, fifth edition, in front of him. He did not get up to welcome us. He did not smile.

Ranjan was gracious and relaxed. Mother brought in tea on a tray.

My father had been reading the eighteenth-century *Britannica* article on India and Indians. Mother must have told him Ranjan's family was Brahman; my father began quizzing Ranjan on his caste.

No matter how gauche or ignorant his questions, Ranjan answered them thoughtfully and intelligently, without a hint of defensiveness. Slowly, my father relaxed with him. Both my father and Ranjan had fathers who were artists—painters of portraits and landscapes.

My mother invited us to stay for dinner. We did. A few weeks later, they came to Ranjan's open house at which he was showing and selling his paintings. The following year, when Ranjan was sick, my mother brought him a flowering plant.

Although my father got used to Ranjan, and to me being with Ranjan, this did not dispel his racism. At the time, I was not sure why it had been almost invisible to me. Perhaps because our subdivision had—as I learned later—covenants on the lots forbidding sales to any non-Caucasian persons. I had never come home with a dark-skinned friend.

Plus, my father had a Chinese friend—a wealthy man who annually invited my parents to a multicourse banquet in Chinatown. They dressed in their finest, stayed late, and the next day my mother regaled us with descriptions of fascinating delicacies. But those friends did not visit our home.

Colonialism, whether in Canada or in India, was—in my parents' minds—a benefit to Indigenous people. It was for their own good.

As were my father's spankings; they taught me, civilized me. It was not until I was eleven and pubescent that my mother finally shouted at him when he was thrashing me: "Stop it! You can no longer do this to her!"

I sobbed and sobbed. I hated being too weak to escape his grip and took my quilt into the toilet and locked the door—the only inside door in the house with a lock. Eventually, I began eyeing the pebbled window that opened at an angle on its chain, wondering if I could escape through it. Run away.

4.

What You Didn't Tell

Elizabeth Templeman

By the time she was ten, any girl growing up in a small town on the east coast in the 1960s would have a cache of secrets she could get lost in.

Growing up in those circumstances, being Catholic to boot, made it hard to distinguish something secret from something sinful from something simply unsafe. It all ran together: one immense surface of forbidden territory to be navigated. You didn't wear day-old underwear, didn't swear, didn't listen to the whispered sins of the boy kneeling on the opposite side of the confessional, didn't walk on the railroad tracks, didn't stare at drunks, didn't rush down to the ocean-side to watch wharf rats fleeing from the old barge when fire struck, and didn't notice when someone's sister stopped coming to school. And since you knew you had done all of those things, well, you just didn't dwell on it. Or tried not to, anyway.

Life was rife with challenge: The goal was to be proper and good (or, in any case, to appear to be good); danger befell those who were not, who dwelled on unthinkable, unspoken things. Not only was there hell lurking but also drowning, tuberculosis and polio, suicide, pregnancy, poverty, and insanity.

Yet I loved the challenge. To carve out a refuge in an existence so fraught with danger was a sweet thing. Sometimes my friends and I found shared havens right in the heart of terror. We ventured in clusters along the dreaded railroad tracks (our forbidden shortcut home from school), past the shacks along the shoulder of the railbed (where children lived who didn't have to be in bed by eight o'clock), past the cat-o-nine tails growing in the swamps (where we had heard that serpents lurked), and to the dank hollow below the railway trestle (through which my older brother had once gotten his head stuck, having pulled himself up to look out for the next train). If we were all there together, who could tell on us? There, under that trestle, we would huddle, tingling with excitement and bursting with courage at unthinkable dangers.

I had my own secret place, too—a private haven. It was back behind the small toilet just off my parents' bedroom. To get there, I had to first pass through the bedroom, that other forbidden place—kids were not allowed in places where they had no business being. Once safely within the closet, I would climb up over the toilet and crawl back to a sort of cupboard place, dark and wooden, where bedding was stored. I remember the coolness of ironed cotton sheets against my legs as I crouched in the darkness, doing God only knows what. Maybe I prayed back there, or daydreamed, making elaborate plans for the future. All that I remember is clean coolness and the sweet abandon of solitude, a gift for a kid in a family of seven.

Because I harboured such a deep and determined faith—itself a secret held tight against the ridicule of older siblings—the church provided a secret place too. My best friends weren't Catholic, so the church was a place to escape even from them. I was safe there, protected by God himself, though I favoured the Mother Mary and spent most of my time below her outstretched arms in the flickering light of the votive candles. Once I turned ten, I could walk to the church anytime I wanted. It was always open to me. And I loved being in there, loved its resounding silence and lofty heights; its muted atmosphere was thick with spirits.

Other secret places were even more intimate, more dangerous, yet also less detectable. Once, standing on the whitewashed porch of our local parish convent, I let my eyes slide down the top rim of the nun's habit when she bent over my catechism book, correcting my homework. Horrified, I realized that she had hair and—far more alarming—that I'd seen it. Her cropped brown hair, barely visible, drew my eyes like a magnet. Too ashamed to confess, I lived with that sin, waiting for God's vengeance to descend. Nothing ever happened—beyond the slightest loss of faith, which I never did manage to recover.

A few years later, when I got to be old enough to start babysitting, the risks began to shift. Wandering around unfamiliar homes, divining new, exotic habits and smells and textures, and beneath, layers of another family's secret life, was thrilling, sometimes unsettling. To be trusted with the responsibility for a beloved first baby, left on our own in a new apartment, altered my sense of self. Loyalties tipped towards the new. Enthralled by a sense of control that came with new responsibilities and intoxicated by the satisfaction of dollar bills earned on my own steam, I was taking steps from childhood to personhood.

I don't think it surprised me to discover that growing up didn't dramatically transform the world for a person. There was no great leap into clarity and comprehension. Fears and secrets were not left behind. Consequences remained puzzling, sometimes terrifying and seldom predictable.

I remember sitting in an upholstered rocking chair watching whatever was on television, delighting in the freedom of solitude, yet dreading the hour when only the colour wheel would remain to announce that even the television transmission station was closed for the night. The house would creak and groan, and all the lurking terror would float at the edges of my mind. I would rush up the stairs to check the little ones, feeling both responsible for their safety and ashamed to be drawing comfort from them in the midnight hour.

Sometimes I would find myself running my finger, ever so gently, around and around the soft spot on the baby's warm head. I knew this spot was terribly fragile and that something awful would happen if it got ruptured. But I couldn't stop myself from circling that vulnerability. Unlike the temptation of the railroad tracks and whatever dark secrets lurked behind the nun's habit and the menace of sins we barely understood, this was a danger so tangible and so easily resisted. I could prove, if only to myself, secretly, that I was a responsible creature in a perilous world.

5.

My Mother's Madness

JoAnn McCaig

About six months before she went down the rabbit hole for the last time, Mom turned to me in the car and said, "JoAnn, if I go bonkers, I want you to know you've been a good daughter."

We were on Crowchild Trail in Calgary, coming back from some outing—a doctor's appointment perhaps or maybe just a shopping trip. I laughed, surprised, and said, "Well thanks, Mom. You've been a pretty good mom yourself."

Truth and Fiction

When I was in my late twenties, I tried to write a short story about my mother's madness. A few years prior, she had gone off the deep end on a holiday with her siblings; they couldn't cope, called for help, and I was the designated family member to fly down to the Caribbean to bring her home, my dad having left by then. I remember little about this trip now, but I must have put some details about it into the short story I later wrote, called "Such Devoted Sisters."

In the story, Franny runs away from home to her sister, claiming that her husband is trying to kill her. The narrator is the older sister, and she says, "Well, we took her in and listened to her story, but we just couldn't keep her there. She was too wild. She paced around the house like an animal in a cage. Sometimes, she'd throw tantrums and break things. And I had to watch her every minute, or she'd slip out the door and run around the neighbourhood. Sometimes she'd tell the neighbours we were keeping her prisoner and would they please call the police." So Big Sis has had enough and calls Franny's kids because the husband has left by now. The doctor forwards a prescription for sedatives, and the kids send Big Sis the airfare and ask her to escort their mother home, they themselves being too busy to make the trip. "But no sooner were we off the ground than she started acting up again and bothering the other passengers. I took her back to our seats, called the stewardess for a glass of water and said, 'Franny, you better have another one of those pills now.' She gave me this look that was supposed to be innocent but just came out mean. She said, 'I can't, I lost them.'"

So the narrator panics. They have a layover, and the moment they land, she drags Franny hither and thither until she finds a medical clinic at the airport. (There really are such things or used to be. I know this for a fact.) She explains the situation to the doctor, and he invites Franny into his office while the narrator waits outside. After a while, the door opens and Franny walks out, saying "The doctor wants to talk to you now, Sis."

The narrator says: "When I got inside his office, I said 'Have you given her something?' and he said 'No, not yet.' So I told him he better not leave her out there alone because she'll run away. He said, 'She'll be fine. Please sit down,' and he started pushing me towards a chair, but I wouldn't sit down, so he walked out and shut the door behind him. I heard voices out in the waiting room but couldn't make out what they were saying. Then he came back in and said it was all taken care of. I sat down and told him all about it, all about Franny and her breakdowns, years and years of trouble and confusion. When I finished, he was quiet for a while; then he said, 'Tell me. What makes you think there is something wrong with your sister?'"

My short story ended melodramatically with Big Sis bolting from the doctor's office only to discover that Franny has fled. And Big Sis freaks out. And the doctor wrestles her to the ground, jabbing her with a big needle. And next thing you know Big Sis is in a hospital. And little sister Franny kindly comes to visit, bringing oranges.

A sophomore piece, it was never published.

But you know how I know that airports have doctors' offices? Because I sat in one once in the late 1970s on a layover with my mom. And the doctor turned to me at length, and said, "JoAnn, what makes you think there is something wrong with your mother?"

I've heard it said that addiction is a family disease; well, I think madness might be a family disease as well. Everybody goes a little crazy when someone in the family has a mental illness. That doctor looked at me—a stressed out and scared twenty-five-year-old, my mom's reluctant and inexperienced keeper—and probably thought "she's the one with the problem, not the mother."

The Bower

Mom confessed to me about the bower one evening after Sunday dinner. It was about a year after Dad died but long before she got sick for the last time.

For years, my sons and I had been coming to Sunday dinner at Mom's. On special occasions, or if my brother and his family were there, we'd eat in the dining room. But if it was just the five of us, we ate in the kitchen. And we had a routine. After the meal, the kids would drift into the family room to watch TV while Mom and I sat with our cigarettes and cups of tea. I'd enumerate my latest grievances against my ex-husband, and she'd say, "Don't let him get to you, JoAnn. He's not worth it." Then she'd bring out items she'd found in flyers, things she thought I'd like or could use. I'd joke to my friends that for Mom, "reading the paper" meant going through the flyers.

It was on a Sunday night like this that she mentioned the bower. "Now JoAnn," she said, checking to make sure the boys were out of earshot. "I know this is going to sound strange but this... thing has been happening at night when I go to bed. These shapes appear on the walls of my room, like tree branches, and they form a kind of arch all around me, all around my bed. And I close my eyes, and they're not there, and I open my eyes, and there they are. So they're real, I'm not imagining them." And then she looked guardedly at me, awaiting my response.

It seems so strange to try to recount this conversation now. Did I laugh or smirk or dismiss? I don't think so. I'm pretty sure I asked respectful questions about what it was that she was seeing, what she was experiencing. In those days, she was still on lithium, still smoking a pack a day, and putting away most of a bottle of white wine a night. (Light wine, she liked to remind us. Capistro Light.)

Anyhow, I like to think that whatever is good and kind in me listened to what she had to say. And whose idea was it to link this apparition to Dad's death? Hers or mine? Not sure. I just know it came up in the conversation. My parents had been bitterly divorced for more than two decades by then. She still spat the name of my stepmother as if it were a curse word, even though Dad was dead and gone. So the idea that this sheltering bower was a visitation from my dad's spirit—did that come from her or from me or from both of us? I honestly don't remember.

You, reader, may be finding this all a bit weird. And I guess you'd be right, it is. But when she shyly asked me to try lying down in her bed to see if I could see the branches, I did it.

While she waited silently in the kitchen, I went into her room, turned out the lights, and lay down. Closed my eyes. Opened them. And I saw only bare walls. Waited a while. Closed my eyes and reopened them. Nothing.

And when I returned to the kitchen, I told her so.

But here's the thing: As I sit here now, writing this down, I can tell you exactly what the bower looked like—not actual branches but shadows of branches twined on the wall and the ceiling around my mother's bed. A little spooky but not menacing. Just this shadowy enclosing. A bower.

How do I know that it looked like that to her? I don't, with any certainty.

But I do know. I do.

Because people have looked at a photo of my mother as a toddler, or as a mature woman, and thought it was me. Though in fact, we don't look actually that much alike.

But we are alike, deeply alike.

Because we are made of the same stuff, my mother and me.

My Mother's Madness

My mother's brand of insanity used to be called manic depression, now renamed bipolar disorder. I no longer say "My mother is bipolar" but that she has bipolar. That way I am not defining her by her disease.

When I was kid, what happened to her was called "nervous breakdown." By my teens, I understood it as depression ("Poor missus, she has the sadness again" was what our Polish cleaning lady said). It was after my parents split up, when I was in my twenties and the burden of Mom's care fell to me and my aunts and uncles, that the term "manic depression" swam up. Then all went quiet for twenty years thanks to lithium. But soon after she turned eighty, Mom's mental illness resurfaced, and her problem was now called bipolar.

In all these years, I had never been given much information about her disease. But this time, in the Rockyview geriatric psychiatric ward, I was given a little booklet. The title was *Bipolar Affective Disorder: A Guide to Recovery*, and it was illustrated with black-and-white photos of people looking sad or of empty hallways. The cover was ghosted with the names of famous people who were mentally ill. No, I mean they had a mental illness. An impressive list: from Thomas Edison to Queen Elizabeth (the first, I presume), from Charles Darwin to Georgia O'Keeffe, from Samuel Coleridge to Mary Shelley, from Charles Mingus to Axl Rose. These names were offered, seemingly, to make patients and their families feel better. The booklet was produced by a group that called itself OBAD: Organization for Bipolar Affective Disorder.

To my frustration, however, the information in the booklet just wasn't that useful. It described various types of bipolar and depression and associated disorders, but no one classification really fit. Nothing really described what happened to my mother.

So what was her bipolar like? Well, when I was kid, Mom was crazy when she got angry.

Think about what it was like to grow up like that: Female anger equals madness. In my twenties, I was stunned to hear my best friend talk of being "bitchy" to her husband. Once I heard her say to him "that okay with you, Pete?" and I just reeled. I thought *You can do that? And get away with it?* Anger in men was called normal. Anger in women was called crazy.

When my mother was anything less than sweet and funny and kind and helpful, she was unwell. She was getting sick again, she was going crazy. The strongest childhood memory I have of being harmed by her madness is the day when, get this, she refused to help me look for a missing piece of my tap dancing costume. And was a bit mean about it. Really. How traumatic.

I know that the grownups—Dad, my aunts, my grandparents—protected us kids from the worst of it, from the extremes. But I also think that Mom herself worked hard to shield us from the hardest edges of her illness. She was, despite everything, a wonderful mother.

My mother's madness was never manic, that I could see. She could be agitated when drunk and was sometimes paranoid. I guess she was sort of manic when she went on shopping sprees and bought things that were in expensive bad taste. But I don't remember ever telling her to slow down. I don't remember her ever staying up all night or being grandiose. Sure, I was vaguely aware of my parents being awake and fighting upstairs during the night when I was little—but doesn't that happen in all marriages? And there was always a lot of booze around. I mean, this was the fifties and sixties.

From my father's perspective, her madness meant hating him. Hating him, hating his whole goddamn family. And blaming him for everything that was wrong in her life. She'd get mad at him and run away to her sister's. And after a while, she'd come back.

The thing about my mother's madness is that it was so... unremarkable. But she was paranoid, no question. My aunt told me how, in that first breakdown in the early years of my parents' marriage, Mom came racing over to her sister's place one night, claiming "He's trying to kill me. He's putting ground glass in my drinks!"

But on the whole, my mother's madness was nothing like the bipolar described in the OBAD booklet. Nor is it like the disease described by Kay Redfield Jamieson in her memoir, *An Unquiet Mind*. But then again, Jamieson is a hyperachieving woman, whereas my mother's goals in life were pretty modest. When healthy and enumerating the good things in her life, she'd list "you kids. And nice things and nice trips." So perhaps it makes sense that her madness lacked grandiosity.

Nor did my mother have any illusions about her powers. What she did have plenty of illusions about was that people were out to get her—my dad, his new wife, the neighbours.

And here's an odd thing: It was only when she was sick that my mother asserted ownership of her body. Mom was generally disgusted by bodily functions. She used to claim that changing our diapers had made her gag; she thought the word "breasts" uncouth and instead said "bosoms." However, when she was having a bipolar episode and was subsisting on cigarettes and booze and rage, we'd suggest that she eat something or maybe get some sleep. She'd huff "my body knows what it wants. My body knows what it needs." And it was so strange to us to hear her even say the words "my body." It sounded slightly racy, even a little obscene.

I don't know how to get to the truth of my mother's brand of insanity. But I suspect that it has a lot to do with being a woman in the 1950s.

Maybe my mother's bipolar was a form of sanity because it permitted her to be angry, particularly at my dad.

And it permitted her to own her own body.

Maybe her occasional paranoia *was* a kind of grandioseness—believing that people were even thinking about her at all.

Sometimes I look at my own life and see what a lunatic I was at various points (grad school, postpartum, divorce, menopause) and realize how because I was living inside my life, it made perfect sense at the time. So I can imagine what it was like for Mom, but what I don't understand is why I can't find a way to describe what it looked like from the outside. A lifetime's training in pretending all is well so that the sky doesn't fall, I guess.

For Mom's sixtieth birthday, in 1988, she got a day pass from the psych ward. The family gathered for Chinese food at her house. Against the advice of her doctors, she had insisted that champagne be served with the meal, and we all sat there amid chopsticks and takeout dishes in her dining room—acres of blue shag rug, the heavy furniture upholstered in hot pink plush, the bell heather china and Waterford crystal glasses—and us kids and the aunts and uncles gathered and Mom holding court. She was so brittle, so broken, and so scary—this tiny deluded little creature defiantly drinking her wine. Our collective silent misery. Was she manic then? I suppose so. I remember only sadness and wanting this excruciating evening to end. I think of her that night, and I see a small, furious woman with blonde curls and big glasses and a mean glint in her eyes.

Yes, perhaps when my mother was like this, she was actually sort of sane. Because she was pissed off and suspicious and selfish. I guess that was what struck me most about her episodes. How selfish she became.

When Mom was well, she was utterly self-effacing. Mild. Kind. Helpful. When I was sixteen, I came home late one night, high as a kite. My parents confronted me, sat me down at the kitchen table. My dad was furious, waving his arms, demanding an answer to the question "Have you been smoking POT?" while Mom sat at the table, hands folded in front of her. "JoAnn," she said. "If we thought you needed it, we would get it for you."

That's what my mother said: "If we thought you needed it, we would get it for you." It was 1970. People still went to jail for simple possession. I remember it to this day, even though I wasn't on pot at all. I was on acid.

And when I decided, at age nineteen, to break away—quit my job, drop out of school, head for the West Coast—she was the only one in my family who wished me well. No one else. Only my mother wished me well.

I don't know how to talk about this. I guess it's because when I ask questions about my mother's madness, I can't help but enter a hall of mirrors. And everywhere I look, there's me, and there's my mother, and there's me.

She's been gone for years now, my mom. But recently, deep in the enforced isolation of a global pandemic, I was driving down Crowchild Trail, and I thought of her. And I said aloud, "Mom, if I go bonkers, I want you to know you were a great mother."

6.

We Had One, Too

Maureen Hynes

But we never thought of burying it in the desert.
 We all knew my father kept it disassembled in his safety deposit box in the local bank branch:
 The Luger.
 My oldest brother (older than his twin by an hour) had the misfortune of inheriting it.
 None of us wanted it in the dismantling of the family home.
 A "cultural difference." How the aggressive NRA spokesman on the radio described the common Canadian discomfort with guns, the much lower rate of ownership, and the smaller number of mass shootings.
 After my father's suicide attempt, social workers swept through his house like a search party. They spotted the antique musket over the studio couch in the basement rec room and confiscated it.
 He thought they were crazy. "The only way I could kill myself with that gun is if I hit myself over the head with it. Repeatedly," said our dad. Lacking powder. Lacking the long stick to stuff the powder down the musket's shaft. It was wide barrelled, so was it a blunderbuss? *Blunderbuss,* from the Dutch, for "thunder" and "tube." And what is the name of that stick?
 Why did I never ask my dad how he got the blunderbuss. Or even why.
 Or ask the social workers what they did with it.
 More blundering.
 At a family wedding after my dad died (not by suicide), one of my aunts told us, "Your dad loved guns!" This astonished all of us.

"Oh yes," she said to our wide-eyed faces. "As a boy, he had a tiny antique replica of that kind of long-barrelled pistol that pirates used." A flintlock gun.

"Tiny," she said. "This big." She showed us two finger joints on her index finger. As a little girl, she'd secretly take the wee gun out of his drawer and play with it. "It was so sweet. It had a tiny trigger that you could pull."

"I loved it," she said. "It clicked so perfectly. But he found out and yelled at me. 'Leave my stuff alone!'"

When we were clearing out the house, we found it. In the kitchen over the stove, there was a holy water font nailed to the wall. The wee gun was nestled into the bowl of that font, jumbled in with old Catholic medals of St. Jude and the Blessed Virgin Mary and Pope Pius XII.

"What?" we said. "This was never here before."

The next time I saw my aunt, I gave it to her. None of us wanted it.

Actually, now I wouldn't mind having it.

I think to hold a real pistol in my hand would make my heart stop. A sensation stronger than distaste or discomfort. Of course, fear. And a metal repulsion.

But the Luger.

I compiled a list of questions for my oldest brother. We had only a vague idea of how it had come into Dad's possession. it. My brother tells me it belonged to our dad's uncle, Edmund, who'd been gassed at Ypres in World War I but survived (sort of). The story goes that Edmund found it on the battlefield, when he was running up a hill in France. Years earlier, my dad had told me that "Soldiers would go through the battlefields and pick the guns off German corpses." Nightmare images.

My brother said that only German officers had Lugers.

Edmund gave it to Dad in 1933, as an appreciation, because my dad visited him in the nursing home for wounded soldiers. And every Christmas, my dad carried a box of Kleenex into Edmund's room. Inside the box, a bottle of whiskey.

According to Wikipedia, Lugers have been used in over forty countries in armed conflict. And that the name for the Luger Parabellum Pistol comes from the Latin: Si vis pacem, para bellum. ("If you seek peace, be prepared for war.")

My brother had a hell of a time getting rid of the Luger. Fifty years later, the registration was iffy and certainly not in his name. He phoned the police, the RCMP, as well as a policeman who said he knew somebody who'd talk to him. But the trail went cold; no one called.

Then many months later, he suddenly got a call. Some gun collector. "I hear you are looking to sell a Luger," said the voice on the other end of the line. That guy went to my brother's house, assembled the Luger in a jiffy. Said it was a beautiful specimen, excellent condition, gave him five hundred dollars. The holster was also beautiful, smooth, and gleaming. Like new.

To me, the passage of contact names sounded like the old tales of how to get in touch with a back-street abortionist.

I've always wondered if the policeman or the RCMP guy was in cahoots with the gun dealer, maybe got a cut.

We told my brother to keep the money—he'd more than earned it.

I never saw the Luger. Just imagined my brother lifting the parts out of the safety deposit box in a brown paper bag, an empty Kleenex box, so the parts wouldn't clunk heavily against each other as he left the bank. Now my brother tells me it was all in pieces when he took it out of the safety deposit box, so he just poured them into his briefcase and got on the subway and went home, full of anxiety.

He tells me that now it's very illegal to store a gun, assembled or not, in a bank's safety deposit box. It took me a few seconds to figure out why.

I never wanted to see it.

But now I would like to.

Don't forget the crossbow.

I think my dad had gotten some kind of kit and made the crossbow from it. Or read the specs in some magazine or book. *Popular Mechanics?* It looked lethal and antique, but I think it was only about thirty or forty years old. It had smooth brass parts. My dad loved brass.

On the last garbage day before we rendered up the house to its new owner, a mysterious network of men appeared outside our house. A half-dozen of them pulled up in cars as I put out the things that we couldn't sell or donate or give away (crockery, books, old picture frames, broken electric tools, and on and on and on). All these things were burdens to us. My other brother cried, putting Dad's old books in the garbage.

How did those men know to come to our place?

They started going through the boxes and containers methodically but quickly because they wanted to get the treasures before the garbage trucks arrived. One man snatched the crossbow, held it up. The wide-eyed, delighted look on his face reminded me of a child who's been given an enormous ice cream cone.

But really, I think he was figuring, "I'll get a bundle for this."

That September morning, I became an upright frozen body on my parents' front lawn.

There was a fourth weapon that I never saw. Another gun, a pistol.

My father had been seeing a psychiatrist. "Suicidal ideations," said the social worker. My dad's live-in caregiver took me aside and told me that the psychiatrist had pressed my father several times about any more guns in the house. My dad finally admitted to owning another one that none of us had known about and agreed to turn it over to the good doctor. And told the caregiver not to tell any of us.

Five years after his stroke—paralyzed, severely depressed, in a wheelchair—my dad got her to find the gun in its hiding place (what hiding place?), put it in a bag or box (what bag? what box?), and he took it to the psychiatrist for his next appointment. He sat in the Wheel-Trans bus with it in his lap. I know he did not return with it.

What did the psychiatrist do with it?

This essay was inspired by "The Family Sells the Family Gun, a prose ballad," in Brenda Hillman's *Extra Hidden Life, among the Days* (Wesleyan University Press, 2018).

7.

The Lost Epistles of Margie

John Barton

we got the dog from her, one sister
said, the other sister who was six
back then, said I remember
Margie, she and Bill stopped
coming to our house after
you came along, neither sister
having known of the letters
she had sent, all postmarked

from Laguna Beach, Calif., during
the month before I came along
on February 7, 21, and 28, script
loose, quick across hotel letterhead
opened, unfolded, refolded, slid
back into envelopes with cancelled
stamps commemorating whooping
cranes, polio, and architects, first

read by a British, recently immigrated
unlikely Edmontonian, who ever since
kept them among the clutter in the top
drawer of his scratched wooden desk
the letters themselves enveloped by
a used business #10 his pocketknife
slit open on its right edge, the right
always his edge, every envelope

he'd ever opened slit on exactly
that edge, more than ten boxes
of slit-open envelopes stacked
in his garage, the envelopes
from cashed paycheques inside
ordered by date, deposit slip
and stubs of utility bills he paid
at the teller slid inside with matching

paycheque stub, a once still-growing
bimonthly reliquary he annotated
with his T-square-level, caterpillar
cursive to leave a straightforward
paper trail, her letters caught under
remnant mid-century routing slips
and a slide rule he used to round up
or down every calculation, her own

reckonings in abeyance but waiting
for new eyes to scan them, my eyes
slipping behind the reading glasses
of a still young man who maybe
married too early, who would
surreptitiously open anything
personal addressed to him at work—
Shell Oil Co., Box 100, Edmonton

Alta., 5—written in a loose, quick
hand on envelopes containing letters
opened, unfolded, refolded, slid
past by a father of two young girls
husband to their mother expecting
a third child no one in her extended
family knew was coming—we only
knew you were here, said an aunt

THE LOST EPISTLES OF MARGIE

on my mother's side, once you had
come—I won't write anything to
make things go tits up, the first letter
promised, jotted down weeks before
my mother's water broke just after
Part I of *War and Peace* stopped
marching towards Moscow, retreating
to Maternity as the lights came up

for intermission and the concession
opened at the Paramount Theatre
on Jasper Avenue—Margie
by the third letter sunning topless
on a balcony with incautious views
of the orange groves she'd toured
with the old folks complained
about for pages in the second

they always took all the deckchairs
around the pool at the resort hotel
where she'd checked in to think
a breeder who'd midwifed our dog
one year before I came along—
I scan the obituaries every day
in the *Journal*, one sister said
as she turned sixty-one, to see if

she's passed—we've had a passable
year together, Margie wrote, but
I've still got a good marriage
with Bill to fall back on when
push comes to shove—I grew up
loving that dog, how he rested his
golden paws on the lowered bars
of my crib, how I learned to walk

pulled along clutching his choker
in my determined fist, a prize
spaniel whose puppyhood kept
her in the ribbons until a visitor
who doffed his hat, his not-yet
unexpectedly pregnant wife
and their two watchful daughters
stopped in at her kennels, she

the owner and signatory of three
letters, the divorce laws balanced
more in his favour until the mother
of his unborn child effected her
own kind of law, how could it be
otherwise, before I came along from
one enveloping void to another, *it was
all new, all over,* I'd later write, only

seeing what this really meant after
I'd read those letters dashed off
loosely, quickly among the orange
groves where I'd have liked to lie back
in a deckchair I hadn't known worked
best if laid flat, let it dawn why no one
knew I was coming, why I am not
named for one grandfather (his

dad) but for the other (hers), truth
an orange to be peeled, scraped
clean of pulp before divided
and eaten slowly, the narrative
unoriginal but common enough
an old story: a man with a wife
meets another woman who breeds
dogs, goes to Laguna Beach, Calif., to

think—a digression undermining
the plot by the time I have put pen
to paper, sheets of hotel stationery
dropping into something as orangey
as twilight when, forty-eight years
later, I first read what someone
named Margie had written of three
times during that year's shortest

month, having guessed she could no
longer sun without her top on a balcony
to ignore thinking things through
before driving north toward the cold
who may now be as dead as he is
ashes laid to rest next to Bill before
or after the top drawer was pulled
open fifteen years ago, her letters

read for the first time in decades
old age and his prostate cutting
short what he added or subtracted
from a shambolically filed
unverifiable history they could have
wished they might be forgiven for not
letting it die with them, a tangent
his desk couldn't give up alone

her letters keeping him company
as he moved from city to city
and desk to desk, from junior
assistant to systems analyst
his arithmetic stack of boxed
date-ordered paystubs in right
edge-opened envelopes packed
so neatly they still overshadow

what he could not account for
leaving him always in arrears
although he'd torn himself free
he hoped, each date-stamped
stub saved after being folded
creased, and ripped down a
pre-existing perforated line to
part himself from what was due

kept on hand to remind him, when
compelled, he knew how to let go
if he had to, and he had to let go
Part II of *War and Peace* still playing
at the Paramount, two daughters still
willing to talk to him while he leafed
through day-old issues of the *Journal*
in the basement, a baby still to be born

pulled out while feeling around an as-yet
unemptied top drawer for something
to write on, not about, the unread
story whose currency I hadn't felt
hold me below the surface all at once
read back in, exposing the holes
I had never known I should plumb
each with a wholeness I can now fill in.

8.

Grief

Frances Rooney

My mother was vacuuming, her back to me, as I went into the living room. She stopped, straightened, squared her shoulders, stared out the window, and said, "Grief is nothing but self-pity." As quietly as I could, I retreated into the kitchen.

I said nothing, but I knew somehow that she was wrong. I was ten, and even if I had been able to say how or why she was wrong, it was never safe to disagree with my mother. And knowing she was wrong didn't help with the guilt, the ugly shadow of self-pity, that since that day has come to me with every loss.

I always protected myself the best I could from my mother. By the time she died (she was sixty-seven, I was twenty-six), I was too tired, too guilty, and too drained of pity for self and others to feel anything but relief. Not a tear. Not then. Not since. When a friend asked if I wasn't grieving, I replied, "I grieved that relationship while I was in it."

My father lived another thirty years, remarried after fifteen, enjoyed his new wife's huge, raucous Italian family and their many dinners and parties. So unlike the isolation, the depressions, the accusations and condemnations, the smouldering, suffocating silences and raging explosions, his and my mother's, when it was just the three of us, they locked in that poisoned marriage, I trapped in the fallout.

After my father died, his wife put his watch on her wrist, packed some of her clothes, handed me the house key as she walked out the door, and said, "Deal with it." She never looked back, never spoke to me again.

In his papers in the basement I found pictures of his high school girlfriends, hundreds of neatly folded brown paper bags, hand tools, a

1930 Louis Vuitton trunk, empty and mouldy.

A birth certificate, handwritten, but nonetheless real:

Girl
b. July 1
Parents: my parents
Date: Ten months after my parents married, fifteen years before I was born
Signed: Illegible, MD
Stamped with a hospital stamp
Scrawled across the bottom:
d. July 4

Irrelevantly, I noted that she lived from Canada Day to Independence Day, days of celebration in my two countries.

No one had given her a name.

My father had kept the paper. Because he thought it necessary to keep an official document, however informal, or did he actually care about this little girl? I could never tell with him. Much of the time, he was the ghost hiding behind his newspaper. Barely there. But then, he kept my baby teeth, so maybe he did notice that he had children. Maybe it did matter to him. Was it possible that this death mattered so deeply that he couldn't speak of it? Was that why he left this one piece of paper out of place, on his workbench, in his otherwise precisely organized retreat?

There in that basement, I named her. Sarah. My big sister I'd never known existed.

This baby, born, died, and never spoken of, could help explain so much. My mother's demands for perfection. Her desperate attempts to protect me from every danger. And every joy. Her campaign to control my every move, my every thought. The hairbrush she pummelled me with. The words she also pummelled me with, many of them before I knew what they meant: Liar, slut, thief, sneak, cheat, monster, fat slob, ugly, disgusting, destroyer of her life, a child she loved but found impossible to like.

Her favourite: I'll make you wish you'd never been born. And its variation: I'll make you wish you were dead.

Her request: Make my life worth living today. Twice I replied to that by saying as gently as possible that I couldn't do that, only she could. The first time she sent me for my father's belt. The second time she shrank into herself and sobbed. The belt hurt like hell. The sobbing broke my heart.

Some mothers whose child dies do all these things.

Probably nothing can explain everything that did and did not go on in that house, and it would be criminal to ask a doomed baby to carry that burden.

But how could *Girl, b. July 1, d. July 4,* my Sarah, not be a factor? How could burying her twice, once in an anonymous hospital mass burial ground and once in my mother's soul, not shift everything? Her child whom she could not even name. Who has no grave, no marker, whose very existence my mother, her mother, colluded in erasing by never mentioning her, denying her own grief, punishing herself for it, writing it off as self-pity. How could trying to do the impossible, how could all the lies, secrets, and silences not drive her half mad?

My world shook, cracked, and split.

I had always thought my mother just hated me. Now I could see, or at least glimpse, her struggle, her vulnerability, her terror, her love for me, so often talked about but almost never felt. And there, protected by the distance of time, the words came: You were wrong, mother. Far from being self-pity, grief is love and tenderness, remembered and cherished. It's a warm blanket. And it's shattered glass shredding your insides.

Finally, I was able to pity my mother (much as I wanted her not to need it). Beyond the pity, that moment let my soul connect me with my lost sister. I have to hope that it also helped reunite my mother with her lost daughter.

And with perhaps a bit less than the usual guilt, this adult, who had been the child my mother so mistakenly terrorized, could grieve. For them, for each of us, for the three of us together, and I suppose for my father too, and for all that we had missed.

9.

Understanding My Face

Michelle Poirier Brown

At the time of my sister's call, there was much I was asleep to. I was thirty-nine and had moved to Victoria from the prairies. I still felt a mild cognitive displacement from the landscape.

That first year, I sometimes drove my car to the lookout on Mount Tolmie, where I could follow the sight lines past the nearby houses, out across the industrial lands and the shipyard, to the Strait of Juan de Fuca. I'd stare at the Olympic Mountains and imagine I could see through to the prairies. I ached to see into a dry horizon.

After ten years, I was no longer startled to hear water fountains during snow falls and knew to expect crocuses in January and towers of chestnut blossoms in May.

And after a recent, homesick walk in a rare thunderstorm, I resigned myself to the permanent absence of lightning.

I wasn't from here, but it was home.

It was evening when my sister called. I was at home, on a sofa I'd bought at Goodwill. I was reading to our five-year-old while my husband was in the bathroom bathing the baby and I interrupted my reading to answer the phone.

"Guess what," my sister opened. "We're Indians."

We are not a close family, and the distance between my sister and me is both emotional and geographic. We grew up in Selkirk, Manitoba. Dad worked in the sewers at the steel mill, and Mom ran an informal kindergarten in space rented in the basement of the Lutheran Church. My father's second job was also at the church, as a janitor. On weekends, he drove a taxi.

Singled out for her striking intelligence and reverent ambitions, my sister was enticed to leave home to attend a religious boarding school in Saskatchewan and had then gone to McGill, intending to become a missionary doctor. She left for school when I was six. We rarely spoke.

My sister plunged into an account of her recent trip from Sacramento, California, to the village of Ste. Anne, set on the spirit-levelling grain fields of Manitoba, where our great-grandmother is buried. My sister, the family genealogist, enjoys precision. She was after a death date and to find it, she needed a gravestone. To her, it was a detail worth the distance.

"I knew I was in the right place," she said. "But I couldn't find her grave."

She said a groundskeeper noticed her and asked who she was looking for.

"Rosaline Curtaz."

"Oh, you won't find her here," he told her.

She protested that she had reliable information that our great-grandmother was buried in Ste. Anne. I could imagine the nature of this protest. My sister draws a fine line between right and righteous.

"She's buried in Ste. Anne," the groundskeeper said. "But she's not here. You're going to have to go to the Indian reserve."

This was news.

I hung up the phone. My daughter had left the sofa to join her sister and stepfather in the bathroom. I followed her.

"You'll be surprised by what I just learned," I said. "My great-grandmother was an Indian."

My husband was smearing the baby's bottom with a honey-scented beeswax cream. He lifted his head to look at me, quizzical.

"This is something you just learned?"

My husband's practiced, measured manner of speaking was one he managed to use with warmth. Tall, bearded, and in need of a haircut, he strove to be even-handed more than handsome. He was as likely to take the children to a rally as to a folk music festival.

I recounted the phone call.

"I don't get it," he said.

"She says our great-grandmother is buried on an Indian reserve in Manitoba. To be buried on a reserve, you need to be a status Indian."

"What I don't get is that this is news." He put the night liner in the cotton diaper and slipped it under the baby. "You didn't know you were Aboriginal?"

I tilted my head at him.

"You did?"

His voice took on a gentler tone.

"I always understood you to have Aboriginal heritage. I wondered why you never mentioned it."

I intensified the question mark I gripped in my expression.

"I grew up in Prince Rupert," he reminded me. "Dad was a doctor with the federal government. We had people from reserves staying in our home all the time."

I felt I was meeting a part of my husband for the first time, as though a familiar stranger were fastening Velcro on my daughter's diaper cover.

"They were waiting to go into the hospital," he explained. "Or they were in town because someone in their family was in the hospital."

My relationship with my husband was not much older than the child he was diapering and I had not met his father. It hadn't occurred to me that he'd been a general practitioner whose patients lived on Indian reserves.

"Why didn't you ever bring it up?" I asked.

"It just felt unnecessary. Like pointing out your shoe size."

The next day, I had tea with my neighbour. I mentioned the story to her and received another blank response.

"It always seemed pretty obvious to me."

Colleagues at work? I hadn't been passing as white with any of them.

I stopped telling the story. It was no longer amusing.

Until my sister took an interest in genealogy, our family history on our father's side was embedded in the stories his mother told us. My father's parents lived in a four-room, basementless house; the plumbing was limited to a kitchen, a bathroom sink, and a toilet. My grandmother did her laundry at the laundromat and washed herself with a cloth. She took great delight in telling tall tales. She would lean in close to us, her voice softened only slightly, and say, "When you're sixteen, I'll tell you about when I was a prostitute in Chicago." It was a jab at our innocence, a joke so she could tell anyone who did not yet know that she had lived in an orphanage run by the Grey Nuns from the time of her mother's death when she was three until her marriage at age nineteen.

That she "grew up in a convent" and that her father was Belgian were the two things that my grandmother insisted the world know.

An oil burning stove in the living room heated much of my grandparents' house. The toilet in the back was always cold in winter, and my grandmother would put a hot water bottle in her bed to warm it for me if I slept over. She kept the door to the second bedroom closed. We called it the cold room. A room-wide closet behind heavy curtains held jars of jams and apricots, stewed rhubarb, pickled beets, and canned beans. Also, an assortment of dime-store trinkets: tiny dolls with immovable legs, a box with three crayons, a tiny plastic man with a paper parachute. We would visit every Sunday night and, occasionally, when we were putting on our coats, my grandmother would ask, "Did you get any rubbish?" It was our cue to go into the cold room and choose from the little items on hand.

We knew our mother hated it when we brought home rubbish. My grandmother didn't care.

Dead relatives are full of surprises. My sister's ongoing search for death dates turned up a very much alive great-aunt Olga, sister to our grandmother, another daughter of the woman I understood to be buried in an Indian reserve graveyard. Olga was ninety-four and living in a care home in Edmonton, Alberta.

The home was operated by the Grey Nuns. Olga had, herself, been a Grey Nun and, according to my sister, had retired only recently and reluctantly. The receptionist made a call to her floor. Olga was at prayers, but I was welcome to wait for her in the dining room. From my table, I watched visitors make their way through the cafeteria food line and wondered if we would have lunch.

I hadn't called ahead. I'm shy and it seemed easier not to. I did not know the status of my great-aunt's health, whether I would even be allowed to see her. I felt I had been propelled here by a question I didn't know how to formulate. Olga was the last person alive who could open the silence that stood like a stone in the middle of our family. What did it mean that our great-grandmother was buried on an Indian reserve? Why didn't we know this?

Olga arrived to the dining room in a wheelchair, her white head bent towards her lap. Her stockinged legs ended in a pair of orthopaedic sandals. She turned her face sideways to look at me.

"Aunt Olga? I'm Michelle. Frances's granddaughter."

Olga acknowledged my greeting with a slight nod, then turned and touched the wrist of the aide who had wheeled her to the table. She wanted the wheelchair foot plates raised out of the way. And a cup of coffee.

"I've come from Victoria to visit you," I said.

"Are you Catholic?"

My mouth emptied. It had not occurred to me I'd be asked this. I was tempted to lie but knew I'd be busted if she asked where I'd been confirmed or made a reference in Latin that I didn't understand.

"No," I said. "We were raised Lutheran. I went to bible school."

My great-aunt grimaced. "That's not going to save your soul."

The aide delivered the mug of coffee and left. I thought I would wait until my aunt was ready for a refill before asking where I, too, could get a cup.

"Well, we can talk about that if you'd like."

Olga shrugged.

"They told me at reception you were at prayers."

"Yes, I still keep the office, you know. Even the middle of the night."

I wished I were Catholic so I could draw on some kind of common reference point.

Aunt Olga looked at me again, taking me in. There was a softness to her, not just the slack cheek and round belly companionate of age but a gentleness that spoke of modesty and tempered habits. Nonetheless, her eyes confronted me with a recalcitrance that seemed directed to me for mysterious cause.

"I'd love to hear about your career. I understand you worked for many years up north."

"It was a profession," she said, emphasizing the word but also warming slightly.

She had served nearly seventy years as a teacher, first in Grand Rapids, Manitoba, then in Fort Liard and Łutselk'e in the Northwest Territories, moving progressively northwards until, in her eighties, she was in Iqaluit, her last post.

"It was our most northern community," she said. "I didn't come here until I was eighty-eight."

"That's a lot of service."

I raised my hopes we would cross soon to territory I knew how to navigate and that her tongue would warm to storytelling—the way my family had always found its way to each other after an absence.

But great-aunt Olga was a reticent storyteller. She talked a little about her life, saying nothing about teaching, but recalled with amusement that as the midwife, she would sometimes be bundled onto a dog sled in the dark of night to attend a birth. Imagining how she must have looked—her long habit tucked beneath blankets as the dog team whisked her across the snow—made her chuckle, her deeply curved back bent even further in amusement. She chuckled, too, at the memory of the mothers who sometimes came to her for parenting advice.

When I asked about her childhood, she spoke with affection about the German couple who raised her. They had lived on the farm next door and childless themselves adopted her. They'd longed for a daughter, she said, and treated her as their own.

Even this line of conversation, though, was cursory. Her overriding interest was in my upbringing, and she returned again to her concern that I was not Catholic.

"Tomorrow, there will be a veneration of the Holy Eucharist," she said. "Maybe seeing the body of our Lord will bring you to Christ."

I assured her I would come.

I tried to steer the conversation back to reminiscences and asked if she had any memories of her mother. She began to speak again about her adoptive German mother.

"Actually," I said, "I'd like to hear more about your birth mother."

"I don't want to talk about that dirty half-breed," she replied. And that was that. She pushed her chair from the table and turned away.

I rose. "Would you like help getting back to your room?" I asked.

She dismissed me with a gesture, walking her chair towards the hall with surprising briskness.

Our visit was over.

Although I did sit next to her at chapel the next morning, we exchanged few words. After the liturgy, she returned to her room and would spend no further time with me.

I went home with the feeling I had come face to face with something that, while not exactly a heritage, was still an inheritance. I still had no words for what had been unspeakable for at least three generations.

Experiences that, before my sister's call, had been mysterious to me began to make more sense. I have a vivid childhood memory of buying candy at a gas station—and the cashier asking if I was Chinese, the face behind the till bright and open, only to collapse when I replied "no," my brow furled with confusion. More recently, I had been just as baffled when on a work trip to Prince George, I had been greeted in the lobby with a cheerful hello and an outstretched hand by a woman in a smartly tailored wine-red suit who assumed I was there to register for an Aboriginal women in business conference.

The most striking of these experiences had been the exchange with a man I knew from work. Garry and I knew each other from the negotiating table for the Columbia Basin Accord. The parties were focussed on drafting legislation to create the corporation that would receive and manage the $515 million endowment coming to the Columbia Basin. My job was to shepherd the document through legal and treasury review and to produce the notes needed for legislative debate. I was to listen, keep track of details, and solve small problems.

Garry's job was to represent the people who had lived in the watershed for ten thousand years, whose lives had been irreversibly altered by the damming and the flooding of the Columbia River Basin in the 1960s, and who had lost the salmon that had been the keystone of their culture, identity, and survival. He was hired by the Ktunaxa-Kinbasket to find them a deal that could right a wrong.

Barrel-chested and soft spoken, he was a thoughtful man, not only well educated but also well-schooled.

I often felt tongue-tied around Garry—if, say, we found ourselves at the coffee creamer counter at the same time. Or, if I did speak, I'd feel anxious about what I'd said.

Once, on our way back to Vancouver from a negotiating meeting in Castlegar, Garry and I found ourselves seated next to each other on the plane. We made awkward small talk.

I stumbled further into conversation, hoping I would learn from this opportunity to hear Garry's perspective on the negotiations. In response to something I said, Garry stated, "Yeah, well, that's because you're Cree."

To me, it was a statement out of the blue. I asserted flatly that I had no Aboriginal heritage.

"Yeah, I know you think that," Garry countered. "And you're Cree."

This thing that people saw in my face. Yeah, I'd noticed.

I'd noticed that there were days when I would look in the mirror and say to myself, "Looks like you're having an ugly day. You look like an Indian."

I'd been saying this to myself for as long as I could remember.

After my sister's call, my husband encouraged me to experiment with identity. When filling out our daughter's school registration forms in September, he answered the question about Aboriginal heritage with a checkmark beside "yes." I signed up for the Aboriginal employee newsletter at work and put myself on the Métis Association mailing list.

Around this time, the BC Government Employees Union distributed a poster promoting greater awareness of the Métis as an extant Aboriginal nation. On the poster were three young faces, beautifully photographed against a bright white background; one was as red haired and freckled as our older daughter. "Métis," the headline read, "The Invisible People."

I brought one home and taped it to the outside of the bathroom door at a child friendly height.

It seemed there ought to be more I should do. I noticed the Métis Association offered Cree language lessons, but I did not feel drawn to them—as though trying to learn a few words of Cree would mean trying to be someone I was not. And besides, was I even really Métis? An invitation to a Métis celebration promised songs I'd never heard, dances I could not dance, and unfamiliar foods I could not name. It invited me to wear a sash I did not own. If I was going to reach into my childhood and revive the cultural practices of an earlier generation, I'd be far more likely to sign the children up for Ukrainian dance classes and try to improve the texture of my perogy dough. If I was going to find a connection to a lost heritage on my father's side, I needed a place I could feel more naturally at home.

I grew up in a craft-oriented family. So when I saw an ad for a weekend drum-making workshop, I signed up.

The workshop was held in a studio space that an Aboriginal art collective rented in Victoria's warehouse area. We used a dried deer hide that we picked up on Friday and soaked overnight in the bathtub. Saturday morning, we gathered in a room equipped with three large wooden, standing-height tables. The studio smelled lightly of sawdust, paper, varnish, and glue.

I was the last to finish my drum. I was pleased with the result. Its sides were smooth, and the skin was an even, fluted edge around the back of the drum. Our teacher, an Elder from Beecher Bay, instructed me on how to tie the lace, crisscrossing it to make a hand hold.

"Tomorrow," he said, "we will learn if this drum has a good voice."

The next day, the Elder lifted each person's drum and struck it with a beater. Some drums had not been stretched evenly, some not tightly enough. A few rang out beautifully; a few were dull.

The Elder raised my drum, struck it, and smiled.

"You have made a good drum."

"Beginner's luck," I said, glancing away.

"This is your first drum?" he asked.

"Yes. I've never made a drum before."

"Then you will need to give this drum away."

I felt stunned.

"Who do I give it to?" I asked, trying to keep the edge of loss out of my voice.

"That's your choice," the Elder answered. "But if this is your first drum, you need to give it away."

I returned to the studio three weeks later for the second of the summer drum workshops. I decided I would make a second drum and then give both drums to my daughters. I wrote my phone number on the signup sheet for a fall workshop the Elder was giving in Beecher Bay for drum making with a fresh hide.

No date was set for it; we would be notified when there were hides. But no notice came. I hung the two drums on the living room wall. I bought deer leather for beaters, but it remains folded in the craft supply box.

My thoughts about inherited identity gradually fell silent. My grandmother's placement in a Catholic orphanage at age three marked a rip in the family fabric that seemed insurmountable. I came to question why it mattered. Eventually, I kept forgetting.

All the same, in addition to the mark on the school form, I ticked the Aboriginal box on the 1996 census as well. It seemed more of a political act than anything else, feeling that counting mattered.

Something in our family had disappeared, and although I felt I lacked the heart to reclaim it, I also insisted, in this small way, on acknowledging our continuing existence. It seemed to me the whole matter would slip into obscurity, a footnote on the family story.

And then, I went to university at Royal Roads.

There were about fifty of us in the inaugural class of the Conflict Analysis and Management Program, among them Carrie Reid, a member of the Coast Salish, and Dave Pranteau, a Cree from Manitoba. Both of them identified themselves by nation and home community during introductions. It was the first time I witnessed this practice.

I sat with Dave at dinner that first night. Carrie happened to sit across from us.

I mentioned to Dave that I'd been told my great-grandmother was buried on an Indian reserve in Manitoba.

"So you're Cree then," Dave said, as if settling a matter.

"Apparently." I said. "I only found out a couple of years ago."

Carrie interjected. "I wondered why you didn't say anything during introductions."

There it was again—a statement that acknowledged something in me that I, myself, didn't recognize.

Yet something had shifted. Both Carrie and Dave had spoken as if I were standing in the rain and could come inside if I wanted. As if the doorway were obvious.

The last weekend of residency, Dave's wife, Bernadette, came to spend time with him at the university. She asked how the experience of embracing an Aboriginal identity was going for me. I said I welcomed it, but that the question of how to introduce myself still perplexed me.

"You could identify as Métis," Bernadette offered.

"Or," Dave interjected, "you could make the whole thing easier and just say you're Cree."

"I'm allowed to do that?" I asked. I was assured I was.

Over the years, I have come to understand that things are more complicated than that. It's difficult to explain. Identity always is.

Yes, I could adopt the practice of identifying myself, stating the seemingly obvious, putting everyone at ease. Except when I did that, I was, true to custom, asked where I was from. A question that instantly revealed what I was not, which is a member of a community, a place I could say I was from. To identify as Aboriginal is to identify, inherently, with specific land and the rights conferred by an unbroken bond with that specific territory. To be Cree is to be Cree from somewhere. To be Cree but without community is to be Cree without Cree culture—which is to say, not Cree at all.

Or so it seemed to me.

Dave had studied for many years with a Cree Elder, a pipe carrier named Peter Ochiese, which included helping Peter run a fasting camp at Moose Lake, Manitoba. Dave said that there was an Elder at camp qualified to lead a naming ceremony. If I came, he would arrange for me to meet with him.

I first flew to Winnipeg, then took a provincial airline a further one thousand kilometres north to The Pas. Dave met me at the airport for the two-and-a-half-hour drive to the camp.

On Dave's advice, I'd brought tobacco and bright lengths of cloth to hang in the trees to mark the occasion of the naming. I brought money, too, but I suspect Dave augmented my payment for the name catcher with money of his own. Dave instructed me that I was expected to send a payment to the name catcher to mark the anniversary. I sent a cheque for the first two anniversaries, but stopped after the third, when the cheque was returned to sender unopened and without a forwarding address.

The weather was dry, but the woods were cool, especially at night. The camp included a large teepee for ceremonies and a sweat lodge, where my naming ceremony would take place. I was apprehensive about how I would find the heat and steam. In the end, I sat through the ceremony outside the lodge. I was menstruating and custom dictated I could not enter.

I was heartsick at this. I'd been tempted not to mention anything about menstruating. But I wasn't there as a tourist. I was there to lay claim to an identity I'd been told I was entitled to embrace. The rules that applied to Cree people applied to me. I was given a place to sit opposite the entrance, near where the firekeeper heated the rocks.

From where I sat, I could not hear the prayers but I could, from time to time, hear the participants call out in Cree to the firekeeper.

In between changing the rocks, the firekeeper engaged me in

conversation. Was I Cree?

"Yes," I said. "At least I think I am. People keep telling me I'm Cree."

"Cree people?" he asked.

"Yes."

"Then you're Cree."

There was no announcement when my name was decided. I learned it in conversational tones. My name was *kîsikakohp*. From Cree to English, *kîsik* translates as sky, *akohp* as blanket. Skyblanket. "Skyblanket Woman," Dave said.

Later, Bernadette taught me that a name is a medicine and a teacher. If I were fortunate, I would learn how to draw on the name when needed. That this would happen was not something I could count on. There were many people who received a name, herself included, who spent many years wondering about its meaning. I would be lucky if a medicine emerged for me.

Several months after my naming ceremony, I had a dream in which I was high above a forest, the treetops like a carpet pattern, a silvery-brown thread of river running through it. At this great height, the sun passed a caress across my back like a warm welcome. The moon, too, circled by behind me, inviting me to turn around, to look outwards into dark space lit with stars.

10.

Paired Secrets

Ann Davis

On Christmas eve, 1916, a Sunday, my uncle Will was found dead in the apartment in which he had been keeping his mistress. It was a scandal, for Will had a wife and two daughters waiting for him at home. An attempt was made to paper over the tragedy. Both the *Ottawa Citizen* and the *Ottawa Journal* ran prominent stories about the sudden death of Mr. W.P. Davis, claiming, in identical copy, that he "had risen about 7:30, with the intention of attending 8 o'clock mass. In the process of dressing, he became suddenly ill." Those details may have been true. What was left unsaid was that he was not at home, at 407 Wilbrod Street, in the house his father had built for the couple as a wedding present. Invariably, the scandal leaked out.

Problems were not totally unexpected. Will's wife, Agnes Scott, had secrets of her own. For six years, from 1897 to 1903, Agnes quietly wrote society gossip columns for the *Ottawa Free Press* and *Saturday Night*. In *Saturday Night,* a Toronto weekly, she signed her articles Amaryllis, a flamboyant flower or a Greek female name that means "to sparkle." In the *Ottawa Free Press,* a daily, she was the Marchioness, after Dickens's cheeky maidservant in *The Old Curiosity Shop,* who Dickens described as "taking a limited view of society through the keyholes of doors." These elaborate pseudonyms were not unusual for the times in which the reporting of society was deemed almost as important as the reporting of politics. In *Saturday Night,* the powerful society editor, Grace Denison, called herself "Lady Gay," whereas Mrs. Alexander McIntyre, in the Ottawa *Daily Citizen* was "Frills." The true identities of these authors were generally known, unlike that of Amaryllis or the Marchioness, for Agnes was careful never to reveal her real name, as protection in small, gossipy Ottawa.

The writer of good gossip columns had to have access to the most tasty news. Agnes did. She was urbane, engaging, and deliciously irreverent. Though not a great beauty, and certainly not rich, she was very well connected. By the 1890s, the Scott family was one of the most consequential in town. Agnes's uncle, R.W. Scott, as mayor of Bytown, championed Ottawa as the best place for the capital of confederated Canada. He subsequently became a senator and a cabinet minister. Her father, Allan John Scott, died young, and her mother, Margaret Heron, with Agnes, moved to a large, austere house at 47 Daly Avenue, where there was no furnace and no bathroom. Despite these reduced circumstances, Agnes, the flamboyant flower, participated actively in society. The centre of the social capital was Government House, when the governor general and his wife—for at the time, all governors general were male and married—were in attendance. Agnes had privileged entrée here. In the Dufferins' time, the 1880s, she was one of the very select group who was invited to participate in evenings of amateur theatrics.

From within Government House, Agnes observed the Aberdeens, who arrived in Ottawa to take the viceregal position in 1893. Lord Aberdeen, according to Amaryllis, had the unfortunate habit "of trying to look as if nobody was looking at him." Lady Aberdeen, in contrast, often acted as if she was the proconsul, for she aggressively used the office as an instrument for social reform. She was upset by Ottawa manners and did not hesitate to make her negative views known. The old select dinner parties for two dozen or so, in which Amaryllis had participated, were replaced by huge, unprogrammed affairs over which Lady Aberdeen presided like a monarch. Amaryllis was caustic: "Her Excellency always had a little page, sometimes two, dressed in the costumes of Louis XIV. They carry her train and run around during dinner carrying notes and messages." Agnes, however, protected her anonymity, such that Lady Aberdeen consulted her about a tinsmith who could make imitation chain mail for a costume party. Agnes recommended Mr. Jolicoeur, the family of which established a much-loved hardware store on Beechwood Avenue.

Lady Aberdeen was justly concerned about the plight of poorer women and children. Her answer was to call upon the women of Canada to form a lobby group, which, in 1894, became the National

Council of Women. Amaryllis, never a great fan of Lady Aberdeen's methods, was a firm and eventually vocal supporter of social reform. At Christmas 1897, Agnes wrote of "the plight of little sick children in the hospitals" and, in late October 1898, just before the Aberdeens left Canada, Agnes was one of the five Ottawa ladies invited to accompany the Countess to visit the women and girls who worked as stitchers and binders in the Government Printing Bureau. That same year, she left no doubt as to her fervent support for the National Council of Women, writing, through the keyhole, that "The best men in the land are the men who admire and help.... It is the man—you know him—who says 'I don't let my wife do this' and 'I don't let my wife do that!' who is loud in his condemnation of the Council. Beware of him."

Agnes found Lord and Lady Minto, the next viceregal couple, to be rather more to her taste. Maintaining her insider status at Rideau Hall, she participated in an intimate firelit tea—"hot toast, muffins and bath buns"—to preview the newfangled apparatus, a gramophone. But for Amaryllis and Ottawa society, the best fun was keeping up with "Minto's Folly," Lola Powell. About half Minto's age, Lola was tall and dark, with blue eyes. She was also an accomplished flirt, known at the time as "chaffing." Minto was smitten. By June 1899, we learn of a splendid canoeing picnic down the Ottawa River. Agnes was not among the party, but one of her sources was.

The young woman who had the honour of being paddled by Lord Minto was Miss Lola Powell. His excellency has a fine little canoe and is as expert with a paddle as any Canadian. He enjoys it immensely, too. While the flotilla of canoes was drifting down the river, some rain fell, but "when you're in the shade with a pretty maid, it doesn't much matter what the weather may do."

Lady Minto, away at the time, was not amused.

Although the goings on at Rideau Hall were endlessly entertaining, Agnes did not stint on reporting the activities of political Ottawa. A Liberal, she quickly celebrated Laurier's electoral victory in 1896: "Le roi est mort; vive le roi." She recorded that Lady Laurier "gives a card party nearly every afternoon and loves best to entertain her intimate friends, all of whom are of the feminine gender." This rather cool assessment is in contrast to her evaluation of Madame Emilie Lavergne, who was either Laurier's mistress or a close friend. She described Emilie as "a brilliant woman called by many the Canadian Lady

Chesterfield." Lady Chesterfield was Benjamin Disraeli's intimate friend and confidante. Were Laurier and Emilie lovers? That was certainly debated in Ottawa society. The story is further complicated: As Emilie's son Armand grew up, he developed an uncanny likeness to Laurier. Whatever Armand's paternity—he never knew who his father was—Emilie was Laurier's central teacher of manners. She taught him how to be graceful, sophisticated, and accomplished, which were important traits for him in his political life in English Canada.

In April 1903, Agnes's gossipy articles ended abruptly and without notice. Surely not coincidentally, it was then that Agnes and Will were married. In *Saturday Night*, Lady Gay unusually assessed her writing companion: "The engagement of Miss Agnes Scott is announced in Ottawa. Miss Scott is the niece of the Hon. R.W. Scott, and she is a person of rarely bright mentality, and *savoir-faire*." As a final journalistic coup, it was probably Agnes herself who wrote the unbylined account in the *Free Press* of their quiet wedding in St. Joseph's Church:

> The bride, given away by her uncle, the Secretary of State, wore a smart and becoming costume of pale pastel blue broadcloth.... The bodice was lavishly trimmed with the Russian lace. It opened over a vest of white lace mounted on chiffon, and the wide bell sleeves were slashed over a bouffant undersleeve of white chiffon. The French hat was of pleated tulle and fancy straw in a Gainsborough shape and trimmed with a magnificent white ostrich plume.

On her wrist, she wore "an elegant Egyptian gold bracelet, studded with baroque pearls," the groom's present. Other wedding presents included a jewel box lined with gold from Lady Minto and silver salt cellars and a mustard pot from Mrs. C.A.E. Harriss. After the ceremony, the couple left immediately for "New York, Naples and an extended tour through Italy and central Germany." While covering the wedding extensively, neither the *Free Press* nor *Saturday Night* acknowledged that the bride was their best-read columnist. Agnes, as well, never gave herself away.

From the bride, we turn to the groom. Who was Will P. Davis and why would Agnes, who delighted in exposing the pretensions she saw around her, marry him? Will's father, Michael Patrick Davis (1849–1932), my grandfather, was widely intelligent, successful, self-assured, generous, and a deeply religious Roman Catholic. With his brother, he ran MP and JT Davis Contractors, a firm that built the Windsor train station in Montreal, 1770 kilometres of track for the transcontinental railway and, famously, the second Quebec Bridge. MP—he was always known by his initials—enjoyed having money and spending it. Family lore recounts that he made and lost three fortunes. With ever an astute eye on politics, he befriended both federal political parties. The night of the 1911 election, Prime Minister Laurier, a Liberal, spent the night with the Davis's in their corner suite in the Chateau Frontenac in Quebec City. In 1932, when MP died, Prime Minister Borden, a Conservative, walked just behind the Davis boys in his friend's funeral procession. MP married and produced four children, one of which was Will. This was known as the first family. In 1910, now a widower, MP married again, to my grandmother, and they had two sons, the younger of which was my father. This was the second family.

Religion was of vital importance in the Davis family. MP's two daughters were sent to the Sacred Heart Convent for school, as was my grandmother. The three girls were good friends. So the fact that Agnes was Irish Catholic, attending St. Joseph's Church as did the Davis family, spoke in her favour. Certainly, in Ottawa in 1897, the talk in church was of the visit of the apostolic delegate Merry Del Val, who came from the Vatican to attempt to help the problem of the Manitoba Schools Question. MP gave a grand dinner party in the young prelate's honour, a party for which MP, in an excess of exuberance, commissioned Birks in Montreal to produce a special set of dinner ware, decorated with the papal insignia in gold. Unfortunately, the plates' slip was defective and many of them broke. I still have a few. Agnes might have been at that dinner, as she wrote perceptively about the Monseigneur, noting that although he "talks a great deal, he says absolutely nothing."

It is certain that Agnes and Will had met by June 1898, for it was then that Agnes spared no ink in describing the lavish wedding of her cousin D'Arcy Scott to the eldest MP Davis daughter, Queen. D'Arcy, a lawyer, was not serious and apparently rather given to philandering. Perhaps Will was a friend of his, since they seemed to share a rather dissolute lifestyle. Will dabbled at being a stockbroker but with little success. One wonders if his father even suggested he work in the family construction company or if MP understood that this would not suit either his offspring or his business. Will was handsome, liked good clothes, as did many of the Davis men, and relied heavily on his father's purse. Sound finances were never a family strength. My grandmother used to say of my father that the only thing he knew about money was how to spend it. When Will died, he left Agnes destitute. Was Will spoiled? Undoubtedly. Amy, a cook for the second family, told me that she used to make two lemon meringue pies because one son liked hot pie and the other cold.

It was well known then, perhaps even tolerated or accepted, that wealthy men had female companions in addition to their wives. Lord Minto had his Folly, and Sir Wilfred Laurier had Madame Emilie Lavergne. MP Davis should not be excluded from this list. When my grandmother set up house with her rich husband, she brought along her companion, Miss Ding. A cousin of mine called this arrangement a mariage à trois. Once when MP bought his wife a sapphire ring, he also gave Miss Ding one. In having a mistress, Will was just following his betters. His family probably knew about his peccadillos, even if they turned a blind eye. The scandal was not that he philandered but that he was caught.

Superficially, Will and Agnes had much in common. They were both Irish Catholics, patrons of St. Joseph's Church, Liberals, and from well-connected Ottawa families. But it can't have been a happy marriage. They were fundamentally different. He was much younger, only twenty-nine when he married, while she was about thirty-eight. He was a playboy, delighting in clothes and fun, while she had to be dedicated about maintaining a covert career as a journalist. Will could rely on his father's generosity, while Agnes had to produce endless text filled with intriguing facts, colourful details, and salacious gossip. She always had to walk a careful line between preserving her anonymity and the trust of her inside social connections. Agnes, like her floral pseudonym, sparkled. Beyond her revealing social reporting, she wore a dramatic hat with a great white ostrich feather. Will, my half-uncle, was not at home often. He was weak; she was strong. They each had secrets.

*For this article, I have relied rather more heavily on Sandra Gwyn's excellent book *The Private Capital* than I would like. All quotations are taken from there. The pandemic closed many archives.

11.

May Her Memory

Nancy Issenman

The day we found out where our grandmother was buried, it was snowing heavily in Montreal. A whiteout day, when visibility becomes next to zero, and nothing is clear or distinguishable. Once the melting snow made a visit possible, my sister, cousin, and I drove up to the Mount Royal Cemetery and found her headstone. There we placed a rock, a Jewish tradition and symbol of her lasting legacy in our hearts and minds.

She was our biological grandmother, someone we had never met or even heard of while we were growing up. The grandmother we did know was Gert, married to Max, our biological grandfather. Gert met Max in a factory after they had both immigrated from Eastern Europe in the early 1900s. She was the supervisor, a formidable and tall woman of peasant stock from the Ukraine, and Max was diminutive, from Austria. When they met, Max already had two children: my mother, Belle, and her older sister, Esther. After their marriage, they had a third child together, Goldie. The narrative could have ended there and did for many years.

Belle, Esther, and her daughter Jane, my sister Susan, and I were all short and petite, despite having ample breasts. Goldie and her two children, Joan and Judy, were taller and more big boned; all had sizable feet also. Although at the time I was not able to articulate it, these cousins appeared to be from a different family than us. They wore functional clothing while we had style (so we thought); they loved libraries and we were more interested in boys and social activities. And despite a lack of religious observance, our Jewish identities were always strong, whereas they seemed to easily pass as gentile. Even their family name,

Cooper, was no give away. My sister moved with a popular crowd at school, and I had my own circle of friends. Jane, by virtue of living in NYC, was cool. Joan and Judy did not fit in that landscape, even though our two backyards joined. Despite the differences, the possibility that we cousins didn't inherit the same genes from our grandparents never occurred to anyone. In that story, we all shared Gert and Max.

The other story begins this way: Records at the cemetery show that my mother's mother passed away at the Royal Victoria Hospital in Montreal on Dec 15, 1912, a little over two weeks after birthing my mother on Nov. 28. They indicate that she was cremated—an absolute taboo for Jews—and, equally astonishing, that her ashes were not buried for another thirty years. So began the family secret that persisted until my mother found out the truth.

By accident.

Early in 1941, a day my mother was on nursing duty, a patient saw the nametag on her uniform and confided to Belle that she had known her mother. Taken aback, my mother asked the woman why she used the past tense, as her mother was still alive (so she thought). Thus, she discovered that Gert was not her biological mother. When we were adults, she finally confessed the secret to us. She recalled how she had confronted her parents but that they never talked about it again. Neither was she willing to talk with us.

So many questions. Why did my grandfather defy the Jewish custom of burying the body within as close to forty-eight hours as possible? Why cremation? Where and why did he keep her ashes for another thirty years? And why did Max and Gert never tell their children about our biological grandmother and her legacy. She must have had siblings, which meant we probably had cousins somewhere out in the world. Where were they? Our grandmother's name was Sarah Bella. Max named my mother after her in the Jewish fashion of naming the newborn after the dead. Why was this important to him even though he kept her existence hidden from us? Why was my mother so complacent about this lie?

Gert was not someone to mess with. She could be sarcastic, sometimes caustic—the one who warned me never to marry a non-Jew because "they could always turn around and call you a goddamn dirty Jew." Naturally, this had been her experience in the Ukraine but perhaps not the best way to talk to a child in Canada. By the time Jane, my sister, and I discovered the story about Sarah Bella and had become interested in her life, Max had died. Gone too were the aunts and uncles who could have shared information with us. Jane had one conversation in which Gert opened up. She learned that Gert had hired Max as a cutter in the garment factory, that she had always "had her eye on him," and that when he married Sarah Bella, she became angry and called her "a nothing." After that conversation, Jane never probed again, and the secret was zipped up once more.

Gert's resentment and mistreatment of Esther was a dark stain in our family. She considered Esther to be an unruly child and a rebellious teenager. The pluck and great sense of humour I so loved in Esther didn't win her any points with Gert. She sent Esther to nursing school in NYC so she could learn a skill and become independent, a daring justification in those days. But it was also a way to get her out of the house, since no nursing schools in Montreal would admit Jews. Esther met and married Harry—an unfortunate alcoholic who Gert and Max strongly disapproved of, resulting in their quasi disowning of Esther and Jane. Yet when Esther was ready to divorce, Gert refused to give her the money (which they could have easily afforded) and shamed her with the adage "you made your bed, now you have to sleep in it." She also forbade Esther to speak to Max, which left little doubt as to who was running that show.

Gert's preference for her own daughter, Goldie, was just as obvious. She adored Goldie's husband, Sidney, a misogynist who was often cruel and demeaning. She doted on Joan and Judy and every summer shared the country house that Max built in the Laurentians with the Cooper family. In 1960, just after Max died, Gert sold the property in private to them for a paltry sum, another secret withheld from the rest of the family. Years later, when Gert was approaching her one hundredth birthday and close to dying, Goldie unburdened herself and revealed the transaction. When she finally sold the house, the value had increased 1000 per cent, and the Cooper family was the sole inheritor. Sadly, Esther lived on social assistance in her later life.

My mother had always had a more accommodating personality as the middle child. She also had the good fortune to fall in love with a doctor of whom Max and Gert approved. After my father's death, Belle remarried, and as a wedding present, Gert offered them the last parcel of land remaining in Max's estate but on one condition—that they build a house on the property within a year. At that point, my mother and stepfather did not have the means or the desire necessary, so Gert withdrew the gift. Oh, how many times my sister and I have bemoaned the loss of a country getaway! But so much more, we feel the sting of Gert's harmful actions and her many betrayals.

As is human nature, I like to ponder what ifs. What if Sarah Bella had not died? Would I have had a grandmother who adored me and supported me unconditionally? Maybe she would have been an ally when I needed someone in my corner. Would I have fond memories of time spent with her and Max, of knowing other aunts, uncles, and cousins? Perhaps she would have shared her experiences with me of the old country. And despite her death, what if her life had been revealed to us through stories and a picture or two on the mantle? I could celebrate her life and not always feel like there is a piece of the puzzle missing—that there's a ghost I still need to meet.

Yet if Gert had not sent Esther to NYC and had my mother not followed her there to nursing school, she might never have met my father, and this story would never have been written.

With each rock placed on her gravestone, Sarah Bella remains alive in our hearts. As we say in the Jewish tradition, may her memory be a blessing.

12.

Roses

Jessie Carson

"Roses," my mother said, while we were at a grocery store looking at bouquets of flowers held in white plastic buckets. "She liked roses."

I picked up a bouquet of the red flowers while I kept half my attention on my son, Shay, ready to catch whatever he might incidentally knock over or to pounce if he escaped through the automatic sliding doors. They were wrapped in plastic; the stems were held tightly with elastic bands. With roses and snacks in hand, we walked towards the checkout. My mother had taken my son's hand, and I paid the cashier. We should have been more prepared than to find ourselves randomly buying grocery store flowers. As we left the store, Shay was desperately reaching up, trying to get his hands on those flowers. I distracted him by offering a fistful of crackers instead.

The cemetery was not too far from where we lived, only a three-hour drive. Neither of us had ever been to their graves, but my mother seemed to know the way. It had taken my mother forty-five years to find them. Once she decided, my older sister found them within an hour, even though there were no gravestones or markers, just the handwritten cemetery records. Like most small Ontario towns, there are several cemeteries, and it only took a couple of phone calls.

My mother doesn't know if there was ever a funeral. If there was one, she didn't attend. At the time of that visit, she still did not know where her other sister was buried. The women in her family were meant to disappear. My mother was too. Although their bodies are gone, their stories linger. They have not been silenced like he thought they should be. We are finding them.

"We just didn't have the words," Mom has said of the language-defying event that she went through as a child. The words took years, decades, to arrive. Hannah Arendt—a writer and political philosopher who studied the topics of power and evil—once said, "An experience makes its appearance only when it is being said." The language needed for this story appeared not because my mother's mother, two sisters, and aunt were murdered but because many women were and are still being murdered by men.

This story wasn't told to me until I was sixteen years old. To describe this event, my mother can now use words that were rarely spoken. It is only in the decades that followed the murder of her family that our English language is now able to grapple with this kind of violent event—although language is not enough to contain this depth of sadness and grief and the reverberation that came after. However, language and this story I write attempt to shape a story that was silent for so long.

Now, we might say:

> abuse
> oppression
> stalking
> femicide
> filicide
> familicide
> mass murder

Yet even now, the word familicide is underlined in red on my screen. The software program I am using is questioning me. Are you sure this is a word? Does the killing of one's own family warrant a word? Does this word warrant a place in the lexicon of experience? Unfortunately, it does.

These words are helpful, but the reality is impossible to capture in its entirety. The story will always remain incomprehensible. How can one ever make sense of the murder of one's own daughter? One's unborn grandchild. His own sister. A six-year old. And his estranged wife.

This family history is confusing. The murderer wasn't my grandfather, as the newspaper articles from decades ago stated. Along with domestic violence, a woman leaving her husband with their baby wasn't acknowledged much either. My grandmother hadn't lived with her estranged husband for well over a decade, yet he never stopped thinking that he owned her and would never give her the divorce she wanted. Over the years, my mother has slowly shared glimpses of her past, the memories that can be conveyed with language, although what I am mostly familiar with is the silence that often exists in the wake of loud, violent, and irreconcilable events. But this silence can be needed too. Until it's not.

We parked the car in front of the black iron fence that surrounded the field of graves. Old, thick trees were everywhere, and the leaves were a lush green. I felt myself slow down to a pace more appropriate for a graveyard.

"Ready?" my mom said.

"Are you?" I asked.

"Oh yeah," she said, rarely allowing herself to make a fuss.

I tore the plastic covering off the roses and passed her the bouquet.

I opened the door to the backseat and only because Shay noticed first was I aware of the trill sound of crickets; males rubbed their wings together from a desire to mate with females or ward off other males.

"Whassat?" he said with a bright smile.

I feigned amazement and only considered later how much we often don't hear and how much children often do.

I unbuckled Shay from his car seat and lifted him out. Even with the air conditioning in the car, his face was flushed and sticky with sweat.

His legs were running before his feet touched the ground. Holding a Ziploc bag of banana chips in one hand, he took off for the grassy open space of the cemetery. We followed him through the gates and walked to the little brick building on the property, not sure if anyone would be there to show us the location of the graves. Shay turned a different way, running over graves and slapping his hand on the tall stones as he passed.

Before we could get to the door of the building, it opened, and a man in dusty overalls came out. He was at least my mother's age, who was sixty-two. He didn't take notice of us at first but walked towards a ride-on lawnmower.

"Excuse me," my mother said.

He looked at us.

"We're looking for a grave, one that's unmarked. My daughter contacted the cemetery a few months ago and spoke to someone?"

"Ok then," he said, "What's the name?"

"Well, there are two names. Florence and Patricia Killins. They share a grave."

"Oh," he said and took a long a pause while looking at my mother. "That was me she spoke to. Give me a minute."

Shay was still happily running off pent up energy and wasn't concerned about where we were. I kept glancing at him to make sure that he stayed on this side of the fence.

The man came back and unrolled a large piece of paper in front of us. He took another look at my mother and said, "I'm guessing you're the one that lived."

She looked back at him then gave a slight nod.

The paper was a yellowed map of the graveyard drawn in pencil. "They're right there," he said, pointing to one of the many rectangles drawn on the map. Written in small printing were the names F. Killins and P. Killins.

"I'll walk you over there," he said. We followed him to the middle of the graveyard.

"The grave would be about here," he said, outlining a patch of grass with his pointed finger.

"And the other Killins grave is over there." He pointed to another empty patch of grass on the other side of the walkway, not too far from where we were.

"Thank you," my mother said without looking towards it.

Before walking away, he said, "I hope you don't mind me saying…" He paused but then continued: "That was just a terrible terrible thing that happened. I remember your pictures in the papers. Nothing like that happens here." Then, he turned again and walked away.

"Apparently, it does," I said.

"Right," she exhaled. "I didn't know his grave was here too," she said, still staring at the spot where her mother and sister were buried. She crouched down to place the flowers on the grass.

My eyes started welling up even though I tried to stop myself from crying.

"Sorry," I said because she had told me that it was not my story. I didn't feel as if I had a right to cry. She had been attempting to bear the weight of it on her own.

"Well, now I'm going to cry," she said when she noticed me, and we both laughed while also trying to stop crying.

"Are you sad?" I asked after a while.

"Oh, it just feels like another life," she said, shaking her head and wiping her face.

Shay came waddling across my grandmother's and my aunt's grave. Can I call them that if I never met them? He began filling his mouth with banana chips, half of them falling onto the grass by his feet.

He looked up at me. "Momma," he said as if it were a question and reached his arms up to me.

I picked him up and felt one of his hands, still gripping the plastic bag, at the back of my neck. His other sticky palm pressed on my cheek. He put his head down on my shoulder. I tilted my head to his, and he started to wriggle out of my arms.

As I planted my son's feet on the grass again, he dropped the plastic bag and began pulling at the red petals of the roses, delighted to finally have his hands on them. We let him. He grabbed the head of a rose, dragging the bouquet behind him until the flower finally let loose leaving only petals on his great-grandmother's grave.

13.

"We Should Talk about This Later"

Sharon Anne Cook

This is a story of family silence, not family secrets. If someone had confronted my parents with questions, they would have readily acknowledged that my father's brother had indeed committed femicide, murdering his family. They would have politely answered any questions posed and closed off the conversation at the first opportunity. Then my father would likely have told the interlocutor what a fine man his brother was, offering an engaging story or two about the many people he had helped throughout life. This would have likely confused anyone seeking information, just as it baffled our family. Profoundly shocked and horrified by his brother's actions, my father remained silent for the rest of his long life about the events of that day. When his brother's name was mentioned, my father was always ready to supply one of a battery of his heart-warming stories about the brother he idolized.

Lest this description sounds like a form of aphasia suffered by my father, there was nothing wrong with my father's mental state. He was a successful animal nutritionist and was university educated in an era when few had a degree. He was also a devoted husband and father as well as a kind, decent, and intelligent man. By his adulthood, he was far and away the most successful member of his original family. Yet in his stories, he was the perpetual slow-learning child, who took instruction from a kindly older brother, without whom he would have perished, if one accepted his analysis. Here he was, at age fifty-six, raising the children his brother had orphaned when he murdered the rest of their family. And without exaggerating the case, he did this well— raising (with my mother) two children, who became admired professionals in their own right and who in turn raised their own loving families. That he was unable to speak about his brother's femicide— instead substituting cheery stories of his brother's prowess or of his kindness and social engagement—says much more about my father than it ever said about the murderer.

My father's big brother was the undisputed star in his family for everyone, not just my father. The assessment by others was that he was fearless, handsome, and admirable in every way. He invented machines to save labour on his father's farm; he excelled in his studies at Queen's University and practiced his French by listening to radio broadcasts; he read widely and wrestled with weighty philosophical questions. My father's older sister, a woman of considerable ability herself, also adored him. She protected and supported him throughout his many personal crises, in the end paying with her life.

My dad, in contrast, underwhelmed his mother and possibly his father. He was the last-born child, perhaps an afterthought, and could never shake the "little brother" identity he had acquired early in life. He did not have the flash and polish of his older brother or the artistic ability of his sister. He was slow to learn to read and had trouble spelling. Extant letters from his school-marm mother ridiculed his slow academic progress, especially in comparison to his able big brother. He accepted this role unquestioningly, thought of himself as a hard-working dullard, and learned early to be humble and to celebrate others before he expected any stardust to fall on him. My father's relationship with his older brother followed from this identity he had acquired of being third best. It is likely that my father shared this identity with many other late-born children; clearly, it shaped his life and his perception of others.

As a child, my brothers and I were treated to endless stories about his brother's vaunted abilities, of his kindness to him, of the respect and awe with which others approached him. There seemed no barriers to his achievements and eventual fame. But in the end, there were more barriers than my father could either acknowledge or overtalk. And the havoc wreaked by his brother was left for my father to clean up, which he did unflinchingly, putting aside his own interests for the welfare of the children, whom his brother had orphaned.

"WE SHOULD TALK ABOUT THIS LATER"

When the femicide occurred in May of 1963, the lurid accounts appeared in more than fifty newspapers across North America: "Five Persons Killed: Youngsters Tell Sad Story," said *The Brandon Sun*; "Evidence of Poison at Inquest," blared the *Regina Leader Post*; and "Berserk Shootings 4 in Family Slain, 3 Others Wounded," intoned the *Toronto Daily Star*. There would be no possible secret about this "berserk" tragedy. The distinctive surname of the murderer, which my family shared, meant that people across Canada made the connection between us and the murderer.

The facts of the case are easily recounted—too easily, in fact. Facts like this mask the horrifying suffering of the victims and survivors, suggesting a tidiness that was belied by the utter confusion during and after the femicide. The mass murderer was a former United Church minister and scholar, factors that put him in an exotic category that piqued the press's interest. Over a few hours on May 2, 1963, in the rural hamlet of Castleton, Ontario, he managed to kill every woman in his family, except one lucky (and clever) twelve-year-old girl and her ten-year-old brother. He murdered their mother before their eyes, their little sister, an aunt, and a treasured older sister. Their sister and mother were both pregnant, bringing the death toll to six.

The murderer (who will remain nameless here, not to support silence, but to deny him public recognition) had been an abuser for years of his estranged wife and daughter. He had stalked the family for more than sixteen years, living in an unheated one-room shack without running water outside their back door so he could monitor their every move. He controlled them by keeping them poor—money that should have supported the family was doled out if they acted as he directed. By the early 1960s, he was a misanthrope with a sense of entitlement and a capacity for violence. He had advanced untreated diabetes, causing gangrene in his feet and open sores on his body. He seems to have regularly dosed himself with strychnine, since it provides a temporary rush.

The murderer wed late in life to a woman unlike him in personality or interests and thirteen years his junior. From the start, he treated her like a child, attempting to mould her in the likeness of an appropriate cleric's wife. The marriage was uneasy at the best of times, and after their daughter was born, his wife finally left him. From that point onwards, he was increasingly unstable. After a series of unsuccessful postings with the church, he finally quit the ministry and took up the building of shacks, one-room hovels. Subsisting mainly on handouts and by the 1950s on welfare, my father was able to explain away every reversal in his brother's life as someone else's fault. In this, he accepted his brother's assessment and gave him support, as his brother became progressively more isolated.

My parents heard about the mass murder on the CBC morning news on May 3. I vividly recall happening on their ashen faces as I bustled into the kitchen to have breakfast that morning. My parents were both sitting, staring at each other, as the CBC Radio National News reported on happenings in Canada and around the world. The radio sat on the end of the Arborite counter, close to the breakfast nook, with a standard Formica-topped table and matching padded chairs in turquoise and chrome. "What's going on?" I asked. Both continued to sit, glancing distractedly at me.

By the time I arrived home from school that afternoon, my parents had already flown to Ontario. They returned about ten days later with two dazed and traumatized children, the only survivors of my uncle's murder spree. They would be absorbed into our family and become my (unofficial) brother and sister. This was not accomplished without the children suffering much sadness at the family, and indeed the life, they had lost. They had been moved halfway across Canada to the unfamiliar prairies without any of their own possessions: no keepsakes from their beloved mother and sisters or aunt, no clothing, no toys, and no friends from their life before. Here, they were dropped into an urban middle-class household from a rural acreage, where life was much more casual. My brother remembers with the clarity of a profoundly shocked child the spotless floors, the unworn rugs, and the order of everything in our Calgary home, including regular mealtimes with Canada's-Food-Rules selections.

I had met my new brother and sister a couple of times on family visits, but I had no understanding of the reign of terror under which they had lived their whole lives, culminating in the horrendous massacre from which each escaped by dint of their wits. That night, my brother had sustained a shotgun blast that just missed his head, singing his hair and throwing him into a dreamy shock for hours; my sister had witnessed the death of her mother and her sister, as she lay wedged under a bed, fully expecting to be murdered next. At one point, the murderer had fallen to the floor in the room where she was hiding, and there he lay for some time, apparently staring at her not two metres away, trapped under the bed. But he had regained enough strength to pull himself to his feet and continue with his murdering rampage in other parts of the house. She then had picked her way through the pools of blood and bodies in the house, running in the night and in bare feet over barbed wire to find help. Through their mettle and nerve, both children had lived. Yet the long road back to normalcy was before them and heavily dependent on my parents' common sense and love. There were no social workers or anyone to provide help: My father and mother were on their own.

It was during the children's slow recovery that my father's silences became obvious to all of us. Long after those years, both siblings told me that they would have welcomed open conversations about what had caused and occurred on that terrible night. Without this verbal processing of the tragedy, the children bore a crushing burden of guilt. They had lived while their sisters, mother, and aunt had died. How was that possible? Were they somehow responsible for their deaths? But if not, why the silence? They were powerless to begin such a discussion, and once I had asked and failed, I did not press the matter either. Instead of quiet discussion absolving them of any fault, what they were given were lyrical stories about the clever man who had murdered their family.

At dinner in my parents' home, lively conversations were common, and we would often sit and argue about politics or ethics long after the meal was done. Very often, too, my father would reminisce about his brother. "When my brother and I were young, he took me to a political meeting at X and taught me..." Always, his brother was defined as the knowledgeable, generous leader of the pack; he always described himself as the awe-struck younger brother who tagged along and learned valuable lessons from this worldly and wise older brother. Pointedly, his revered brother-the-mass-murderer never came up.

My sister and I shared a room, and before she settled into a restless sleep that first night, she began to recount her memories of that day when she lost her family. This became the nightly ritual: The light would be turned out, and she would tell me another part of the horror. Somehow, this comforted her, although it is difficult to understand how this could be. I would ask a few questions, struggle to imagine what that life had been like, and fall asleep, too. That was almost sixty years ago, and when we travel together these days and share a room, we fall right back into the old pattern with another memory, another snippet from her massive stash of personalized horror stories. It has always been clear to me that both my sister and brother (who had no one to tell his dreadful memories to at night or otherwise) were made of far tougher stuff than I could claim.

On my parents' return home with them, the focus in the household was to settle the children into a loving, stable home. I followed my parents' lead as they picked their way through each day, trying to maintain an environment in which the children would be comfortable but also challenged to rise above their misery. Soon after their return, I tried to engage my father in a discussion about how he understood why this dreadful thing had happened. "We should talk about this later," he said, as some other more pressing matter took precedence. My mother spoke very freely about it to me, but she didn't know much. My father was the font of information about what in his brother's past could possibly have brought him to this. Having my sister's stories at hand each evening, I was curious about how my father saw the causes of his brother's rampage.

But if I thought my father would confide in me or anyone, I was wrong. I slowly came to realize that my father was utterly unable to process what his brother had done. Whereas all of us wanted to hear him rage against this despicable man, there was only silence about his brother's final act of revenge. "Later" never arrived for an important conversation with the children or my mother and me. And in following my parents' lead, I also never encouraged my brother to talk through his trauma—to my everlasting regret. Somehow, he came through that fiery furnace, in large part because he had his sister in whom to confide. Both emerged as sturdy, capable, and deeply empathetic adults. I can only stand in admiration of their strength.

Even more remarkably, they were able to see beyond my father's inability to condemn his brother's cowardly and vicious acts. Because of my father's unwavering admiration and love for them, the siblings eventually responded in kind to him and to my mother, as they formed a warm second family once my brothers and I had left for university and jobs. My parents lived well into their nineties, and both regarded these two orphaned children in miraculous terms—that they were so stable, smart, and successful was an enduring point of pride for them. My father took enormous pleasure in introducing my brother, the medical doctor, and his sister, the college instructor, to his neighbours in the retirement residence: "And these are my brilliant nephew and niece!" he would say with a booming voice to ensure that everyone had met and welcomed them.

So there was mainly a happy ending to this story. But one ending that did not change was my father's inability to ever publicly face his brother's decision to destroy innocent lives but rather to see the massacre as one big mistake in an otherwise unblemished life. When he was in his seventies and my brother and sister were in their thirties, and long since living independently, my father wrote them a letter: "Dear Peggy. These are a few notes regarding your father and my dear brother, Robert Ivan." [The murderer was not their father; it is unclear if my father knew this or not. It would not have mattered to him in either case.] In his careful handwriting and phrasing, he listed every kind, clever, and generous act he could remember that had been carried out by his brother from the time he was a small child until he was in his forties, at which point the material deserted him. He acknowledged the immense loss my brother and sister had suffered from his brother's cruelty. Yet he felt the need to recoup his brother's reputation more than twenty years after he had massacred their family. My father ended this catalogue of sweetness and goodness by saying, "I once met a man in Welland, who said Bob had helped him and got him into his first job. No doubt he helped many people. Peggy, I know that you will agree that he was a good man." Clearly, my father had never given up in the hope that the two children he had sheltered and raised, and who had made him so proud, would forgive his brother and further, would declare him a good man.

As wrongheaded as my father was in pleading with my brother and sister to join him in admiring his brother, I know that this last effort to eulogize his brother was as much to assuage his own grief and guilt, undimmed after all those years—that he had been unable to stop his brother from murdering defenceless women—as it was to recoup his brother's reputation in the minds of the survivors. Unable to break his silence through authentic conversation with anyone about the case, he was reduced to pleading his brother's case through a letter; he worked from weak evidence but with a powerful desire to somehow erase the unspeakably sad circumstances of their family's massacre.

14.

I Should Have Known (A Found Correspondence)

Blaine Marchand

1. Between Us All These Years

August 23, 1937
744 Champagneur Ave
Outremont, Montreal, Que

Dear Dorothy,

You will be surprised at this letter, its Montreal postmark. I've been meaning to get in touch for such a long time, but with circumstances beyond my control, I was unable to do so. Up to now.

I am delighted to hear you married. Now the barrier between us all these years can be broken down. I am not sure how much you know, but due to Auntie, our hands were tied. Mother and Dad did not wish any unpleasant scenes between Auntie and Uncle's parents who raised you.

I was born April 2, 1911, a year and nine months to the day before you—I in Montreal, you in Ottawa, on January 2, 1913. I work in a stockbroker's office. Dad works for Tip Top Canners, travelling in the Maritimes for six to eight weeks. He returns for a short stay before he is gone again.

When Auntie Kathleen lived in Ottawa, I used to spend my summers with her. Now I stay home and look after the house while Mother and Dad go to visit her. But I go to Ottawa once or twice each year. I have an invitation for some weekend next month.

Even though we did not correspond with you, we have been hearing of you all these years. I enclose a photo taken a short time ago. If you happen to visit Auntie, you will see it in a small frame, beside the one of Mother and Dad.

I am not letting Mother or Dad know I am writing you. I do not want Auntie Kathleen and Uncle Jimmy to have words. I would rather you say nothing for the present.

I will close for the time, wishing you and your husband a successful married life. I am hoping for a reply in the near future.

Your brother,
Bob

2. I Should Have Known

"I want to know the truth," I demand of Aunt Kathleen, holding the letter in my shaking hand. "Is this Bob really my brother?"

Aunt Kathleen busies herself with making tea. She clears her throat over and over but does not look at me. She rearranges the teapot, the cups and saucers, and the pitcher of milk on the table until they are just so.

"Yes, Dorothy, he is," she says as she pours the milk into my cup. I watch the hot drink cloud. "Let me explain."

And she does—my parents separating, my mother putting me and him in the orphanage, and then fleeing to Montreal. Aunt Kathleen took us out to raise us, but the neighbourhood gossip was too much to bear, so she gave us to her fiancé's parents. Bob was a handful, and the Irishes put him back in the orphanage. After the war, my parents reunited. Aunt Kathleen heard about this, took Bob to Montreal, knocked on their door, and said, "This is your son. You should raise him." "But we are about to go out," my mother protested. "Well, take him with you," Aunt Kathleen snapped and stormed off down the stairs.

"That's enough," I say. "Let's just enjoy our tea."

When he comes home from the office, Ed and I talk about the letter and my afternoon with my aunt. I am uncertain what to do. Do I really want to meet these parents who chose to abandon me?

I decide to let things be. We both agree.

3. The Happiest Day

September 25, 1939
326 Lyon Street #1
Ottawa, Ontario

Dear Mother and Dad:

Yesterday was the happiest day of my life, as I got to meet my own mother, dad, & brother, Robert. The barriers of twenty-six long years have now been broken, and I sincerely hope that we shall get to know and understand one another better.

Ed and I sat by the fireside until three talking about the wonderful parents and brother I should have known years before. I am proud of the fact that I have such a mother, dad, & brother like you three, and I know that I always will be. I am looking forward to the day in the very near future when you three may meet my friends.

To say thank you for everything seems so weak, but perhaps someday, in some small way, I may have the opportunity to do something to prove that I really do mean thank you.

I hope Bob's cold is all better today. May he never have to go to war because I am looking forward to having many visits with him. I sure think he's swell and only wish I had known him and answered his letter sooner.

Hoping to hear or see you in the very near future.

Your loving daughter,
Kathleen Dorothy

4. Torn Fragment

(undated, in your handwriting)

I learned last week they drove to town to visit Aunt Kathleen. I guess they did not want to come the extra mile. I understand. I mean why would they want the wear and tear on their car's rubber tires.

Family Portrait

(unknown garden, Montreal, circa, 1939)

At your back, like swords,
stalks of cannas are rigid.
In black and white, no clue
as to the actual colour
of the exotic blooms concealed
in the furtive leaves. Only

that this growth emerged
from swollen underground stems,
rhizomes, taken in, wintered over,
hidden from light in sawdust,
brought out, planted when
the earth and air were promising.

Perhaps it is early October.
The four of you pose stiffly,
the wind at your backs
—you in a dark car coat
beside your parents
who stand side by side
but angled away, not touching,
while your brother smiles.
His hands clutch a wide-brim hat,
its crown dented and pinched.

A path leads somewhere out
of frame, out of sight. On either side
the family's posed. Soon the cannas
will be brought down by frost.

15.

Frozen Air

Linda Briskin

Be vigilant. Protect yourself. Find a safe place. Expect the worst.

My white skates, tied together and flung over my shoulder, swing with each stride. The blades brush rhythmically against my red down coat.

I'm eager to skate on Grenadier Pond in Toronto's High Park, frozen smooth for the first time in five years. It's nestled at the bottom of a slippery hill. The city vanishes amid the trees, their branches laden with snow. Not a burden, I imagine, but a lacy protection.

At the edge of the pond, I sit on a log and remove my mitts, then my winter boots. I finger the white leather of the skates, appreciating the scuffs. The decades-old memory of buying them used at Newson's Exchange surfaces. "These are for 'serious' figure skaters," the young clerk said. Sadly, my skating skills never lived up to these skates.

As I lace them up, a sign, frozen at a tilt, catches my eye:

NO SKATING ALLOWED

I ignore it.

Impulsively, I surrender to risk. I place each foot tentatively on the pond. Feeling Precarious, I steady myself before gliding cautiously off to the right.

But I'm afraid. I'm always afraid.

My mother's voice is ever present, haunting:

Be vigilant. Protect yourself. Find a safe place. Expect the worst.

Sometimes, I sympathize with my mother. As a Jewish woman born in Montreal in 1921, my mother encountered window signs that read "Pas de juifs." As a girl of fourteen, her beloved father died suddenly at forty-nine. Her relatives in Kyiv and Brest-Litovsk, who she only knew by name, disappeared during the Holocaust.

My mother had a right to be afraid.

But she also wanted me to be afraid. Maybe to assume the burden of her fear. Her warnings, an unwelcome inheritance, buried themselves deep in my psyche. They were not a caring gift. They did not protect me.

And my mother did not protect me from my father's arbitrary rules or his rage.

"You cannot," he said.

"Why not?"

"Because I say so." His fury explosive but predictable.

My mother left the room.

Maybe she was afraid.

Sometimes I tried to have conversations with my mother. But she was not a teller of truths, and we never got to the heart of our family history. With a childlike ability to slide away from reality, she offered only imagined versions of her past, and of mine.

"Why do you think I left home at sixteen?" I once asked her.

"You were such an adventurer," my mother, then seventy, said with a smile.

The day I moved out, my mother said nothing.

My father said, "I don't care what you do."

It was not an adventure.

The erasures, her complicit silences, hardened my heart against her.

Now on the tenth anniversary of her death, I light a Yahrzeit candle, a soul candle. The dancing glow flickers. A Morse code memory.

I remember the photograph of my mother at eight, dressed in her Russian costume, one hand covering the other. She told me that just hours before this photo was taken, she had suffered a bee sting on her finger. Her smile was enigmatic for one so young. It's 1929.

In my high school graduation picture, the same half-smile. Like my child mother, I turn towards the camera, distant and aloof. We're almost twins, she at eight and me at sixteen. It's 1966.

Here, my mother is twenty-two. It's 1943, the year she married my father and six years before I was born. The photo was taken during the war, yet she seems carefree, smiling for the camera, flirting with danger. She is perched on a railing, likely at the Parc du Mont-Royal in Montreal, poised at the edge of a precipice.

I never knew this woman. She bears no resemblance to the mother I remember who was deeply disappointed, angry, resentful, fearful.

When I left home, I took my books, a single peacock feather, and small blue cobalt bottle, and the money saved from years of babysitting, to pay for a rented room.

I was determined to leave behind her warnings, her disregard, and his rage and bullying.

I did not.

I skate—tentative, vigilant. I yearn to embrace the freedom of movement. To welcome the challenge of danger. I long to hush her warnings with the whistle of the wind and the singing of the blades on ice.

In the distance, an expressway breaks the circle of trees surrounding the pond. Cars whiz past recklessly. I turn away from the road and skate towards the far end of the pond, where reeds caught fast in the ice are sentinels standing tall. Beckoning. My arms swing in concert with the measured stroke of each leg. My skates leave a trail of waves.

Holding my confidence like a banner, I skate as if I were safe, pushing myself to gather more speed, then coasting with the air at my back. The delight of continuous movement. The exhilarating cold.

Surrendering to desire, possibility.

Then the whisper grabs my attention. *Be vigilant.* Watch for those pockets of air, frozen white just below the surface. They might fracture under my weight, grab the picks on my skates, and trip me.

I no longer take in the black treetops etched against the sky or the circling raptors. I no longer look at what lies in the distance.

Now my wary eyes track the marks on the surface. My breath strangled and shallow—never deep enough to dispel the clutch of fear in my stomach. My skate touches the edge of a crack. My arms come up to balance against a fall, and my mind imagines my knee striking hard ice. Caught in the catastrophe of a broken limb, I'm gone from the park and the pond, already planning how to survive weeks of pain and a clumsy white cast.

With gritted teeth, I bring myself back to the ice, heart staccato. I hum "Swing Low, Sweet Chariot" to silence the mantra of *danger, danger, danger.*

Lying in bed that evening, finally calm, I remember the sheen of the ice, the span of the frozen pond. In my imagination, I skate fearlessly, without caution, permitting the joy of it. I embrace the wind in one direction, battle it affectionately in the other. I delight in the dance of the trees and race the clouds as they travel across the sky.

As sleep descends: *Be vigilant. Expect the worst.* My skate hits a crack, and I hurtle into the air. Arms elegantly wide, I land with grace. With muted elegance, I create a perfect figure eight. I twirl and spin with abandon.

In my dream, I mail a postcard to my mother.

I went skating yesterday. I did not fall.
Your daughter

16.

Shangri-La

Donna McCart Sharkey

I grew up accustomed to secrets, instructed to not tell. And to not ask why I shouldn't tell.

Many of these were microsecrets. Don't let your father know how much your shoes cost. Others more important. Don't tell your Protestant aunts and uncle that this year you will be going to a Catholic school.

Larger secrets still lurk—at my mother's family cottage.

My mother's youngest sister, Grayse, visited the cottage infrequently. When she did, she played crazy eights with my sister and I and read Harlequin novels in a room overlooking the lake. She was our provider of chocolate bars, Pepsi, and barbeque potato chips. But despite her gifts, I was cautious. Although I was unaware why, she had a meanness towards me, as like her, I was the youngest sibling.

Grayse claimed that my sister and I were equal. Presents from her to us were often a different version of the same gift. When given small figurines, my sister received an angel with pastel wings. The red devil lying menacingly on his side was for me.

My father called the cottage Shangri-La, although he was never more than barely welcomed there by his in-laws. He too, rarely visited the cottage—perhaps two or three times over the summer—and when he did, if my mother's sisters were there, they would bait him until his temper exploded. He, like them, possessed fast-firing emotions.

But my mother's brother appeared mellow, laidback. My sister and I passed summers at the cottage mostly with my mother and him. We kids also had friends on the island: Diana, Francis, and Debby. We rowed, swam where we chose, bicycled along the road, and returned to the cottage in late afternoon to watch Zorro on television. In the evenings, exuberant sunsets magnificently took over the sky and lake.

The year I turned eleven, mum told my sister and me that we wouldn't be going to our cottage for summers anymore. No explanation was provided, and we didn't ask. Our next several summers were spent at a community swimming pool and tennis court near our home.

Years later in retirement, mum's brother moved permanently into the cottage. The summer following his death, the cottage empty, my daughters and I spent time there. The first night and continuing on, the same nightmare cursed my sleep. In it my uncle appears suddenly, threateningly, outside the cottage. He chases me, catches up, and pulls me into the house and behind the wood stove in the kitchen. Each night at this point, I wake up.

That summer, I found the deed to the property and discovered the sale of my mother's part ownership to her brother for one dollar, the year I turned eleven.

17.

Sabbath

Wendy Donawa

Every Sunday before church,
Mum puts a roast and potatoes in the oven,
and when we get home, it's all brown and crispy.
"We're holy and hungry," says Dad.

Dad polished my shoes, and I have clean white socks.
Clean panties, too, because Granny says
"What if a bus hits you?"
I have a Sunday purse, but when it's not Sunday,
you can put gum in your pocket.

Sunday school's over early, so I wait
in the vestibule with its big wooden doors.
I could go inside, but the doors squeak clunk,
and people will look at me.

The priest drone and drones
and all the people rumble rumble
and here's a man in the vestibule
maybe waiting too, a Dad-ish man
with a big overcoat and hat.

"You're a big girl," he says, but I don't know
what is the polite answer, and he
picks me up with his hands on my bum.
It's rude to say "bum," but I think it,

and he turns, so I'm squashed against the wall,
and his hands on my bum and his fingers
poke poking and hurting, and now they're singing a hymn.

When he puts me down he takes a hankie
out of his Dad-ish coat and wipes his fingers,
and I don't know what I'm supposed to say.

On the drive home I say "Mum, I don't want
to go to Sunday School anymore," and
Mum says, "Don't be silly dear," and
when we get home,
the potatoes are brown and crispy and
"Yum," says Dad, "we're holy and hungry."

18.

Drawing Out Shadows

Caroline Purchase

My grandmother and I sit at her green Formica kitchen table. She shuffles playing cards while I sip milky tea.

"Now you're almost twelve, I'll teach you how to play two-handed Hearts." She winks. "Enough of the Crazy Eights."

I force a feeble smile, but the dark question hanging in my mind swings loose. "Amma?" My eyes tear up.

She drops the cards. Her nimble fingers tilt my face to meet her eyes. "Elska," loved one, "what's wrong?"

I know things I'm not supposed to know, things I don't understand.

Amma stands and beckons me into a hug, her solid warmth radiating through my lanky body, swathing me.

I lean back in her arms and anchor myself in her sea-blue gaze until my quivering stops.

"When I'm grown up, will I have a nervous breakdown?"

From age five, I savour weekly visits with my grandparents. No Mom, no younger brother or sister. I dash into Amma and Afi's house and smell roses and lavender, freshly-baked cakes and cookies, musty books, and mothballs. I find puzzles, games, dolls and dress-up clothes and hats to play with whenever my grandparents host members from their Icelandic-Canadian community in Winnipeg. I listen to them speak Icelandic, lulled by Afi's soft pitch and nurtured by Amma's more vibrant voice, which brims with warmth like her oven-baked kleinur or pan-fried pönnukökur filled with jam and rolled up and sprinkled with icing sugar. When adults congregate in the living room, Amma serves them china cups filled with strong coffee and offers delicacies on china plates. I stay for one round of treats, then Amma winks at me, and I'm free to raid the goodies she stores in cookie tins on the stairway to the attic—my play area and sleepover spot.

I aspire to be a detective, like Hercule Poirot, Miss Marple, and Sherlock Holmes in the mystery novels in my grandfather's den. By age eight, I scale Afi's wooden bookshelf ladder, scour through his collection, extract books, and open pages. The dusty smell tickles my nose and makes me sneeze. I nestle in Afi's squeaky oxblood-leather armchair and dive into stories where the hero pieces together clues, solves the mystery, and restores order.

At home, I practise spying. I hide behind the couch before my parents sit down with their predinner drinks. I eavesdrop when my mother talks on the phone. I snoop through my mother's dresser drawers.

One day, I uncover a tiny black-and-white photo of a blonde lady. She wears a black gown with a white collar and cradles a bouquet of roses. I know her eyes must be blue. My heart pounds as I tuck the photo back in its exact place.

I love it when Amma sings songs to me while playing her piano or accordion. She fixes me with her luminous eyes. "Beautiful, beautiful brown eyes... I'll never love blue eyes again." Her gaze and her words ease the ache inside me. My mother and younger sister own Afi's classic Icelandic features—grey-blue eyes, blonde hair, and aquiline noses—which I yearn for and will never have. I deduce if I looked more like my mom, she'd show more interest in me.

My parents' bedroom door is ajar. I'm nine, and I know Mom's code: I may rap on the door and ask permission to enter.

My beautiful and perfect mother stands before her dresser mirror, brushing her sunlit hair. Her steel-blue top and skirt match her eyes.

I scoot into her shadow and perch on the bed's edge. Her top dresser drawer hangs open, and I spy the corner of the photo. My heart races. "What's that picture?"

She glances at me, removes the photo, and shows it to me. "My mother."

I frown. "But Amma's your mom."

"Your amma is my stepmother." She taps the photo. "This is my mother, Verda Viola." Her composed face blanches. Her frosted-pink lips pinch closed. She turns away, reburies the picture, and snaps the drawer closed.

The sad part in me screams and wants to cry. I hold my breath and suffocate it.

"Off you go," Mom says.

I scamper out.

Her crisp skirt swishes, and her heels click behind me.

Throughout my childhood and adolescence, I sniff out snippets of Verda's story, incrementally grasping how Verda haunts my mother and me. My amma, my aunt, and occasionally my mom—when I sensed it was safe to lightly probe—are my sources. Who provided exactly what detail is jumbled in my memory. However, specific phrases the three women repeated verbatim over the years are etched in my psyche.

Verda Viola had two daughters: first Evelyn and then two and a half years later my mother, Dorothy. But Verda wanted a boy. Ron was born five years after my mother. Mom pronounced to me over the years, and Aunt Evelyn and Amma parroted it too: "Verda got her wish, but it cost her mental health."

Verda had a nervous breakdown and was institutionalized for the next eleven years at Selkirk Hospital for Mental Diseases. I imagine my five-year-old mom, eyes frozen onto her mother while attendants restrain Verda in a straightjacket and yank her from the house.

Once or twice, my mom mentions visiting her mother at the mental institution on Sundays. I picture the scene: A five-year-old girl scurries down a fluorescent-lit corridor alongside her father and siblings. Patients lurch and shriek. Dour-faced doctors and nurses in white stride through the halls with instruments and clipboards and medicines while solemn workers push trolleys of pungent-smelling laundry and supplies. The girl peeks into large antiseptic rooms filled with tight rows of white-sheeted beds fitted with metal restraints. One such bed confines her mother. I can't imagine mother and daughter ever exchanging loving glances.

My aunt and my mom tell me Verda regularly endured shock treatments. More devastating, she underwent a lobotomy. I envision each must hold an image of their mother restrained, dragged down the hall, and forced into a room for treatment.

From my research, I ascertain that in the 1940s, Selkirk's inpatients regularly received seizure-inducing electrical shocks without a general anaesthetic or muscle relaxant—and without consent. Prefrontal lobotomies, where surgeons excise connections between the prefrontal cortex and frontal lobes, were also common.

When I ask Aunt Evelyn's son, a lung surgeon and researcher, whether I could track down our grandmother's records, he shrugs and says, "Why track down outdated documents, even if they still exist?"

I'm thirty-seven and living in Vancouver when I travel to Toronto to visit my parents. Mom and I clean up the kitchen after dinner.

She pauses from scrubbing the roasting pan. Her glassy eyes fix on me, and she recounts a past incident between us.

I remember. I grit my teeth.

I'm seven. Mom is supposed to pick up my friend Jan and me alongside Pembina Highway in Winnipeg, where the bus drops us off after day camp. She drives by, doesn't see us—apparently our fault because we aren't at the exact right spot—and can't figure out how to switch lanes and loopback. My mom returns home. A couple of hours later, Jan's father finds us sitting beneath a billboard sign.

I listen to Mom's words. I play witness and catch a glimpse of vulnerability, even remorse. To my wonder, my long-nursed hurt dissipates. I can comprehend how her anxiety propelled her to flee.

My mom adds information I hadn't known at seven: "Jan's father, who usually fetched you, was furious with me." She wrenches in a sharp breath. "He's a psychiatrist."

She needed to blame me to halt her tidal wave of shame.

My mom is nine when the hospital doctors deem Verda stable enough to return home for the first of two occasions. But Verda isolates herself in her gloomy bedroom until recommitted to the mental institution. Then, I imagine, my mother's flood of grief carries an unsettling sense of relief.

When I'm nine, I hide mystery novels under my pillow. I wait until Mom says goodnight and then raise the blind and read under light cast by the streetlamp. To help myself fall asleep, I make up stories where

I'm the courageous crime solver. But those nights I hear ambulance sirens I fear they're coming for me, the victim hiding under her blanket.

That summer I play the villain, causing another aftershock to hang between Mom and me.

"Time for bed!" Mom summons me at 8:00 p.m. from the front door of our house.

The neighbourhood kids snicker.

I feel my face flush. Although I stall, I obey.

She sits in the den, posture erect, on a tan upholstered chair.

"Not fair!" I say. "Everyone else can stay out."

She raises her eyes from her book. "I don't care about everyone else. Get ready for bed—now!"

"I hate you!"

Mom's face darkens, and her lips lock. She lifts her glass from the side table. Ice cubes clink as she raises her glass to her mouth.

My heart thrashes. I run upstairs and prepare for bed. When I creep down to the living room to kiss her goodnight, Mom turns her face away.

For a week, she ignores me.

Ten years later, the incident still reverberates between us. One Sunday evening at the dinner table, I silently seethe at my mother's nailed-down etiquette and how she controls the conversation.

I interject: "A friend's coming to get me in an hour."

"It's ridiculous how you expect others to give you rides." She sips from her crystal wineglass. "One would presume you'd be more independent by now."

I glare at her, and she glowers back. I bolt from the house and run down the driveway.

Mom chases after me. "Into the house, young lady." She clamps my wrist. "The dishes, now!"

"Leave me alone!"

"You hate me," she says, releasing her iron grip.

I shake my head. "I don't hate you." My wet eyes fix on her. "You hate me!"

When I'm sixteen, I study a sample of Verda's handwriting. Was it my mom or amma who showed me? Line after line of elegant yet shaky handwriting repeats instructions about how to catch the bus. My lasting impression is how Verda's anxiety is exhibited in the content, perhaps because I also possess a low threshold for anxiety. To drive someplace new or catch a plane, bus, or train is nerve-wracking.

My mom is sixteen when Verda returns home from Selkirk. "But then she felt herself slipping." The few times my mom repeats this odd phrase to me, her expression and her voice appear disembodied. Apparently, her father instructed her to look after her mother's hygiene. Armed with a shampoo bottle, my mom opened the door to the dark and oppressive room but lost her courage. She placed the shampoo on top of her mother's dresser, skulked out, and closed the door. "If only I'd washed my mother's hair," my mother would say.

Given Mom's fixation on cause and effect, I surmise calamity occurred a day or two later. Amid grade eleven final exams, she returned home for lunch. Did she check in on her mother only to find Verda wasn't in her gloomy bedroom? Did my mom call out, "Mother?" Did she race around the house before descending the basement stairs?

She found her mother hanging by a rope from the rafters.

How did my mom, then sixteen, react? I can't hear her shriek, wail, or keen.

Not the invulnerable woman I persistently scrutinize. Not the woman whom I cannot seem to emulate. Not the woman who never cries or yells or laughs out loud.

I surmise my mom froze inside and strangled her emotions to protect her own sanity.

"If only I'd washed my mother's hair," Mom chants.

Her words, laden with trauma and guilt, perpetually shred my heart.

I deduce my mom called Afi at work.

"Father, come home!"

Afi, a WWI and WWII veteran, declared, "She went out like a soldier." I hear reverence: Verda was brave enough to take her own life. The tone carries through when Mom first utters Afi's line to me when I am sixteen—the same age Mom was then.

Mom says Afi forbade her to tell anyone about the incident. She failed her grade eleven exams. When Afi informed the principal that her mother had just died, he allowed her to rewrite them. The secret of Verda's mental illness and her suicide was perpetuated, the shame, buried. But secrets worm their way out of the earth.

Flaxen-haired, blue-eyed, and petite Verda had a fine mind, both delicate and robust. Undoubtedly, her exquisite looks and intelligence captivated Afi. He met Verda—his friend Daniel's younger sister—when they were students at the University of Winnipeg.

When I'm seventeen and attending the same university, Aunt Evelyn gives me more details. After he graduated, Afi received a scholarship to Oxford University. From England, Afi wrote letters back home to his sweetheart. During his absence, "Verda started showing signs of instability," Evelyn says. Then, apparently, Daniel composed typed responses to Afi's letters and instructed Verda to sign them. Evelyn states, "It was the onset of schizophrenia."

Verda's mind breaks after her son is born, and her family shatters. Later, Afi and Verda's three grown children gravitate towards professions to repair and strengthen minds and families. My aunt Evelyn becomes a social worker, and my uncle Ron, a prison psychologist. My mother considers social work, but her humanities professor dissuades her from "such heartbreaking work," she tells me when I'm the age she was then. Perhaps her professor sensed a fragility that I cannot see. Instead, she becomes a high school teacher.

But then Mom marries at twenty-seven, nine years after Afi marries Amma.

"Your amma brought life into the house," Mom says. "But she could be difficult."

At twenty-nine, my mom gives birth to me.

"You were the first to take away your mother's freedom," a psychotherapist points out when I'm thirty-four. "That's why you're the target of her hostility more than your brother and sister."

Disillusioned with motherhood, my mom pursues a master's degree in educational psychology when I'm ten, followed by a degree in textile arts when I'm nineteen.

I, too, cannot find contentment after I finish graduate school in English literature. I marry at twenty-two and work in retail advertising. At twenty-five, I divorce. At thirty-two, I move to Vancouver, in part to escape from my mother and an emotionally abusive boyfriend fifteen years my senior. I strive to be stoic like my father and mother. Still, I believe something is wrong with me because I cannot shove my unhappy feelings away.

Months after settling into an apartment, I spot an advertisement for an introductory session at the Vancouver Art Therapy Institute, two blocks away. I remember painting mountains, ocean, and sky. As usual, I judge my work as no good.

The school director examines my painting. "Can you tell me about the heavy application of red across the sky?"

My face burns. I burst into tears, flooded by inchoate feelings. I rush home, shove the artwork into a closet, and forget about the session and my artwork for two years.

At thirty-four, I quit my management job in advertising and try chiropractic school. But I can't stomach the formaldehyde stench that permeates the school and adheres to my clothes. I hang back from the cadavers on stainless steel tables as their liquids drip into plastic buckets.

"Your turn," says a student, thrusting the scalpel towards me.

I refuse his offer to dissect. When the anatomy professors in gore-stained lab coats power-saw through ribs and stick their ungloved hands into chest cavities to poke at hearts and livers and spleens, I hold my breath and plug my ears.

At lunchtime, I run past groundskeepers digging fresh graves in the Catholic cemetery bordering the chiropractic school. I whiff the scent of newly turned dirt. I see plumes of smoke rise from the incinerator's chimney and catch the noxious odour of burning bodies. Today, I puzzle over why I subjected myself to a year of trauma. I do recall that instead of homework, I read mystery novels—my one guilty pleasure and source of sustenance.

The brain is the only part of a corpse that does not repulse me. We students are forbidden to touch it. Instead, we watch the lab instructor pull a brain out of a bucket, cradle it in his hand and point to fulcrums and fissures, cranial nerves, and all. I lean in, mystified by its intricacy.

I feel certain I want to be a psychologist. However, rather than repeat undergraduate and graduate school—this time in psychology instead of English literature—I figure out a short cut and enter art therapy school.

The unconscious reveals itself in art. In group art therapy sessions with five other women, my bright and abstract paintings portray my sense of disconnect from my nuclear family. Soon, the paintings focus on my mom and me. I portray my mom as an iceberg with me cut off from her and surrounded by blue.

Our art therapy group also triggers nuclear family dynamics. When one woman processes her art regarding a suicide attempt, I muffle my tears and then sob, usurping the group's attention from the artist. When the youngest member—who sits at the head of the table beside me—constantly shows up ten minutes late and grabs the pots of paint I'd gathered for myself, I hide my irritation.

Within months, I paint images of my mom's mother hanging by a rope, progressing from abstract to realism as my emotions became less amorphous and my understanding of them more exacting. When I process my art with the group regarding Verda's nervous breakdown and eventual suicide, the art therapist postulates Verda likely suffered from postpartum depression at a time when—tragically—treatments caused more harm than good.

The art therapist suggests I make art and then journal about my relationship with my mother—specifically my repressed anger. I can release some hurt, but rage is impenetrable.

"Use art to explore your connection with your birth grandmother," the therapist urges.

I balk, for I feel no relationship with Verda at all.

In our second year, the group confronts me. "We're concerned you're not expressing your anger," one student says.

"I'm worried she's unprofessional with her practicum clients," the youngest one says. "All she does is cry."

My body shakes. I feel unsafe and betrayed.

Yet she is right. I remember melancholy consuming me during those two years of art therapy training. No matter how hard I choked back tears, they overpowered me—in school, in cafes, on the bus—wherever and whenever it felt most humiliating.

The art therapist steps in. "Just because Caroline is sensitive, it doesn't mean she cries around clients."

Meanwhile, in our diagnostic categories course, we learn about society's harmful penchant to label and categorize individuals with mental illness. Our professor, a psychiatrist, believes a primary caregiver's lack of attention is a determining factor. We discuss schizophrenia, bipolar disorder, depression, and anxiety. I sit spellbound, compelled to understand mental illness as best I can. Shyly, I approach the professor. "My birth-grandmother had mental illness and died by suicide when she was around forty." I describe the timing of possible onset and recurring episodes. "Do you think she had schizophrenia or bipolar disorder?"

He shrugs. "I can't say for certain." His kind eyes peer over his reading glasses at me. Perhaps he's waiting for my more ominous question.

"Do you think I'm at risk?" I scrutinize his face, catch his slight nod.

"It seems unlikely," he says. "But you need to take care of yourself." He removes his glasses and focuses on me. "And I do caution you: Before you have children, check with your partner whether mental illness runs in his family."

His words are a knife twisted into my navel.

I'm twelve. Amma and I stand in her warm and fragrant kitchen, with me nestled in her arms. My ear rests against her beating heart.

"Elska, don't worry." She kisses the crown of my head.

My racing heartbeat steadies.

"You won't have a nervous breakdown when you grow up." She rocks us back and forth.

I look up into her loving eyes.

"If I have kids, will I have a nervous breakdown?"

"Elska."

Her high forehead crinkles. Her eyes grow moist behind her bifocal lenses. She offers me a big and assured smile.

"You'll be a wonderful mother."

I have no children. Nor do my brother or sister.

19.

Umbilical Noose

David Pimm

"Seal up your lips and give no words but mum."
—William Shakespeare

"Time moves in one direction, memory in another."
—William Gibson

We all have secrets, even—maybe especially—the ones that we hide from ourselves.
Among other ways, secrets can simply leak; they sometimes secrete. And they can occur even at the cellular level.

I had secrets that I kept from my family, and my other family members had secrets that were kept from me. But times change, as they do. We all got older, and some secrets surfaced (though not all of the closet-crowded skeletons), and a few were even explicitly presented (though the conversation often ended with "but please don't tell so-and-so").

It started, I suppose, with an Enid Blyton story mentioning a family conference where they were all sitting as a single group, discussing what had occurred and planning what still was to come. This was something my sister and I had never experienced in our family. My mother later said to me that, when she was a child, her parents had been open with discussing anything in front of her and her three siblings, regardless of how young they were or what was being said. But they had been firmly instructed not to say a word outside of the family of anything that had been discussed. The house's walls were there to keep the words inside. Strict boundaries. Locked doors. Silence.

Once she had her own children, my mother went the opposite way and told me little as a boy, although she did gently complain that I stopped telling her things when I was about ten. Nevertheless, my neck still knew things that even my brain's memory seemingly did not. My neck remembered. And later on in life, my neck started to secrete secrets.

Here's one of my secrets, a smallish one, but one that I never told my mother about. I had given up on school lunches at the age of nine. (They were dreadful lunches and, even though the teacher supervisor said you could say how much of whatever you wanted, you then had to eat it all; the generous servers would give you what they wanted you to have, regardless of what you said.) I'd asked my mother if I could come home for lunch, or maybe have a packed lunch, but she said no to both requests.

So I lied. I told the school I was going home for lunch while not letting my parents know anything had changed, which left me dealing with the five shillings (two half-crowns) that I was handed every Monday to pay for the school lunch.

It was about a fifteen-minute walk to and from school, and half-way along, past the park, was a large Wall's Ice Cream factory (in Acton, in northwest London) with a small café attached, where workers had their lunches. And this was where I ate a fried egg and chips five days a week. But it cost a shilling and threepence, and I only had a shilling. I was pretty short then and could barely reach the counter. I'd eat quickly, never talking to the working adults I sat alongside, in case they would ask why I was there each day. Then I had to kill time, as I couldn't have gone home for lunch and got back to school so quickly, so I wandered around the streets mostly looking at cars. In order to eat this lunch every day, I ended up not just embezzling the school's lunch money but also thieving coins from my sister's money box on occasion, in order to make up the difference.

It nearly blew up when my friend Charlie Lawrence, who lived nearby on the same street, got run over as he and I walked together to school. I ran back to tell his mother and also told the school. Because the school believed I went home for lunch—sigh—I was asked to check in on how he was. This meant I had to go close to my home and risk being seen by my mother and hence have to reveal my secret. But I got away with it because my mother didn't see me (as far as I know).

As I got older, I became increasingly self-contained. I was able to keep some secrets simply through silence. My older sister pretty much stopped talking to me when I was about eleven or so. It turned out later there were several significant issues occurring in her mid-to-late teenage years, about which I had been totally oblivious. I only later realised that I was being sent away on long school trips (to France, Austria, Switzerland, and the West Indies) as, among other reasons, a way to keep secrets from me, although at the time I was neither aware nor concerned.

Time passed. My sister left home, I left home three years later, off to university. I visited and talked with my mother. My father, who was generally quiet, had been a Lancaster bomber navigator during the Second World War in his early twenties, including the bombing of Dresden in 1945. I had a German girlfriend for a couple of years in the early 1980s and, once she and I parted, my mother told me that, although my father had liked her, he was nevertheless happy I was not caught up with a German woman. Another secret revealed. And a couple of years ago, I went to Dresden to give a talk and also planned to explore J. S. Bach's involvement in Dresden and Leipzig. When the talk was done, I weirdly managed to sprain my ankle severely, which prevented me going to Dresden's old centre that my dad had helped destroy. It seems that was a generational avoidance.

My mother started to tell me other things, too, like this: my father's Irish cousin, who worked for MI5 (not that I knew, of course), was killed in a plane explosion when it was taking off from Heathrow Airport. A visitor informed my parents that he thought the explosion was deliberate. But then my mother said I was not to tell my sister. And I didn't. And even more significantly, my mum's mum came to live with us near the end of her life. After she died, I was told that my grandmother's father had sexually abused her in her teen years. Keep it to yourself, my mother requested. Yet in the telling, it seemed that she wanted it remembered.

And then there are the secrets we keep from ourselves. One day, I trudged in for massage treatment, feeling as sunken as a shipwreck. Flat on my back, the massage therapist's practiced hands haltered my neck as my upper torso tried to rewrite its wrongs (not that I was aware what they were). I started thinking about my consistent flinch as my lover's thumb dared to caress my throat; then I recalled that, when I was young, I overheard a teenage girl's slight as I walked away from the tennis club: "I just saw him ape down the road." Another hunch. Something with my neck had been around a long time. So, I talked about this to my mum. She mentioned her early concern regarding my sister's green-eyed grip around my neck, with me still in my crib. And even earlier, I heard (which a part of me clearly already knew) about a fetal slipknot, an umbilical noose even before I was born.

Secrets can be a hiding place for safety. A final resort. Even now, in writing this piece, I feel a certain reluctance to reveal some of what my mother revealed to me—and this despite her death several years ago at age ninety-three and a half.

20.

May 31, 1934: My Grandmother Writes to My Grandfather

Maureen Scott Harris

Hospitalized, feeling *there is an experiment being made on me,*
my grandmother writes a love letter. *My darling Walter, I don't know*

just what has happened to me. Or how she came to be where
she's scolded for weeping when she thinks of him. *Have I lost*

my memory or was I knocked down? The doctors are indifferent
and give her sleeping powders. She asks *who is minding*

the children? She wants her glasses. *Don't let them keep you
away from me.* Signs herself *your own ever loving wife / Joy.*

He called her that though her name was Kathleen. They were thin
and strict and loved me. He held my hand when he walked me

to the library, she kept children busy and organized everyone's lives.
Scant, scant, scant the details … no one living knows what happened

or why she was there. But here they are, my childhood's gaunt
giants, firmness overturned, aching with secrets and longing.

21.

Fireflies

Soriya Turner

She and her brother walked in silence over the familiar dirt roads of an abandoned tree farm. In the June dusk, the signs of unraveling land were less visible, and her sense of time teetered out of sequence. They stepped across rutted passages and leathery mud in the low-lying intersections of truck lanes, brushing against waves of bolting oat grass at home in the disturbed earth. The black cypress windbreaks still stood, but there were no tidy rows of plantings stitching the earth to the horizon. Soon developers would erase all signs of this fertile bottomland.

This was the place they had learned to ride bicycles and build dams over the creek that flowed from the irrigation pond. There was a huge pile of long metal piping for the irrigation system that they would clamber over, clanking the pipes together and bouncing on the long arcing stretches of metal, despite being forbidden. Then they would stand, one at each end of the pile, and try to spot the other's face framed in the round window of the far end of a pipe. They called spooky sounds down to each other and kept switching from one pipe to another, and neither one could keep up. That was the whole point: never be caught and seen by the other one at that far end of the long tube. But it still happened often enough, and their voices would meet and tangle in the echoing tube. They could keep this going for hours.

In this twilight, more than fifty years since the last time they had played on the pipes, where was that pile now? Time had accordioned up tight as it always did when she was home, especially with her brother, whom she saw rarely. So when they did anything together it was a return to their games and thoughts as children. They had never developed much of a history from spending time as adults.

She had a gut sense of wading into the past as they filed through the oat grass and smelled its crisp greenness that was like watermelon or a snow cone the way it made her nose prickle along the inside. Her throat ran with juices from her tongue.

This was like no other walk they had taken, as children or adults, ever, since when would they have gone out so far from the house at dusk? By the time they would have been old enough to do this, her brother was probably out smoking with his buddies or driving the secret MG he had bought and stored in town.

Wading out of the world and into the sea of oat grass, she knew it was certain: There had never been this many fireflies in the early summer when they were kids. The popping and glimmering lights kept multiplying, thick as sparks from a leaf fire. When was the last time, if ever, that she had stepped so carefully through a field of grass with her brother, afraid to disturb the fragile light show?

But then she saw it was not just in the field. Looking to the tops of the Norway spruces up the hill, and back toward the pond, she saw every space against the indigo sky was flickering with swarms of tiny moving lights. They never seemed to land but kept rising once they had launched up out of the grass, soaring on a looping ascent that rose higher and higher, each one a daredevil flyer carving up the dark. For every cloud of lights that swept upwards, there were still more billowing from the grass.

She and her brother made a few monosyllabic comments about the display, but as it intensified, there was no place for words. They kept walking along the road, in and out of the grass, circling a large meadow that reached down to the irrigation pond, bordered by the creek on one side. There really was no point in going anywhere but here. The tree farm was just a small point in the background now that they were swept into this multiplied world. Perhaps this was a special phenomenon of early summer, lots of rain, but in any case, it did not feel like anything she had ever experienced down in these familiar woodsy parts.

It was as if she and her brother's internal beings were x-rayed by this light, made to shine like the cold light of fireflies, except it was not so ghostly a light. It was red and electrical at the edges, a warning, like downed power lines whipping and snaking across the road. Something was being raked away to expose the inside, and they could not let each other see this.

Walking with her brother in heavy dusk, over roads they didn't need light to see, such a walk could never be unencumbered. Even before they could really remember much, their spirits were damaged by the babysitter. Why can't she think of any other word for him than evil?

She and her little sister had pounded on the locked bathroom door and screamed, demanding to come in. Her brother never answered, only the babysitter: "We're having man talk in here, no girls allowed." They had gone to sleep crying. It didn't occur to her to tell her parents.

Who taught the babysitter to do these things? "My brother" is what he said when the story unravelled. But which one, and who abused the brother? Was the handyman father the source of all of this? And who abused him? This was a chain that went back generations, she knew now.

She longed for a simple walk among the shadowy grasses, a walk by children enraptured in the dark, fireflies brushing their bare arms in the settling dusk. But tonight, it felt like ash from a city on fire. Even among fireflies more plentiful than they had ever seen, the air soft as down, lush grasses trailing over their wrists, even here, in the most innocent place she knew, the bruises between them from the babysitter would never be lifted.

It was overwhelming, this twinkling night, the whole night, the fields as far as they could see, everything rupturing with sparks. Just touching the grass sent up clouds of fireflies. They were dazzled, silenced. They walked round and round the field as if it were the whole world. Could they walk long enough to erase the harm done? Could they just keep walking this field, not talking? She always felt her brother's unspoken warning between them: "I know you want to talk about it, but I am done with it, it's long ago, and I live now."

What she longs to say: "This thing wounded me too, in a different way from you. It never goes away. Sending that predator to jail would feel great, I have to admit. How has he gotten away with so much? You and the other neighbour boys were just the start for him. He is still getting away with it. How many more are there?"

She can't put her arm around her brother, she can't stroke his hair and look into his face with compassion. He would edge away from such direct expressions of caring. She carries all this by herself. Some of it their younger sister knows, but in the end, she, the eldest, carries the constant twilight in her heart.

Her brother can't feel what she is holding, all of this chill that the cold light of fireflies can't warm. She prays for the fireflies to speak for her, to make a net and lift them both, to swarm around them like a blazing blanket. But fireflies, magic as they are, are pale soldiers against the damage done.

How long does a firefly live, anyway? As long as a night, maybe less? How long was there a real childhood for her brother and his friend before they were molested? Barely six years. Would it have been stolen some other way, if not by the babysitter? Her brother has lived to adulthood, not hit by a car, not blown up by the grenade he found in a garage, not disabled in a bike accident, or drowned. But the boy she played with in the sandbox, climbed the cherry tree with, and shouted through pipes with is dead.

How did the babysitter learn to suck the life from young boys like the worst kind of parasite? What did it ever give him? There would never be enough from the young boys to fill his void. She imagined he could never stand himself, with or without them, and the brief moments of escape with them were the only thing that made it bearable. How else to explain it? How he came after the two boys repeatedly, her brother the more vulnerable. How many more times was her brother abused than his friend who blew the whistle? The friend had finally said to his parents, "I don't like it when L goes wee-wee in my mouth." But she and her sister thought this babysitter was so funny, always requested him, while their six-year-old brother cried and was told to be a man.

In the twilight and this night of the trillion fireflies, she imagines that she and her brother have entered a different dusk, an infinity of dusks, in the tree farm. All the familiar paths are waiting for them. The fireflies greet them like a meteor shower. They do not expect this beneficent welcome; they hardly know how to accept it. They don't talk except in the most concrete terms: "Look at this, see the pond, are the irrigation pipes over there? Remember when we ran away and camped in those trees?" Still, he doesn't step inside this twilight she carries. She knows he is horrified that she still thinks about something that happened over fifty years ago. Another door closed between them.

Whether open or shut, the door stands to remind her of what she did not know at the time. What her parents could never have imagined and then had to accept had happened while they were out socializing, trusting a male babysitter against the warnings of busybody friends. They were concerned for the girls. How had that babysitter appeared to several families so reliable and kind? How did he do that? This was not something parents of the 1950s ever thought to worry about.

While she treads the hard and crumbly dirt roads, kicking stones, running her hands through the grass on either side, she wants to seize the babysitter's throat and snap it open. A mild evening in the twilight for her is never free of murder in her hands. She longs to see her brother as he was before, the boy playing in the creek, prying up rocks, building a dam, not this circumspect man who sleeps with a crowbar under his bed. How would he be if nothing had happened? A trillion galaxies of fireflies will not bring him back, not in her eyes, not in the depths of her rageful heart.

When she looks over at her brother his face is clear, smoothed by the softly pulsing lights. He lifts his fingers to touch the fireflies. He would never crush a single one. They land on his arms, the little feet tickling among his arm hairs. The greenish light illuminates them faintly. He looks closely to see exactly how the thorax pulses. His arms are glowing when he holds them out to her.

22.

Just a Story

Deborah Yaffe

"If you ever tell anyone, I'll beat you half to death." That's how my father introduced the story. But my father has been safely dead for over forty years, so he can do me no harm. And most of the people involved are also dead, so what the hell.

I have no idea who else, if anyone, knows the story.

The bare bones are safe to tell: My Uncle Jerry was shaving himself one morning and died of a brain aneurysm, aged forty-two. My Aunt Sharon was left with three children under ten, the youngest an eight-month-old baby.

We all lived in Los Angeles. Sharon, one of my mother's younger sisters, was under five feet tall. Jerry, at roughly six feet, towered over everyone else in our family. When he came home from the war, he resumed his education under the GI Bill of Rights. They lived in a Quonset hut in Rodger Young Village, in Griffith Park. You can look it up on Wikipedia.

They were poor. They had two children in short order, both sickly, plagued with allergies. Once Jerry finished his studies—I presume in criminology—he worked as a probation officer with young offenders, and they were able to buy a modest house. I'm sure he was good at his work. He had a warm presence and was interested in jazz. I was always very fond of him. (I know that doesn't exactly make sense, but somehow in my mind, it all went together.) He didn't make much money, and they scrimped along. They couldn't afford to keep kosher; they didn't have the same access to middle-class amenities as even my cash-starved parents had. They were all very thin, and somehow, I thought of their family life as thin.

Finally, Jerry got a well-paid job working at a residential school for wayward boys in another county. He lived there during the week and came home at weekends. By this time, the new baby had come along. My older cousins adored their father and ran to meet him when he arrived for Friday night dinner. Jerry and Sharon thought about going to a fancy restaurant to celebrate their good fortune.

But he dropped dead instead.

Now here's the forbidden part. My father went out to the residential school to clear up Jerry's things and a woman was living in his apartment. Turns out doting husband and father had a plumper life during the week than at the weekends.

Jerry's death would have been as much of a shock for that poor woman as it was for my Aunt Sharon, and I doubt my father was kind. He had a horror of female sexuality and nothing but insults for female bodies. ("Bouncy, bouncy" he would leer at the breasts of women crossing the stage on 1950s television, dressed in strapless gowns as the times required.)

After the funeral, everyone gathered in our house. I've kept the memory of my aunt sitting in the living room, vacant and gutted, holding the baby on her lap. Older relatives twitted about, telling my cousins they must be brave.

More recently, I had been going to Los Angeles to help my cousin look after Aunt Sharon, who died at ninety-seven. She was four foot, five inches and weighed forty-five pounds; she could barely see, hear, or walk, and constantly lamented her useless state. That frail, wisp of a thing had kept things going admirably until well into her nineties. She was ready to join Jerry in heaven as well as their son, who had been killed, at nineteen, by a hit-and-run driver.

My cousin always talks of her Papa—how much she loved him and how good he was. It doesn't seem as though she could know he'd been unfaithful. My father wouldn't need to threaten me now; I'd chomp right through my tongue before I'd breathe a word to her.

From time to time, I've idly wondered what would have happened had Jerry lived. Would he have kept on his double life? I can't imagine he would have left Sharon and the children. Would he have needed to find a different job, to live full-time at home, and to end the burden of his split loyalties? Did the aneurysm have anything to do with his mental anguish? Was he, in fact, anguished? Maybe he happily compartmentalized his two lives. Maybe he was delighted with his arrangement.

At this point, it's just an anecdote, of no particular significance to anyone. I wonder why my father chose to tell me the secret. Did he tell my mother? And now, it's not even a secret, just a locus of unanswerable questions.

Afterword

Anxieties creep in. What if my cousins somehow see this piece?

The baby grew up never knowing her father. As a young woman, she went to Israel, met a young man, and has since lived in a fairly closed, ultraorthodox community. She has had maybe ten children. I doubt she reads any secular literature, and she is unlikely to come across a Canadian anthology.

To my knowledge, my older cousin doesn't read for pleasure or relaxation. She has had little of either in her life, especially since her brother died. Again, she is unlikely to stumble across this volume.

But what if?

Can I risk exposing my cousin to unwanted knowledge? Am I being frivolous in telling this story? Does anyone need to know it? More unanswerable questions.

Maybe self-doubt is one of the legacies of family secrets. Maybe they create an underlying tension between saying too much and saying too little.

Adults in my family always stressed the dangers lurking in the outside world. My response was often to deny the existence of any danger. I took way too many chances. I am lucky to be alive.

So although the well-behaved side of me urges restraint and advises me to consign this essay to the metaphorical back of the bottom drawer, I can't resist throwing caution aside and daring reality to spoil my fun. But if by chance, dear reader, you should come across my cousins, please don't say a word.

23.

A Mysterious Death on the Family Homestead

Renee Duddridge

I do not know how my great-uncle's scavenged, maggoty body came to be left dead on a secluded path among scattered canned goods and paperback novels. No one knows. Yet.

On July 15, 1977, RCMP detectives did not come onto Marcus's Lac du Bonnet land to examine his place of death. Nor did yellow caution tape mark the location of the dead body. It was said that Marcus's wallet and cash were not on his body or in his log hut. Who identified him then?

A neighbour alerted my Winnipeg grandmother, Nettie, by a phone call that a corpse, maybe that of her brother, was found. Nettie cried so long that my grandfather became very worried. Marcus was two years younger than my grandmother and her only sibling. She knew the found body was his. Her attempts to contact her brother all late spring and summer had been to no avail.

Marcus and Nettie were children of a Norwegian father, Ole, and a Swedish mother, Carrie. Ole and Carrie followed their dream and emigrated from Norway to the United States less than a year after their July 11 1896, wedding. They received a land grant on October 8 1901, signed by President Theodore Roosevelt. Ole and Carrie homesteaded on 160 acres in Roseau County, Minnesota, for only fourteen years. Just after Christmas Day 1903, Marcus was baptized and declared "in fine fettle."

Marcus became hard of hearing as a child. As a youngster, he was ill with scarlet fever. Children's gravestones in the Roseau area from 1904 to 1910 mention scarlet fever and leave evidence that Marcus was lucky to survive. Did the scarlet fever epidemic cause the family to move out of the region? The June 24 1915, edition of the *Brainerd Daily Dispatch* reports letters remaining unclaimed in the post office at Brainerd, Minnesota, including letters to Ole.

Marcus lived in a stone or log hut all his life. In 1911, his Canadian life began on a homestead near Lac du Bonnet, Manitoba. Under the Canadian Homestead Act, commonly called the Dominion Lands Act, 160 acres were given free to any male farmer who agreed to cultivate at least forty acres and to build a permanent dwelling within three years. The only cost to Ole was a ten dollar administration fee. During the first of many mosquito-and-fly-plagued summers, eight-year-old Marcus, ten-year-old Nettie, and their parents cleared large rocks, planted vegetables, and grew grain on the land. The rocks were used to build their first small stone-house. The Homestead conditions were met. Later, a slightly larger log hut with a gable roof was built. The scene of Marcus's death included the ransacked log home and the path to it.

Did Marcus die there on the path near his log home? It is assumed he died outside. Or was the unconscious body dragged from inside to outside? In any case, because his body lay on the path, black blow flies arrived within minutes, as they do in an outdoor death. The female corpse eaters laid hundreds of eggs while eating his decaying flesh. Although investigators did not calculate exactly how long his fly-covered dead body lay there, the day of death was noted on paper as July 15. I did not see my great-uncle's body as I had just travelled to Saskatchewan to purchase a house for a later move. I was told by my dad that his body was barely identifiable. It is suspected Marcus did not die peacefully on the land on which he lived.

In 1914, three years after a young Marcus, his sister Nettie and his parents cleared the Lac du Bonnet land and established a garden and crops, World War One started. The Canadian government encouraged farmers to increase their output. The government message "Food Will Win the War" persuaded Marcus and his father to farm more acres. In his developing years, Marcus worked many back-breaking hours. From 1914 to 1918, the family garden, farm, and Marcus grew. The family benefited from high prices for their produce due to the demand for food. In 1920, Ole signed for his hard-earned homesteaded land. The deed of land was part of a land grant issued on behalf of the Government of Canada in the name of King George V.

At the end of the war, Marcus lost his best companion. His sister moved away to work as a house cleaner. Nettie hated black flies, mosquitoes, and outdoor work. She found work as an indoor helper in a Moose Jaw home and found love. Marcus accompanied his parents to attend Nettie's 1921 Winnipeg wedding. Nettie left the work of growing and harvesting the vegetable garden to Marcus and their parents.

When Marcus was twenty-one, my father, Nettie's child, was born. Marcus was delighted. Marcus was the silent, hardworking type. Being hard of hearing, he was shy and never married. In the cold and snow-filled Lac Du Bonnet winters, his favourite pastime was to sit by the wood stove and read. He encouraged his favorite nephew, my young father, to read. Later in life, my father also became an avid reader. My father told many stories of his summer visits to his uncle.

Marcus's life was mostly ruled by the work on the land, and the land became more difficult to work. Just prior to 1926, the Province of Manitoba expropriated a strip through the northwest corner of the family's 160-acre parcel to build a highway. The right of way divided the family land into two parcels, which made farming complicated. Equipment had to be moved across the Provincial Trunk Highway 11. When seventy-one-year-old Ole retired in the fall of 1932, he sold the remaining southwest quarter of section twenty-five for "natural love and affection" and one dollar to his twenty-nine-year-old son. Being hard of hearing affected Marcus and his family. It likely determined his death.

Marcus lived alone in the log home and worked the land until the Winnipeg River waters enticed him to a different lifestyle. His home was only one mile from the Winnipeg River. Marcus slowly reduced the outdoor farm work and began to canoe and fish. He posted an advertisement in the Springfield Leader. The July 19, 1949, notice read: "FOR SALE 1938 Massey-Harris 10-foot Dumprake. God (sic) condition." In the summers, Marcus was known to be away from his log home for weeks at a time. He paddled, harvested wild rice, and fished. He harvested wild rice along the river and its tributaries with his Indigenous friends as a combined job and hobby. He was able to earn some cash and at the same time have the companionship of his friends. My young father met many of Marcus's friends and tells of some of their escapades.

Marcus did not always stay home reading and chopping wood. On April 28, 1959, my seventh birthday, at a regular session of the Lac du Bonnet police court, Marcus pleaded guilty to charges of being intoxicated in a public place. He was fined ten dollars. From the 1960s to the 1970s, Marcus continued to live a bachelor life until his unexpected death at age seventy-four.

Did friends of Marcus find the body? Whoever found him and the trailed cans of food and novels assumed that Marcus had recently shopped at the grocery store in Lac du Bonnet. There were also remains of spilled food boxes. It was surmised by those who found the body that Marcus planned for provisions for at least one month. Except for the many stacks of chopped wood, the tagged hard covered books and raided remains of Marcus's home, there was little evidence left of his daily life. The raided remains maybe evidence of the reason for death or were caused later. Most of the many hard-covered books were left open at random as if someone had searched all. No cash. No will.

What caused Marcus to die? Perhaps a thief quietly followed my deaf great-uncle up along the path and then knocked him unconscious to steal his cash. Was the thief at the grocery store and noticed a wad of money as Marcus pulled it from his pocket? My great-uncle carried a roll of cash and liked to pull a bill or two off the roll to pay. Or maybe my very-much-alive great-uncle, arriving with an armload of groceries and possibly fresh fish, was attacked by a hungry bear that was not heard. Because my great-uncle did not own a car or drive, the question remains: How did he get home? Did a taxi driver or a friend drop him off at the highway's edge? Did the effort of carrying too many groceries along that long length of path cause chest pain and arm pain in the seventy-four-year-old? Did my great-uncle have a heart attack? A lot of maybes.

After Marcus died, did a wild animal or bird scavenge his body and drag away the groceries? Most of his few friends did not have phones. There was no 911 operator then. In the late seventies, cell phones were not in popular use. Marcus did not have a landline in his rustic home. And because he was hard of hearing, he could not hear a barking dog or a person coming from behind.

As a youngster, visiting with my sisters, parents, and grandparents, I romanticized my great-uncle, the original stone house, and the log cabin. Marcus had created many special summer visits for his nephew and the stories my father told were those of an idolizing young man. Marcus had a shaman friend who dream travelled. The two of them and my dad shared delicious wild rice and fish meals and their fishing stories.

Later, I realized the harsh reality. The log cabin became a real shack, with no electricity, sewage, or water. And dirty. My youngest sister recalled being scolded for dropping a pail down the well. My other sister recalled being quite shocked about how Marcus lived and about how he kept his food in a cold well in the ground. The only heat was a wood stove. There was an old horsehair couch. It was dark in the log hut with only one small window.

My great-uncle promised that Dad would inherit his land. Days after notification of Marcus's death, my parents, sisters, and police officer brother-in-law, who is experienced in examining death scenes, went to Marcus's property. When they got there, the log cabin had been raided. My parents, sisters, and family then searched through Marcus's books, kitchen stuff, and personal items looking for a will. They looked outside in the well and woodpile for a hidden container that could hold a will. It was never found. My sister recalls clearing out the hut and gathering some of his personal possessions, including a pocketknife once owned by Marcus. My sister did not think the land was worth much at that time. Her memory is of fields full of rocks and stones, not good for crops.

My eighty-two-year-old grandfather, Nettie's husband, who had grown up impoverished in Scotland did not have a sentimental attachment to the land. He and my grandmother rarely visited Marcus or the homestead. They did not drive a car. My grandfather had constantly worked and travelled as a CPR valet for thirty-five years. He was anxious to sell the land quickly because it was the property of his wife's family, and taxes would have to be paid. But the land was worth something to the next-lot neighbour who had been renting and farming the land. A 1977 real estate agent's advertisement in the Springfield newspaper listed the property. The land was sold to the neighbouring farmer by my grandfather for less than nineteen thousand dollars.

In those days, a woman had little say in land matters. My grieving grandmother did not have the strength to stand up to her husband and argue that she did not want to sell so quickly. Many years later, she revealed she had enough money to pay the taxes for several years after her brother's death but was discouraged from keeping her family homestead. She was also unsure whether my father would need future monetary help.

Because the will was not found, my fifty-three-year-old father did not inherit the land. He was heartbroken because he could not afford to purchase it. At age thirty-four, my father became blind with detached retina resulting from a war injury of shrapnel in his left eye and head trauma. His vision was partially repaired by many surgeries. But he was unable to work full time until he was forty. His illness and lack of income resulted in six years of dated and unpaid bills. The death of his uncle caused a life-long sadness. My dad's inability to own the family's homestead was a lasting regret.

I am still sad about the mystery of my great-uncle's death and lack of will. As the oldest granddaughter, I wanted to buy the land homesteaded by my great grandparents and keep it in our family. It has beautiful trees on one side, as it borders next to a provincial forest. But the timing was wrong. My new husband and I had just bought a house in Saskatoon. We could have afforded it but had just taken out a mortgage; we would not be living close to the property for awhile. The sale to a stranger of our family homestead is a huge loss to my family.

My great uncle's exact date of death is unknown. Although his body was found around July 15, 1977, there is an historical record that notes a different date. An August 2, 1977, obituary in the Winnipeg Free Press stated the cremation of Marcus's body had taken place. The Springfield Leader reported a memorial service date of August 6, 1977. To this day forty-four years later, what happened to my great uncle, his ransacked log home, and missing will is not discussed in my family. Someone does know what happened on our family homesteaded land in Lac du Bonnet. But who? It is a secret kept by a stranger, and it has become our family secret.

24.

Spectral Stories

Lenore Maybaum

"In this pause, I suddenly saw something very clearly. Whatever it was I wanted from my mother was simply not there to be had. It was not her fault. And it was therefore not my fault that I was unable to elicit it."

—Alison Bechdel, *Are You My Mother?*

I remember my mother's books. I collect them on my shelves and carry them in my mind. Many I took under the auspices of borrowing but then kept to run my fingers down the margins of their pages and to feel the ghostly hollow of her pen's inscriptions.

As a young theatre major, my mother accumulated shelves of hardbound Shakespeare anthologies, British literature, and well-worn paper play scripts. Although she no longer studies literature nor performs on stage, not for decades now, I like these reminders of her previous self—a person I would have liked to know, one who had not yet endured the string of betrayals, failed marriages, and debilitating insecurities that would come to mark most of her next few decades. Even more than the stories on the page, I am struck by my mother's annotations: maps of a life before mine that hinted at her impassioned relationship with language and literature, traces of a romantic young woman before her long, burdened days of raising four young children alone. I piece her inscriptions together to trace the shape of her loss. I piece them together to trace the shape of us. Growing up, as now, my mother was an enigma, a woman who kept her personal life private and her past life guarded. Yet preserved in her annotations is a spectral connection to another narrative, one unnamed yet known to me.

Somewhere, there is another story.

I was in search of these spectral stories—first my mother's, then those of strangers, and, much later, those of lovers and friends. As a child, I collected old postcards and letters from flea markets, books from my grandparents' basement, and notes discarded in school hallways. I would keep them and organize them, take them out and reread them, and create narratives in my head of the lives of the people who wrote them. Despite growing up in a small house with five other people, my most formative childhood memories are of private interactions with other people's correspondences.

Perhaps like many children, particularly those of large families, I felt alone most of the time. Whether this was the cause or the result of being a young reader, a bookworm, I'm not sure. But I remember little outside of being alone, reading, during my elementary years.

When I was nine years old, I went into our basement and found myself digging through old boxes, one of which contained dozens of love letters written to my mother a decade earlier. I recall the beautiful cursive lettering that decorated them, calligraphy of delicate, swooping curls across the yellowing pages. Although I did not recognize the last name of the return address, Maybaum, I was drawn to the postage written in German. I tucked one of the envelopes into my pocket, and by the end of the night, I had written a letter addressed to the return address listed on it.

Weeks passed, and I had more or less forgotten about the letter I had sent, until one night, after my younger siblings had gone to bed, I was called in for a family meeting. My parents' expressions were grave as they sat me down to the dining room table. "We received a letter," my mother began, "from Germany." I could tell it was serious, yet inside my heart leapt. My letter had been not only received but responded to. I could hardly contain my excitement as my mother proceeded.

Over the next half hour, it was explained to me that the address belonged to my biological paternal grandmother, and that the man who I knew as my father—the man sitting across the table from me and whose last name I shared—was actually my stepfather. My mother warned that I was never, ever, under any circumstance to write to that address again, not even to speak my biological father's name. For sending the letter, I was grounded for the following two weeks.

Over the next decade of my life, random fragments of information came to me about my biological father—that my mom met him when she was a foreign exchange student in Germany when she was only seventeen, that he was finishing his PhD in Chinese philosophy and poetry when they met, and that he and my mom had eloped, eventually moving together to the US where they lived with my maternal grandparents for two years. The stories of how it had ended vary. According to my mother, my biological paternal grandfather had a heart attack, and when my father flew to Germany to be with him, she promptly filed for divorce. There was little emotion in this narrative of hers. My maternal grandmother's story is the same until the part when my father flies back to Germany: "Your mother tried and tried to reach him, but he never responded. Eventually they divorced."

These pieces of his life and my mother's former life came to me sporadically and inadvertently over the years and clearly weren't expressed as invitations to a longer conversation. I was thankful for them but careful not to pursue additional information, as the topic of my mom's elopement and eventual divorce—to a foreigner, no less—was taboo in my conservative extended family.

Several years later, one late afternoon in high school French class, our teacher played an audio recording of the children's book *Le Petit Prince*. While the students around me continued to work through their French grammar exercises as the narrator read, I was immediately captivated by this story, drawn to tears in parts, and couldn't wait to get home from school to tell my mother about it. When I did her jaw dropped: "Your biological father was obsessed with that story. He sent me pages from it while we were separated, and he quoted lines from it when he proposed to me."

When I was nineteen, after I had moved out of her house, my mother gave me the letter written to me by my biological father a decade earlier. She also told me she had destroyed all of the letters from the box in the basement. "Too incriminating," she said.

Around the same time, I found a funeral announcement for my paternal grandfather, Wilhelm, in my grandparents' basement. On the back of the announcement, in the same beautiful cursive I recognized from years earlier, was written, "Any sign of life will be kindly and quietly appreciated."

My mother's handling of her history, of my history, was problematic on many levels, though the news at age nine that I had a different father felt immediately validating. At once I had a narrative to frame what had, up until that moment, been an unnamed longing. It confirmed what I had intuitively felt for as long as I can remember: I was not at home in my home. The news I had another father, perhaps another family in Germany, rationalized my strained relationship with my stepfather and half-siblings, with whom I seemed to share very little in terms of interests, appearances, and personalities. This new knowledge also strengthened my identity as a collector of correspondences, a scholar of stories. Suddenly, my own inner aching to connect the lines and histories of others took the form of a more embodied search for meaning in my own life, for a direct line to the place I am from—a place to which I feel intimately connected without ever having physically experienced.

And so it began, at age nine, the acknowledgment of a sense of loss in my own life and the drive to reconnect to something I had always known and never known. I sought out lessons in German literature, language, and culture as a way of strengthening this burgeoning sense of myself as different, even European, and quite possibly intellectual. Through reading, I could recuperate a relationship to a father and, in some ways, to a mother I never knew, all the while encompassed by the family silence that obscured so much of my sense of myself and my history.

But this experience also taught me an important lesson, which was that reading, unlike writing, could be a safe way to do identity work. Through reading, I could escape the chaos and turmoil of my parents' marriage, the crying babies, as well as the palpable sadness and regret that characterized my mother's interactions with me when I was a young child. Reading was a way of escaping that public reality and connecting to another, more private, reality, which included my fantasies of myself as a European and the daughter of a German intellectual and the fantasies of another version of my mother—unfettered and happy. But writing included risk. It had for my mother, and it had for me. It left a trace of our inner desires and those shadowed identities—as wayward, naive, romantic teenage mother and her fatherless child that were clearly not welcomed into the family's public space. "Too incriminating," one might say.

Since I had already been punished once for writing, I never wrote to my father again until I was in my twenties, and by that time, the return address to my biological grandmother was defunct. It was a lesson I'd have to learn again and again my childhood years—the ways that reading alone could serve as entry into those past lives and spectral stories of my family's history in such a way that speaking or writing could not, or should not.

25.

Uncle Fred's Secret

Ruby Swanson

My soul was being destroyed. I didn't know why it was a secret. I didn't know why I couldn't talk to anyone about it. I lived in dread worrying that telling my mother could mean that her reaction might make me have to choose between having a relationship with her or supporting my son. I couldn't put it off any longer, I had to tell her.

Simply looking at the phone had made me cry. As I dialed her number, my heart slammed against my ribs. By the second ring, tears bathed my face and neck. I couldn't speak when my mom picked up the phone. All she could hear was me sobbing.

Quietly she said, "What's wrong?" I didn't answer. She waited and asked again, but I still couldn't answer. The third time she asked, she too was crying. In a whisper, she pleaded, "Tell me, what's wrong?"

"Carl's gay," I blurted.

"That's it? That's all? Stop crying. He's not sick. There's nothing wrong. They told me my brother, Fred, was gay."

A shoebox overflowing with tattered old black and white photographs sat on a shelf in my parents' basement stairwell. I loved looking at the pictures despite not having a clue who most of the people were. Buried in the collection were a couple of shots of my uncle Fred from when he visited us on our farm in Saskatchewan, just a few months before he died. There was Fred wearing a three piece suit and spats with a fedora perched at an angle on the side his head. He brought my seven-year-old brother a shiny red toy metal tractor and a bride doll for four-year-old me. The doll was almost as tall as I was. I had years of fun doing her long blonde hair. There was hardly any hair left on that poor doll's head.

In my mid-twenties, my Vancouver cousins told me Fred was gay. Since all I knew of him was the old, faded photos and the memory of my bald bride doll, I was only politely interested. And besides, my mom had never talked about her half-brother Fred.

Fedor (Fred/Frank) Sopotyk was a baby in 1903 when his family left Ukraine, heading as far west as they could possibly imagine in search of a better life. Canada was giving away land. Posters and pamphlets flooded Ukraine tempting peasant farmers: "Over 200 million acres of land in Canada is waiting for new settlers 160 acres for $10."

One hundred and sixty acres was 32 times the amount of land Fred's family would ever own in Ukraine, where their house, barn, chicken coop, dog house, vegetable garden, blacksmith shop, tools and machinery, and a few animals were all packed onto a tiny five acre plot. It was a sliver of land that would have been divided again and again with each new generation.

With fifty dollars in his pocket, my grandfather and his young family escaped poverty and oppression in Ukraine in exchange for isolation, extreme weather conditions, and mosquitoes on the Canadian prairies. They left Ukraine with a few sacks and wooden chests filled with grain, vegetable and flower seeds, farm tools, household utensils, clothing, and a couple cherished mementos. By train, they crossed Poland to Hamburg, Germany. It took two weeks to cross the Atlantic to Halifax in steerage, the least expensive section of the ship. It took over a month to complete the eight thousand kilometre journey to Saskatchewan.

My mother, Lena, and Fred came from a family of thirteen children. My grandfather, Ivan, had five children with his first wife, Fred's mother. She died a few years after they arrived in Canada. Ivan married my grandmother with whom he had eight more children. Lena was the second youngest, and Fred was the second eldest. The seventeen year age difference meant they hardly knew each other. Fred moved to Toronto before my mother could have had any early memories of him.

I didn't ask my mom anything more about Fred being gay, and she never brought it up again. I became curious about Fred only after her death and called the few living relatives, who were then in their eighties, that could tell me anything more about my uncle.

As the eldest son, Fred had the privilege of attending the Saskatoon Normal School, a place where high school graduates trained to become teachers. Fred left Saskatchewan for Toronto in the early 1920s. He never taught school after he left Saskatchewan. Some cousins said Fred fell in love with a woman, who was a circus performer, but it hadn't worked out. Things got interesting when I found out he worked as a vaudeville female impersonator, had a stage name, and spent a short time in the United States playing female roles in films. After World War II, Fred moved to Vancouver.

While researching Fred, I worked with LGBT historians and archivists in Vancouver and Toronto. They were eager to find and piece together lost history of the gay community. Before homosexuality was decriminalized in 1969, anything resembling a gay newspaper or magazine rarely existed, and if any sort of record about anything did exist, it was well hidden. Alan Miller, a retired librarian and archivist at the Canadian Lesbian and Gay Archives in Toronto, spent days searching back issues of *The Globe* and *Toronto Star* newspapers, published between 1920 and 1945, looking for information about Fred and Toronto vaudeville female impersonators. I was at work when an email arrived from Alan telling me he found a report about Fred/Frank and another man in *The Globe,* dated July 11, 1928. He attached a scanned copy of the newspaper clipping:

> CHARGE OF DISORDERLY
> Frank (Fred) Sopotyk and Eberton Shunk were arrested last night by the police of Cowan Avenue Station on charges of disorderly conduct.

At the time, there were "comfort stations," much like the public restrooms we have today at subway and train stations, along the streetcar route. "Perhaps Frank got caught up in a washroom bust. All of this was before there were gay bars or clubs, so nothing to be embarrassed by. Poor Frank though, to have his name appear in a local paper," wrote Alan. The bust likely wasn't an example of the police calmly writing a ticket and telling the young men, "Time to go home, boys." Arrests often included a beating and a night or two in jail where additional punishment was readily handed out.

When I first learned about the vaudeville performer part of Fred's life, I was thrilled. It was a novelty. Not many people have relatives in vaudeville shows. My husband's great uncle, Jerry Burke, was a professional musician in the Lawrence Welk band, and my Fred was a female impersonator in Toronto—fantastic. The afternoon I received the email from Alan about the disorderly conduct charge, I naively hoped maybe Fred and his partner were embracing or possibly walking arm in arm and were charged for that. But even something as harmless as holding hands would have been impossible. Two men could never have openly displayed any kind of affection in 1928, when gay men were forced to meet in dangerous places. Tragically, nearly a century later, in many countries, this still remains the case.

As I held a photocopy of the newspaper column, a profound sadness nearly suffocated me. There were no gay clubs or bars in Toronto in 1928. When Fred and his partner wanted to be alone, there was nowhere for them to go. Rooming house owners watched everyone coming and going on their premises, and rooming house walls were paper thin. They would have been forced to meet in a public washroom. This was my dear sweet uncle who thirty years later brought lovely gifts for his little niece and nephew when he visited his youngest sister's family.

He was twenty-six years old when he was arrested. Fred escaped rural Saskatchewan to try to make a life for himself in Toronto, three thousand kilometres from his home and family. What happened instead was that the poor man was made to endure the humiliation of being named in the local paper and singled out as a criminal for committing the crime of being who he was.

On a quiet sunny Sunday morning in the fall of 2013, Alan, my son Paul, and I set out to find the locations where Fred had lived around St. Patrick's Square in downtown Toronto. Most of the old buildings in the area had been demolished. We skulked around loading docks and back lanes clutching Alan's list of addresses and an old street map and glanced at maps on our phones. We found a few cornerstones with construction dates from the 1970s and some that were from a bit earlier. Office towers and provincial government buildings, hospitals, and retail shops replaced rooming houses and parking lots.

After wandering around the area for a couple of hours, we took a streetcar down Queen Street to Cowan Avenue to see if we could find the police station in the area now called Little Tibet. A weathered bronze plaque on a metre high stake had an image and short history of the original Police Station #6, a dour looking small brick building with a warehouse type addition at the back. A line of tiny rectangular windows, just below the roof line, ran the length of the rear building. These must have been the holding cells. The original police station building, just west of Queen and Cowan, was demolished and had been rebuilt in 1931, using mottled red and brown brick with tyndall stone trim. In 2014, it housed a centre for newcomers to Canada and more recently an arts co-op. While we were there, three young men stood smoking outside the front door. The comfort stations were gone. No one spoke. There was nothing to say. I imagined how awful this would have been for Fred. Who was there to talk to and what could he possibly have said? To survive, he had to hide everything.

For the next twenty years, Fred stayed mostly in Toronto. He lived in the United States during his short film career. In Toronto, he continued performing and had odd jobs working on and off as a baker in a bread making factory. After World War II, five of his brothers and sisters followed him to Toronto with their own families. Fred immediately pulled up stakes and moved to Vancouver.

My cousin Stella knew Fred well. She was eleven years old when he arrived at their house in Vancouver in 1947. Stella's mother, another one of Fred's sisters, was worried he was going to have a nervous breakdown. He had lost interest in life. Uncle Fred slept on the couch in their living room for a month before he found a place to live in a rooming house a few doors down the street from the restaurant where he worked in the Downtown Eastside, already then home to the poorest of the poor. Slowly Fred settled into a new life as a waiter. He regularly had Sunday dinner with Dora and her family and left a Gladstone bag in Dora's closet for safekeeping. Every now and then, in private, Fred would add and remove items from the bag.

Fred was a heavy smoker who didn't drink much. He was always well dressed and immaculately groomed. He had a fancy silver cigarette lighter/case that was one combined unit with his initials FJS engraved on it. Fred was in his mid-fifties when he died suddenly. No one did autopsies in those days, leaving us to believe he had a heart attack due to a congenital heart condition on that side of the family. After Fred died, Dora and Stella opened the Gladstone bag. "We found items and articles about homosexuals, confirming to us that he was gay," said Stella.

In 2013, I called Qmunity, the Vancouver LGBT community centre, hoping to speak with someone who could tell me something about early female impersonators and what life was like for gay men in Vancouver after the war. Qmunity immediately put me in touch with Ron Dutton, founder of the BC Gay and Lesbian Archives. Ron quickly located the addresses where Fred had lived and worked. He told me about Vancouver, the port city, during the first half of the twentieth century. Even then, Vancouver had a reputation for tolerating marginalized groups, including gays. The city was booming, needed workers, overlooked personal lifestyles, and likely provided Fred with some freedom that wasn't available in a Saskatchewan farming community or even Toronto, where he would have had to be even more careful with the arrival of his siblings and their families.

Ron rode his bike through the area to match the current building addresses with the information he had about Fred. Just as in Toronto, many of the Vancouver buildings had been replaced, and the street numbering had changed.

A few years later, Ron took me and my high school friend Harry on a walking tour of the Downtown Eastside. "The area hasn't changed much since the 1940s and 1950s," said Ron. The streets were lined with abandoned buildings. Some had been vacant for decades; a few others had scaffolding and the odd construction worker milling about. Around the corner on East Hastings Street, we wound our way through a block long sidewalk clothing exchange. Dozens and dozens of people who lived on the street sat and slept on the bare concrete sidewalk. Bits and pieces of used old clothing were laid out beside them. A giant tent and trailer complex housed a mobile clinic and safe injection site. I had never been to Vancouver's Downtown Eastside before.

Surprisingly, both rooming houses where Fred had lived were still standing. Fred worked as a waiter at the Busy Bee Café, across the street from the New Horizon Rooms at 45 West Cordova Street, his first home. In 2017, the building had been renamed the New Horizon Shelter.

Our last stop was 56 East Cordova Street. Ron struck up a conversation with a resident who was outside having a cigarette. She invited us in to see the modest upgraded rooming house run by the City of Vancouver. We walked up a constricted stairwell and were greeted by a security officer—instead of a rooming house owner—who sat in a tiny office monitoring a bank of security cameras. Still no privacy. The long narrow hallway was lit with glaring fluorescent lights. The floor was visibly warped and sloped downwards. Residents no longer had to share a bathroom at the end of the hall, and each room had a small area for food preparation.

On May 4, 2017, I stood inside the rooming house at 56 East Cordova Street where Fred lived in Vancouver. Sixty years after my uncle's death, I honoured his memory by walking through the neighbourhood where he spent the last few years of his life and where he died in 1958. Alone.

*The excerpts reprinted herein are taken from the memoir *A Family Outing,* by Ruby Remenda Swanson, published by Cormorant Books Inc., Toronto. Copyright 2016 © Ruby Remenda Swanson. Used with the permission of the publisher.

26.

The Road Leads to Crosby Beach

Amanda Hale

I wrote the first words by hand in a London pub in January 2000. I imagined a girl called Mary Byrne, fresh from Ireland, presenting herself for the job of narrator in the fictionalized story of a family, (mine), whose father was interned in Britain during World War Two for his fascist loyalties. But it was only in 2012 that the story truly surfaced and began to write itself in the voice of the imaginary Mary Byrne.

When we were children, our mother had hinted at half-siblings, never clearly explained. "There may have been one, two, possibly three, with one or two different Irish women," she would say in her offhand manner. In our family there is a streak of romancing. My mother and her sister Mary, my grandmother, Great Granny, and Great-Great Auntie Maude Middlewood were all storytellers. "Liar, liar!" they would trill at each other, breaking into giggles. They were always telling tales about our family, creative nonfiction word-of-mouth tales.

While researching for that book begun in the London pub, I received a newspaper article through the mail, sent by one of the many people who wanted to help. People love to help writers unearth family secrets. We all have a truffling instinct—a yearning to be in on the dig, a fellow archeologist. I opened the large brown envelope, hand addressed, and found a sheaf of newspaper cuttings, including a yellowed column from 1953, reporting a court order for my father to pay child support to a Miss Brennan for their infant daughter. There was no photo, so I immediately began to imagine the child. She would have been my little sister. For me, the youngest of four and the so-called spoiled brat, this was an attractive addition to our family, cinching me up a notch.

I posted the relevant details on Genealogy.com and heard nothing in four years. Then, in April of 2016, with a sixth rewrite of my fictionalized novel out in multiple submissions, I received an email from an astonishingly named Mary Byrne, resident of Dublin. I suppose I had chosen a common name for *my* Mary Byrne. Nevertheless, this message caused a dramatic collision in my mind between fact and fiction. I felt that my character had written to me, her creator. "I am writing on behalf of my adopted cousin Anne," she wrote. "My apologies if this unsolicited message is upsetting, but I have reason to believe that you may be half-sister to Anne." She went on to tell me that there was also a half-brother, Liam Michael, born two years after Anne. This living-breathing Mary Byrne turned out to be an internet sleuth who had learned much about my father, the fictional Mr. Brooke of my novel, and also about me from my webpage.

Mary Byrne and I became fast email friends. She put me and my two sisters in touch with our new sister, who travelled from Christchurch, New Zealand, to meet us in England in the autumn of that year. I went with Anne to the agency that had dealt with her brother's adoption, and there we learned of yet another half-sister—Nuala—born to a different Irish woman. The clerk, a Mr. Jenks, distinguished by sparse strands of grey hair raked carefully over his skull, showed us the adoption documents for Liam Michael, Anne's brother, born three months after our father's suicide. Mr. Jenks extracted from Liam's file a double spread newspaper article. On one side was a photo of our father holding baby Anne and standing next to her mother, Vera Brennan, who showed an advanced pregnancy. On the facing page, he held another little girl and stood beside a different woman. The focus of the article was clear in the headline: "He bred 'master race' children but did not wed their mothers."

My mother had it exactly right—three children with two different Irish women. Clearly, she had seen this same article from what she called "the gutter press." In wartime, when our father was interned for three years, Mum had developed a hatred of such journalism.

I tracked down Liam's adoptive family only to learn of his death at age thirty-five in bad circumstances. They took me to see his grave near their home in Southport. I photographed the headstone and sent an attachment to Anne, who had already returned to Christchurch.

We had "family sessions" once a week in our mother's bedroom. She loved having us gathered around her with no outsiders to interfere. I slept in my father's single bed, inches from Mum's bed. Our father was gone; we didn't know where he was. He'd come back from the war a different man, Mum said. Uncle Jimmy (who had been a major in the war), said he'd been a traitor and a coward, but Mum shushed him and said, "Not in front of the children!"

Sally and Bridget sat in the corner, squished in the big chair, while Jimmy balanced on the arm, swinging his leg back and forth with a bedroom slipper flapping against the sole of his foot. They were in pyjamas and dressing gowns. I was in Jimmy's old cast offs, sitting up in bed with the eiderdown draped around me. It was always cold in our bedroom, but I was shivering with anticipation, waiting for someone to reveal a big secret. I felt as if everyone knew something that they were keeping from me, and that they might drop some hints this time, some clues that I could follow. But week after week, I was disappointed. There was nothing, just a lot of drivel about what our baby cousin had done and how funny he was, how Grandpa was poorly again with his heart, and how Granny wanted to go shopping in Manchester tomorrow and had invited us all to have lunch at Kendal Milne's, but we must be on our best behavior, and I'd have to wear my new red shoes that pinched my toes.

"Bridget painted her toenails!" I burst out. Mum glared at Bridget who was blushing like a beetroot. But it didn't work. I thought if I was the first to tell a secret then they'd all come pouring out, all the things I longed to hear. Because I felt them, I knew they existed, the silence was so loud in my head.

I cried a lot, not knowing what I was crying about. "You have to stop," Sally would say. "You'll make yourself ill." But once I started, I couldn't stop. It all welled up in me, and the more I cried, the more my sisters clammed up because I was embarrassing them. Jimmy just smirked and kept silent while Mum shouted, "Stop crying, or I'll give you something to cry about!" which only made it worse. I was the family tap that nobody could turn off. We were drowning in secrets.

When my siblings went away to boarding school, I began to create my own world. I became a storyteller like Mum and Gran and Auntie Mary—but a secretive one. I had a book to write my stories in, hidden in my father's desk next to my bed. For decades after we left that house, I remained in that room, sitting up in bed, scratching in my notebook, with Mum's portrait of Jesus staring down at me.

My mother instilled in me an early feeling of perpetual surveillance. "God is watching you all the time," she would say as we motored around the countryside, visiting my siblings at their various schools. "God is watching you. He knows everything you do and everything you think." What a terrifying thought! I wondered if he also watched my brother and my sisters and how he could be in so many places. Perhaps he knew where our father was. Mum taught me the Lord's Prayer as I sat beside her in the passenger seat, repeating the words, trying to hold back a feeling of car sickness: "Our father who art in Heaven, hallowed be thy name." But my father was named JL for his initials. It was only as I learned to read that I realized his name was different from "jail," where he'd been locked up for three years during the war, which I had missed, being born near the end of it. Bridget told me they'd had family sessions almost every night during the war, in the air-raid shelter.

When Mum remarried, we moved to my stepfather's house, where I had a whole wing all to myself. No more family sessions. Mum was very busy with her new husband, and eventually we all flew the coop—to Canada, to London, and me to drama school where I played Joan of Arc declaiming, "I will dare, and dare, and dare, until I die!"

During my research for the book, I travelled to Llandudno on the north coast of Wales and walked the Great Orme. When news had come of our father's suicide, Mum said he'd jumped from a cliff on the Great Orme and had drowned; that his head had been dashed off on the rocks, and his body washed up on a beach. I imagined this scene over and over, his arms flung out, his body suspended on the wind like a giant seagull, as his hat flew off, spiralling downwards, and his body plunged after it.

The Great Orme is a limestone headland jutting into the Irish Sea, a sleeping sea serpent, two miles long and a mile wide. I started at the parking lot and headed for the cliff path, all my senses alert, seeking the exact spot where my father had launched himself into the deep, leaving us forever. I found a delicate white bone nestling in the grass and recognized it, from postwar school lunches, as a rabbit bone. I placed it carefully in my pocket and kept it as a talisman. Jimmy had told me that Mum once called our father "a frightened rabbit." He was a hatter. They moulded hats in those days out of felted rabbit fur. No pun intended, but my thinking was fuzzy from that early feeling of vital information withheld. The talismanic nature of the rabbit bone may sound fuzzy, but it felt (again, no pun intended), important as a signpost to lead me on in my quest.

I was guided across the Great Orme by my imagination, investing every move and thought with a significance they did not deserve, as it turned out. All those years of imagining my father flying from a clifftop dissipated when I learned through academic research, that in fact he had jumped from the Mersey ferry and had been decapitated by the paddles. I had been pursuing a metaphor, investing it with all the passion of my misguided quest. There, on the white page of a history book by A.W. Brian Simpson (about wartime Regulation 18B, under which internment without trial became legal in Britain), was written the plain fact, accompanied by the text of my father's suicide note. A slip of paper found where? Not on his body which had been washed up two weeks later on Crosby Beach, not in the forgotten pocket of a fellow ferry passenger. No, he had apparently sent that slip of paper to a newspaper to be printed for all to see: "My work here is complete. I follow the Fuehrer to glory and eternity. Through the sacrifice of the Aryan martyrs our world victory is assured. Heil Hitler."

I have spared my sisters this detail. Our brother is dead, our last family session having been held at his bedside in a Toronto hospital, when our mother was still with us. We three sisters remain, elderly now. And I am the holder of this particular family secret.

Excerpt from *Mad Hatter,* the novel I began writing in a London pub in January 2000:

A young woman was out walking with her four-year-old daughter. They lived in the nearby town of Crosby, north of Liverpool, and would walk across the sand dunes and down to the beach almost every day. The countryside around Crosby was flat and sandy, and in some places very marshy so that deep ditches had been dug to drain the fields. A broad stretch of sand dunes extended along the northern half of the coast.

The woman looked back and saw her little girl crouched, prodding at something with a stick.

"C'mon, love, what ya doin'?" she shouted.

The child looked up but didn't move Whatever it was, she was intrigued. The mother smiled to herself, sprinting back up the beach to fetch her little beachcomber. Shells crunched under her feet, and her shoes left damp imprints in the sand that dried slowly in her wake. She was almost there, reaching out her hand to the child when she saw what it was she was poking at. There was no smell. The waves kept washing over it, refreshing it, but it was clearly a putrefied body. There were the arms, the legs, a bloated torso, and where the head should have been there were jagged edges of spongy whiteness, more like seaweed than flesh.

"C'mon, darlin'. C'mon, take Mummy's hand." She heard the tightness in her own voice as though from far away, and she tried to control herself, not to frighten the child. "We have to go and get help, Sweetheart. Somebody's drowned."

The girl looked up, her brow furrowed.

"Drowned? What's that?"

The mother felt panic rising in her now, a desire to run away before the grisly sight imprinted itself on her.

"Come on!" she insisted and grasped her child's hand firmly.

As they walked down the beach, the little girl kept twisting around to look back, all the way until they were over the edge of the sand dunes, descending to the town of Crosby.

My mother chided me for my curiosity. "Why are you always delving into the past?" she would ask angrily. I suppose she was trying to protect me from what I might find with all that delving.

Of course, I had to go to Crosby beach—to walk across the dunes in a bleak wintery season, with sharp grasses lashing at my legs. The beach was covered with razor clam shells—those long, sharp, brittle, grey shells that litter the coast. I brought some home and kept them for years, with the rabbit bone. Recently, I transferred bone and shells to my garden, mixed in with bulbs and shrubs, returning to the earth like my father, although his skull still travels with the tides, or is perhaps rocking somewhere on an ocean bed, wedged between coral formations that imitate the pattern of a brain.

I have his death certificate, dated 12th October, 1955, photocopied by a frizzy haired woman at the Crosby registry office.

By road, Llandudno is 67.6 miles from Crosby. Liverpool is 7.4 miles from Crosby. How far out was the ferry when he threw himself into the water, three months before his second son was born. It took my father's corpse two weeks to arrive on Crosby Beach, his body washing in and out with the tide—limbs perhaps flailing, or stiff with rigor mortis—finally arriving, to be discovered by whom? I have imagined a mother and daughter, perhaps me and my mother.

The internet reveals new secrets every time I consult it. My father apparently wore size nine brown Oxfords with rubber soles

On September 29, 1955, his body was washed up on the foreshore of Crosby Beach. So it took thirteen days for them to register his death, during which time there must have been a postmortem, with my mother called in to identify the body, which she did by a mole on his chest.

Such details are vital. This is the kind of information I needed as a child. I imagine my bare childish feet firmly planted on those brown Oxfords, the laces making patterns on my soles. Dancing on Daddy's shoes, his big hands reach down to hold mine as we dance.

27.

Pistol Packing Momma

Phyllis Shuell

pistol packing mommas
pearl hart annie oakley
and calamity jane's
first shooter was a 22 single shot rifle
like the one mother laid on our green arborite kitchen table

the offensive defensive weapon she says
is not a toy
there will be no shooting
gophers   weasels or coyotes unless
white saliva is dripping from their mouths
and they are staggering like john swetana
coming out of the beer parlour on saturday nights

we are to shoot   men only
like the ones who followed us home
leering out the car window
"want a ride kids"
"save shoe leather"

mother reported the creeps to
neighbours and police they said
a widow and five kids need protection
buy a gun

she taught us how to load the rifle
shoulder the stock
look through the sight
aim and pull the trigger
and knock tin cans off their perch
ten tin cans in a row
ten weird men   bang
nine freaky men bang bang
keep that old Winchester blazing
'til all perverts like rats in alberta
are exterminated

instead of now I lay me down to sleep
or counting canadian arcott sheep
I count bullets that ricochet rattle my dreams

a man jimmies the backdoor lock
I tiptoe to the basement
get a ladder
reach the gun on the wall
find the bullets under mother's mattress
load and lock
aim to maim bang
thankful not to be dead he leaves
beet juice fingers clutching his right shoulder

pearl says "should have grabbed his wallet"
annie oakley says "sharp shootin kid
that 22 is a good ole gun"
calamity jane pats my hand and whispers
"put that gun down girl
put that gun away"
together we purse our lips
blow gunsmoke from our fingertips
and hum
pistol packing mamma

28.

Cover Story

Betsy Warland

Under Cover (When)

I sent a copy of my first book, *A Gathering Instinct*, to my parents in 1981. I also mailed a copy to my brother who visited my parents soon after. During his visit, when the topic of my book arose, our mother indicated that she was upset about a suite of poems in the book regarding the breakdown of my marriage. Then she showed him her solution. She'd removed those first twenty pages with a razor blade. Needless to say, I never mentioned my subsequent books to my parents.

After writing the above, I suddenly felt an urgency to clean the bathroom. This could merit analysis but I will resist. During that activity, I recognized what needed to be said next. I've previously told this anecdote in two of my books. The above rendition, however, differs.

In those two books, our mother threatens to do her razor blade delete, and my brother persuades her not to do so.

Recently, he corrected me.

"She did cut those twenty pages out."

Heart & Soul: Stories for Skeptics & Seekers, Betsy Warland, anthology edited by Susan Scott (2018)

Cover Up (Thirty-Three Years Later)

My second memoir was narrated by my chosen given name, Oscar. In *Oscar of Between—A Memoir of Identity and Ideas* (2018), I first mention my discovery in the late 1970s of another author in the family.

—9—

He was born December 23, 1918, in Ft. Dodge, Iowa.

Oscar was born December 27, 1946, in Ft. Dodge, Iowa.

After the attack on Pearl Harbor, he enlisted and was stationed on a Navy supply ship for fourteen months. Utterly bored, he repeatedly requested a transfer to a destroyer, but his commander repeatedly denied his request. To counter numbing monotony, he began writing vignettes about the small dramas being played out on ship.

Discharged in December 1945, he returned to New York where he'd worked as an editor for *Readers' Digest*. Began writing *Mr. Roberts*. It sold over a million copies: he became the "toast of the New York literary scene." The 1948 stage version staring Henry Fonda "was a smash" success.

[WRITER'S BLOCK]

He died in his bathtub a year later.

[the family's shame]

His name was Thomas Heggen. He was an excised relative. Here, Oscar thinks of her mother's plan to take a razor blade and cut out the first twenty pages of Oscar's first book.

....

Oscar gets the book. Inhales it.

Her facial resemblance with Thomas is startling.

Comprehends her parents' distrust of books.

Books can kill.

—10—

ross and tom was published in 1974.

Oscar was married in 1969.

Her husband of eight years' name?

Thomas.

Oscar of Between—A Memoir of Identity and Ideas, Betsy Warland (2016)

Cover Over (Coming Apart)

My brother Steven was the first to discover John Leggett's 1974 double biography, *ross & tom,* about "two authors who achieved sudden fame and fortune and then self-destructed." Now, four-decades later, I check John Leggett's book out of the library to reread it.

As I reread it, I discovered that we had another author in our very extended family—the well-known author Wallace Stegner. Wallace was Tom's first cousin, and he actively supported Tom in his writing career. In the early 1990s, when I was the writer-in-residence at the Saskatoon Public Library, I visited Stegner's home (now an artist's retreat) in Eastend, Saskatchewan. Within our very extended family, Stegner—to my knowledge—was never mentioned.

Thomas's family and relatives knew about his success. He often visited his parents in Minneapolis, Minnesota, just three hundred miles north of where I grew up. My only remaining cousin, Dale Warland, saw the touring *Mister Roberts* on Broadway starring Henry Fonda, when it was performed there. By the time I began writing in the Sixties, Thomas Heggen had been dead for eleven years, but within our extended family, it was as if Thomas Heggen had never existed.

Take Cover (until 2013)

One reason for this erasure of our family authors is that our extended family members were not bibliophiles. Books were for educational, practical knowledge, and religious purposes. Also, books captivated people. What was between the covers was unknown territory that could change people—open up entirely new ways of perceiving and being.

The postsecondary education of my two brothers and myself led us permanently away from the Midwest: my brothers to the east coast and myself to Canada. In the life of books, narrative becomes far more complex, unpredictable, and dangerous—but also illuminating.

"Books can kill."

Break Cover (Breakage)

For the past couple of years, I have been writing a long essay to accompany the second edition of my 2000 memoir about the final year of my mother's life, *Bloodroot—Tracing the Untelling of Motherloss*.

In this essay, I investigate what *Bloodroot* revelations have arisen during these past two decades, including a pivotal aspect that I had unknowingly covered up. At the time, it appears that I had convinced myself I didn't know about this relevant story when I wrote the memoir. How did I catch myself out? In preparation to write the second edition essay, I decided to review my previous thirteen books for any bits of narrative about my mother and me.

When I arrived at my 1990 book of essays, *Proper Deafinitions*, I was in for a shock.

Flipping through the book, I abruptly stopped at my poetic essay, "mOther muse:|<<mousa, mosaic>>." That poetic essay evokes a pivotal situation that profoundly defined my mother's and my relationship.

> how do I (w)rite you
> you i have protected myself from
> for so long
> even in my crib
> listened intently
> how you moved from room to room
> not wanting to agitate turn turn tension tighter
> you were my mOther
> so foreign mater-: <<mater>>
> though the world said the opposite
> in every book & greeting card
> that we were intimates
> in( )mates
> crying in the basement
> dark walls of depression
> closing in after I was born
> snowless black fields surrounding...

Cover Me (as in a Dangerous Situation)

Thomas Heggen's wildly successful book became a wildly successful play on Broadway, then a wildly successful movie. He was embraced by his family and the literary community but tortuously rendered unable to write and ended his life.

My writing career has been the opposite: forty years of pursuing a challenging but fascinating writing quest, embodied in thirteen books sans nomination for awards or establishment acclaim. And, for me, the absolute necessity to move away from my family—to another country—in order to write.

I have been sorely tempted to abandon this essay. I even wrote an entirely different ending that left the angst of the cover story quietly in place. I'm now the only surviving member of my family and haven't anyone to cover me, but then again I never did have anyone to cover me. I just agreed to hide.

What comes to me just now is that Thomas Heggen's and my trajectories—if fit together—offer what the other of us each lacked as authors. And like two missing pieces in a jigsaw puzzle, Thomas's and my stories complete the picture of our family's missing authors.

29.

Twelve Red Letters

Jean Crozier

Sometime in the mid-1960s, my older sister ordered a new birth certificate, the long-form version, more detailed than the wallet-size certificate she already owned. Since my husband worked close to the government office that issued birth certificates, he agreed to pick it up. That evening, I watched as he stepped from the car, threaded his way around our children's tricycles and toys on the sidewalk, and climbed the back stairs. His shoulders slumped; his usually tanned face was grey. He thrust a large manila envelope into my hand and hurled outrage along with the document: "They were never married. Your mother and father. What the hell."

The long 8 ½" x 14" form carried the details of my sister's date and place of birth as well as my mother's name and marital status—innocuous words in small black type.

A twelve-letter word was stamped in brilliant red ink, crosswise, over the entire page: Illegitimate.

Our mother's secret was out. After years of my sister and I having been subjected to disparaging comments about women and girls whose behaviour didn't meet my mom's standards, the word "hypocrite" swirled through my head and about my kitchen. The image in my husband's eyes replicated his words: scorn.

My siblings and I chose to not confront our mother: Nothing good could result from such a discussion. That secret further fortified the barrier that had existed, for as long as I could remember, between Mom and me—and the even more impenetrable wall between my older sister and our mother.

The shiny black and white photograph from my mother's collection shows a man and woman standing in a garden; both are smiling, clearly enjoying each other's company. She is young and beautiful, perhaps in her mid-twenties. The waves of her short dark hair reflect the sun, and the pleats of her silk dress fall gracefully along her slender body. He is an older gentleman in fine clothes, his three-piece suit impeccable: the tie and pocket handkerchief, the polished shoes. Bare-headed in the sunshine, only a fringe of grey hair.

When I look at that photograph, my heart aches for the way life played out for this young woman. As an eleven-year-old in Wales, she had won a scholarship to a private girls' school, placing second out of two thousand candidates. She learned to play violin and piano. She mastered cutwork embroidery, and spent gymnastics classes climbing ropes and playing floor hockey. Her life was ahead of her, but on the day of that photograph, standing in the sunshine, looking so happy, I doubt if she had yet become a secret keeper. She couldn't have known how cruelly her dreams would be dashed, the barricades she would have no option but to surmount, the depths she would be forced to plumb for energy. Who can know such things when one is young, carried away by dreams—and words—of love? He was unlike the men she'd met since arriving on the Canadian prairie, more like the Welshmen of her childhood. Men who spoke and dressed well, men who knew a fish knife from a fruit knife.

She'd been teaching in a tiny rural school for four or five years, eight grades, eight children, each of them there because the law mandated school for children between six and fifteen years of age. Her weekday home was a room in a farmhouse, part of the parents' contribution to the school's budget. Her packed lunch often consisted only of ketchup or jam sandwiches, for the Great Depression was in full swing by the time she'd graduated from teachers' training at Normal School. She was fortunate to get a job at all, but her dream of passing on her love of learning to the children of poor and marginally literate parents would never be realized.

She was Ellen, my mother, born shortly after the Victorian era, a time when women's behaviours were harshly controlled and judged, although men were subjected to no such constrictions. She outlived her brothers and sisters and most of her friends, and died just short of her 103rd birthday. My siblings and I are the only ones left who know her secret. Had our mother been born fifty years later, there would have been no need for secrecy.

My story is a tale of the grief my mother's secret caused, and its interference with the mother-daughter relationship for which I believe she yearned. As did I. Instead, her secret's legacy is one that knocked askew my own relationships as a daughter, a wife, and a mother. This too is a secret, my secret, emotions that I have hidden for years. I am eighty now, with only a few years left and fewer fears. My heart overflows with sadness for my mother. I believe she would have broken the barrier her secret erected if she had known how or if she had been able to risk uncovering her vulnerabilities.

She never forgave herself for her mistake—for falling in love with a man more than twice her age, a man who was already married. I wonder if he ever felt guilty for transgressing society's norms and boundaries. My mother and father were not the only people to have been caught in a web of untimely love.

That's the thing about secrets—we can't talk about the events because they're secret. Since we don't tell anyone, we can't hear others say, "Oh yes, my sister's experience was just about the same as yours." A woman's shame is hidden from other women, closeted from criticism, shrouded in layer upon layer of words and images: subterfuge.

I find it odd that as a young woman, I hadn't guessed her secret, although everyday life was different then. There were no photographs on my parents' walls or in frames on a desk. My mother had bought a good camera when she was teaching; her collection included photos of her students playing in the schoolyard and of her siblings on the farm. But there are no photographs of my parents during their early years together, in the late 1930s, before World War II ended the Depression. Buying and developing a film would likely have cost as much as a day's food.

Perhaps it's no wonder my older sister and I never felt like wanted children. We were not the centre of our parents' attention, not the light of their lives. Years later, Mom remarked that her firstborn had never been cuddly, didn't want to be held, squirmed and screamed whenever Mom tried to comfort her.

When Mom eventually talked about those early days, pain had etched pathways around her mouth. The day she had tried, unsuccessfully, to pawn her beautiful camel-hair coat. Boiled rice was often their only food, and she hated it for the rest of her life. She described the single room she and my father rented above a retail shop in a poor section of town. It was a far cry from the two-storey stone house in which Mom had grown up or the hotels my father's family had operated, with their dining rooms whose tables sparkled with Irish crystal goblets, Doulton china plates, and sterling silver cutlery.

Mom sewed the dresses my sisters and I wore in the 1940s, made our costumes for the neighbourhood festival, baked bread and gingersnaps, taught us to tie our shoes and to play Snakes and Ladders. I don't remember our father playing with us; he would occasionally offer to drive my sister and me to school, if the day was exceptionally cold, but my sister always refused the offer. Perhaps she was ashamed that our father didn't look like the other fathers—that he and the car he drove were old. "This Buick weighs a ton," he told us. "The best quality."

My mother did everything to keep our father happy. Late in the afternoon, every day, she washed her face and re-did her shiny auburn hair into braids that encircled her head, put on a clean dress, and made sure the house—and we kids—were tidy. If our father was going to be late home, Mom would feed us then send us to bed early, with a candy to keep us quiet. In later years, she denied the candy giving, but I was the one over whom the dentist shook his head and scolded. My siblings and I were expected to behave properly, especially when our father was at home; misdemeanours meant a wooden spoon to our bottoms. We knew we shouldn't get in the way. I don't recall our parents bickering. Our father was 'lord of the manor'.

When I was ten, he suffered a broken leg in a collision that wrecked his car. Four and a half months later, he died from a heart attack in the middle of the night. On the day of the funeral, my siblings and I remained with a neighbour while Mom, her parents, and brothers and sisters attended the service. Although children weren't usually taken to funerals in those days, I suspect we stayed home so we would not be subjected to the stares—and possible vilification—of my father's first family, the wife and half-siblings about whom my siblings and I would know nothing until years later.

My poor mother, suddenly alone, had no choice but to reveal the secret to her family: Did she tell them before the funeral? Or had she tried to avoid the revelation? Had she been confronted before the service, or at the funeral, by the other wife or her children? After the service, my mother lay sobbing on her bed. Her family sat in our living room, heads bowed and hats in hand. No one talked to my siblings and me, and we sat silently, encased in our own shroud of confusion. We didn't, couldn't, understand the depth of our mother's despair or the turmoil felt by her family. Within days, my youngest aunt, who had been boarding with us and whom my siblings and I adored, followed her father's orders and moved out. As if contact with us would contaminate her.

We never spoke of my father again.

Within two months, Mom had found full-time work with the provincial government and often held one or more part-time jobs as well. She'd catch the 7:30 a.m. bus and return at 10:00 p.m. or later. The government was allowed to pay less than minimum wage. The Rotary Club delivered hampers to our home at Christmas time. In those days, a destitute woman had to produce a valid marriage license to qualify for welfare support, regardless of the urgency of her need or her children's hunger. My grandmother sent chickens and eggs from the farm, quite possibly without my grandfather's knowledge. We planted vegetables over our entire spare lot; my siblings and I hoed and weeded, then picked the produce. After Mom got home from work she canned the vegetables, a three-hour hot water bath process—regardless of her fatigue.

Soon enough, my sister and I became adolescents and our house evolved into a nightmare of angry screaming matches. Like our mother, my sister was brilliant, creative, and talented. Unlike our mother, and with increasing vehemence, my sister's temper was a firecracker, ready to explode at a moment's notice. She bullied us younger siblings and resisted our mother's rules and pleas. She forged notes so the storekeeper would sell cigarettes to her before she was twelve. By the time she was fifteen, she'd found her own place to live; she and her black-jacket wearing friends went to bars long before she had reached the legal drinking age of twenty-one. Years later, after she died, I sought a psychologist's help in understanding my sister's behaviours, her addictions, and our relationship. At one session, the psychologist instructed me to visualize my sister standing in a field of flowers, reaching out to receive the gifts I offered her but surrounded by a plexiglass tube, clear but impenetrable.

My mother also enclosed herself in a protective barrier to keep herself safe, placing us outside, away from her and from her love. For if we pierced that wall, we just might have uncovered her secret.

Occasionally, in the 1950s, after my father's death, his older brother, a bachelor, came for Sunday dinner. He rode the bus to our house, always dressed immaculately in a three-piece suit, a hat, and polished shoes. His conversation was peppered with the activities of this person and that—names I didn't know. "Who's he talking about?" I wondered, but I knew better than to question our uncle. After he left, I'd ask Mom about these people, and she'd say she didn't know who they were and to "never mind" them, just "let him talk." Another subject not open for discussion.

Probably the terror of every adolescent girl's mother during the mid-1950s was that of unwanted pregnancy. My mother's edicts were strict and, I felt, both puritanical and unreasonable: no boys if she wasn't at home, no late nights, and no sleepovers at a girlfriend's house if the parents were not at home. I was to speak softly, to walk not run, and to always dress conservatively. She disapproved of Protestant girls dating Roman Catholic boys, cars, snug sweaters, form-fitting slacks or skirts, lipstick, eye makeup, nail polish, dangling earrings, black leather jackets, Elvis Presley music, jiving, and anything else that would make a girl look "forward"—behaviour which could be perceived as a precursor to wanton behaviour and pregnancy. Sales of birth control products were illegal until 1969; the Pill hadn't yet been invented. Every city had homes for unwed mothers; the young women's babies were taken immediately after birth, and paternal support was nonexistent. I had no intention of letting that happen to me.

In a fit of adolescent fury, probably after some argument, I hurled hateful words: "I didn't ask to be born, you know." I didn't understand the truth, then, of her response: "I didn't ask for you either."

Mom and I didn't share confidences, didn't or couldn't laugh or cry together about boyfriends, teenage hormones, dreams about the future, marriage or careers or goals. I yearned for the love and pride I could see between my friends and their mothers. Was I truly unlovable?

Three or four years after my father died, when the postwar babies began entering school and teachers were in short supply, Mom attended a summer university program and returned to teaching. Her little students drew pictures of her, always with a smile. She and her fellow teachers were a tight-knit group; for the first time, Mom felt she belonged.

With the naiveté of an eighteen-year-old who was going to be the best wife and mother in the whole world, I married a divorcé with two children. Together, we would create a home of love and laughter, a rose-covered cottage with a white picket fence, just like those described in women's magazines or in the love songs of the day. Or so I thought. My mistake. And his. My mother disapproved. Deservedly so, I soon came to realize but by then it was too late. I had four babies in rapid succession. Neither their father nor I knew how to create a peaceful home.

My mother remarried, returned to teaching, attended church, led or supported her community and its projects, and baked apple pies and roast chicken for her husband.

Her students worshipped her, and her neighbours and peers awarded her their approval and respect. She decorated wedding cakes with intricate swirls and flowers, produced award-winning photographs, and created delicate handcrafts, finely-woven grass baskets, and flower-bedecked millinery for her granddaughters. She and I talked about recipes and child-raising. Nothing intimate.

Mom was unable to offer understanding or support when I ended my marriage and when I left a steady job to set up my own business. But the day I graduated with a Bachelor of Science degree, after nine years of part-time study, she and my stepfather came to my graduation. Finally, I'd achieved something worthy of their approval. The clock they gave me, embellished with a small plaque, still hangs on my office wall.

Over a decade passed before I found my own sense of peace: I'd remarried by then, to a widower who understood life as a partner and who gently shared his wisdom. We laughed and worked, travelled and played, and built a life together unlike anything I'd ever known. Together, we had respect and acceptance, love and joy and mutual support. With that security came confidence. I wrote a note to my mother. I told her that my siblings and I had known her secret for years, that none of what had gone before mattered, and that she was our mother and we loved her for herself and for all she'd done for us. She didn't respond, but the next time I visited her, we talked about my father and their years together. Her words seemed to come easily; she spoke of their love and of her shame and embarrassment. The tension that had threatened to strangle us disintegrated. She allowed me to hug her goodbye.

I had begun to research my father, scanning *Henderson's Directories* for details of where he lived, when, and with whom. The issues from the 1930s first showed him and his wife living together, then he at one place and she elsewhere. Their children were grown, all but one living independently. By 1937, as the Depression continued, my father was in the boarding house his brother ran. Two men who had been used to professional success, social standing, fine food, sartorial finesse—the good life —had now been reduced to commission sales on vacuum cleaners, stock-market sales, mortgages, and whatever else they could find.

"Your dad told me that his wife just walked out on him. He said he came home one day, and she just wasn't there," Mom told me as we washed our supper dishes.

Another day, over a cup of tea, Mom mused: "Your dad was so good to me; he always took care of me and you kids, too."

A different day, another conversation: "I don't know what I was looking for. Your dad was so much older than I. Maybe a father figure." Although my siblings and I adored Mom's father, our grandfather, I'd heard the tales of his harsh parenting: the footsteps on the stairs when his kids didn't settle down to sleep, the pain of his slipper on a child's bottom, the siblings' fear of him even after they'd grown and had families of their own.

For a few years I was angry at my father. What right did he have, I raged, to father my siblings and me at his age? With no means of supporting us? Why didn't he even have any life insurance when he died, I asked my mother. Her response was simple: he couldn't afford it. Life insurance for a man his age would have been expensive, and who expects to have a vehicle collision followed by a heart attack?

"We never went out when you were kids," Mom said. "Your dad always said we'd have lots of time for that when you were grown up."

Each time I visited, Mom dropped bits of remembrances: "His kids begged their mother to give him a divorce, but she wouldn't. She just wouldn't." No-fault divorce, or divorce following two year's separation, would not become a reality for another forty years.

When my father died, intestate, neither Mom nor we children had a legal right to any of his property, his belongings, mementos—anything that had been his. His youngest son sued for and received damages from his father's vehicle collision; from our home, he collected the belongings to which he felt entitled. It wasn't until the 1970s, as a result of the famous Irene Murdoch case, that property rights were equalized in Alberta and ultimately in all of Canada.

"But what about the house?" I asked Mom, and she told me our father had put title to the house into her name. "At least he did that right," I thought.

Secrets. I was fifty-nine when I wrote that secret-revealing note to my mother. She would have been eighty-five. Two lives spent in a tussle of wanting to care but unable to do so. Years wasted. But now, when I look at my parents in that black and white photograph, I view them with compassion.

30.

I Found a Picture of My Great-Aunt

Heather Ramsay

My great-aunt Winifred rode a steed, her back straight, her short hair like a helmet. Joan of Arc. Why did a girl on a horse on the wide-open prairie make me think of an armour-clad warrior in medieval France?

For the longest time, the only image I ever saw of Winnie hung among a collage of photos on my mother's wall. Winnie, with her tight auburn curls and a lacy white dress, clutched a parasol beside my grandma, then a chubby-faced toddler. Their two brothers squinted at the sun. I had nothing else to fill in the blanks about my great-aunt's life. I'd always assumed she'd died young.

Then my sister subscribed to Ancestry.com and began filling in the details of our lives. She gave me her log in information, and I snooped around the branches of our family tree. I'd heard stories about Charlie Brown, Grandma and Winnie's dad, who came from England and ranched by the Bow River, near Calgary. Later, he sold his leased land and cattle and moved the family to Victoria, where my grandma was born. When he lost his money in bad investments, they all trooped back to Alberta around 1915. In 1926, his wife, Daisy died. My grandma was seventeen and Winnie, twenty-five. Two years later, Charlie died too, in one of the first car fatalities in Calgary.

My grandma used to say she was an orphan, but I'd never really thought much about it. Looking at the family tree, I could see it all in a timeline. Her parents first and then her brother, Victor, in 1938. The eldest boy Gordon and his wife had died in a plane crash in Tokyo in

1966. My grandma died in 1990 at eighty-two—the only one of her family to live to that age. Or so I'd thought.

What about Winnie? In the picture on my mother's wall, she'd been around ten years old. I scrolled to her section on Ancestry and found her birthday: November 1900. Then I looked at her death: 1975.

This floored me.

She'd been alive six years after I was born. Was this a secret? I phoned my mother to find out.

Grandma's sister, did I ever I meet her?"

"No," she said.

"Why not?"

"Because she lived in a mental hospital," my mother said.

"What? Why?"

"I don't know."

"How long was she there?"

"Most of her life I guess," my mother said.

A secret so easily shared once I'd asked. I hung up and scrolled the internet. The history of mental health treatment in the Western world is not pretty. Prior to the 1800s, those considered insane may have been imprisoned or left on the streets. Then in the Victorian era huge asylums were constructed, and people who appeared problematic often got shoved in.

I did not want to believe that my family had a story like that.

"Did you know her?"

"Not really," my mother said.

"But she was your aunt."

My mother went quiet. "I remember one time," she finally said. "I was alone in another room. I don't know where we were or why we were there, but I heard my mother say, 'snap out of it.' And I knew she wasn't talking to me."

By the time my grandma had died, I was nineteen years old, and I'd moved a province away. Years went by before I began to wonder about things past. Then one day I started commuting in the darkness between Chilliwack and Vancouver and would often chat to my parents on the car phone. The rain would pummel my hatchback, and I'd grip the wheel to pass a transport truck.

"What was wrong with Winnie?" I asked my mother one night.

I FOUND A PICTURE OF MY GREAT-AUNT

"Maybe something like her mother had? I think it was ALS," she said.

Spray from eighteen tires folded onto my windshield, and I am white-knuckled into the phone: "Lou Gehrig's disease? That would be awful. And possibly genetic. Wouldn't Grandma have known?"

"I don't know," my mom said.

"Why not?"

"I never asked."

I called my mom's seventy-year-old cousin, Stephen, to see if he had any idea. He didn't. "Children were seen and not heard. We weren't encouraged to listen to adult conversation. Or even be in the same room," he said.

Our family shared some stories. Like the one about Stephen's dad, Gordon, and his wife, Frances. How she became so wearied by the lack of electricity and running water on the Brown family farm (in the 1940s!) that she took her kids by the hand and left on the train for her mother's house in New Westminster.

"Who could blame her," Stephen said. "Mom was incredibly bright. She didn't want to be stuck out there. She had kids in diapers. She wanted them to go to a proper school." But this story had a happy ending—for a while. Gordon followed her to New Westminster and convinced her to come back. "Only if they lived in the city," she said. They compromised and bought a house in Calgary where Frances and the children lived during the school year. And so it went, until they died in that plane crash in Japan.

When Stephen finished that story, he said: "Why don't you ask Harold about Winnie?"

Harold Tipper, another of Mom's cousins, lived in Grande Prairie for years but now he and his wife Maxine are in Edmonton. I'd only met them once and had to think about how he fit into the story.

Grandma's nephew.

My mom's cousin.

Oh my God. Harold is Winnie's son.

"Call him or better yet, go visit. And hurry up," said Stephen. "He's almost ninety."

I asked my mother if she'd ever talked to Harold.

"Of course I have!" she said. "But not for a long time. And not about his mother."

So we arranged to meet. I flew to Calgary, met my parents, and we drove to Edmonton— the city where I was born. January's grey clouds warned of a storm, and the hard snow crunched underfoot. I felt nervous about prying into Harold's mother's mental health. So much shame around it, still. In Winnie's day people were put away—out of sight, out of mind. Today, treatment may be better, but society can barely face the topic.

But Harold smiled as Maxine took our coats. "Call me Hal. I'm so happy you've come. It's not too often that anyone wants to talk about my life."

I had questions prepared. Easy ones first, to break the ice. But Hal just launched right in. His dad, Bill Tipper, came from England and worked as a hired hand for Winnie's parents. That was before the Brown family moved to Victoria and before the war. Somehow, they met again after Winnie's family moved back to Alberta, and in 1921, they married. With funds from a soldier's settlement and a gift from great-grandpa Charlie, they bought land just down the road from the Brown family farm in Gopher Head, midway between Big Valley and Byemoor, two small Alberta towns.

Everything went well for Bill and Winnie for a time. They had parents and siblings in the area and enough money to buy a tractor. Charlie had given Winnie (and her siblings) Model A cars. In 1924, their first son, Bob, was born. Hal showed us pictures of the happy family at a picnic; by a lake; of Winnie smiling at Bill; and of Winnie twirling a parasol. But around the time of Hal's birth in May 1928, things started to go wrong.

Hal called it the Brown family curse. Daisy had died first, in 1926, of a mysterious neurological disease. Then Charlie was killed in a taxi in one of Calgary's first traffic accidents. Bill's parents had come to live with them too, but just five months after Hal was born, Tipper died. They buried him on a hillside and Bill's bereft mother returned to England.

Hal remembers bits and pieces from those days. During the drought, his father ran the Byemoor dray service, so he could bring money and supplies back to the farm. His mother baked wonderful bread. Winnie and the boys had to wait for the weekend when Bill got home to power up the radio with the car battery. Blizzards sometimes trapped his father in town.

He remembers the rabbits they snared for stew that tasted like willow bark. His mother cuddling him as she read. How she'd run outside when Bill got knocked down by lightning on his way back from the barn. The time she'd rushed around during a hail storm, holding pillows up to the glass so the stones wouldn't break through.

But in Hal's most troubling memory, his mother held her sons' hands on the railway platform at Big Valley some forty kilometres away. He doesn't remember how they got there, but his father arrived before the train to Calgary did. Somehow Bob and Hal got home, but his mother didn't. Later, he learned that was the day Bill drove Winnie to the Alberta Hospital for the Insane.

Alberta's first mental asylum was built in 1911 in Ponoka, a small town in the rolling hills halfway between Red Deer and Edmonton—the middle of nowhere, really. According to the philosophy of the time, that's exactly why they chose to build it there. Troubled minds needed fresh air and immersion in nature. Today, this might sound idyllic—it wasn't.

"First you hate it, and then you get used to it." A forty-one-year-old man from Vermillion spoke these words, recorded in *Political Asylums*, a book about the history of mental health treatment in Alberta by Ronald A. LaJeunesse. The man had lived in the asylum at Ponoka since the age of twenty-two. He'd wanted to go home, but his parents thought he'd be better off in the hospital. Over time, they visited him less and less.

Hal told us his mother didn't stay very long at Ponoka, maybe a few months. That was in 1933, he thinks, although he wasn't sure. "Your grandmother picked her up, took her to Vancouver to visit relatives. Tried to snap her out of it."

I pictured my grandma screeching her Model A to a stop in front of the asylum—Winnie running out, the two of them flipping the doctors the bird, and my grandma pressing the accelerator, creating a giant cloud of dust.

In reality, when Winnie got home, the public trustee had frozen the couple's assets and would not release them again until after she had died. Hal still does not understand why. With no access to the sizeable inheritance her father had given her, the family sank into poverty.

"I wish I knew more about what happened," Hal said.

He and his brother hadn't even noticed their mother was different until they moved from the farm into the tiny town of Byemoor around

1936. At first, she took part in stage plays; the Anglican minister came by for visits, but as time went on, Winnie retreated farther and farther into her shell.

"Much of the time, Mother stayed in her room," Hal said.

Hal left at fifteen to go to high school and spent little time at home after that. Several years later, he was living in Grande Prairie when a letter came from his dad. Bill had been transferred to a job in another town and didn't think Winnie could handle the change. He took her to another mental institution—in Claresholm this time. The tone of his letter seemed almost apologetic, Hal said, worried that his son would criticize him for not being able to take care of Winnie. Hal didn't.

Before we left their house, Hal showed us more pictures and said we should take some home. My mom and I flipped through, making piles. Then she held up one. "That's my favourite," he said.

Winnie riding a horse.

When I got home, I couldn't stop thinking about her. Hal had swirled so many stories, backwards and forwards in time. She'd been in Ponoka so briefly, around 1933 or 1934. So when had she gone to this other place? I looked up the Claresholm Mental Institution online, and although much has changed since Winnie's time, the place, an hour south of Calgary, still exists. Could I learn more about my great-aunt there?

The woman on the phone tapped at a computer. "Winifred Tipper: admitted in 1953, discharged in 1975," she said. That meant she'd been at home with Bill for over twenty years. The more I found out about her, the more questions appeared.

Hal said that after she'd been to Ponoka, she used to talk about shock treatments and was terrified of having more. He said his dad chose Claresholm because they didn't do interventions like that. But in Lajeunesse's book I read that Superintendent Dr. Randall Maclean introduced insulin shock therapy to Ponoka in 1937 and bought an electroshock machine in 1945 and had been cautious in its use: "The patients would suffer violent convulsions and frequently break bones, often in the vertebrae. They would choke, tear muscles, and lose their memories for months or even years."

That sounded bad, but I checked and rechecked the dates. Hal thinks he was around four years old when his mother was first hospitalized. If Winnie had only lived in Ponoka for a short time in 1933 or 1934, she could not have endured this. Lobotomies weren't practiced until the

1940s. Had she been sterilized? Ponoka embraced Alberta's 1928 eugenics legislation and practiced involuntary sterilization of people considered mental defectives, as long as they had the consent of the next of kin. Would Bill have agreed? By 1937, the government amended the act to allow sterilization without consent.

"What was she there for?" I had asked the lady at Claresholm, but she couldn't say. The records had been destroyed. "If it helps, almost everyone was diagnosed with schizophrenia back then," she'd said.

Did that help? I thought of Superman's girlfriend, Margot Kidder, hiding in the bushes in suburban Los Angeles—screaming at the police to shoot her. The world tittering when the police arrested her instead. To this day people associate the condition with violence and uncontrollable behaviour. What would someone have thought back in Winnie's day?

Thanks to Hal, I had so many other pictures of his mother in my head. Winnie with bobbed hair wearing a Japanese dress. On her wedding day in the back seat of a dusty car. In a tam o'shanter, looking at Bill with a flirty smile.

I wrote to Hal about the day his mother took the boys to the train.

Could she have been pregnant? And her breakdown related to the death of Gordon's first wife, Harriet, whose daughter, I found out, died at birth in February 1934? Harriet herself died a month later from complications. Winnie and Harriet were neighbours, sisters-in-law, young moms. Maybe she was terrified to meet Harriet's fate?

Hal wrote back: "You've touched on a subject that I have always wondered about. Mother and Dad never talked about it to either Bob or me, and since everyone involved is long since gone, I'll never know." The next summer, I went back to Alberta and drove through the prairies with my parents. We passed dried fields of canola along the now paved roads to Big Valley, taking only a couple of hours to get there from Calgary. In my grandma's day, the journey could have lasted two days. At the little museum, we found an old newspaper that reported Grandma taught at the nearby Ozark school in 1928, the year Hal was born. We found a 1937 picture of Grandma with her Big Valley class. I realized that she taught at one of those one-room schools in the district every winter until 1938. She lived near Winnie all that time. In 1939, she moved north of Edmonton. That same year she got married at thirty years old.

LaJeunesse wrote that back in the 1920s, University of Western Ontario professor Madge Macklin, Canada's foremost geneticist, called for the sterilization not only of all patients with schizophrenia but of their parents, children, and any other relatives—in case they carried a latent gene that could spread the disease again. My grandma, who took me to Woodwards for lunch. Who taught me how to knit a scarf. My grandma who never once mentioned her sister to me. Did she know about this?

Her parents had died, and her sister had been in a hospital for the insane, and all I'd ever thought to wonder was why she'd waited so long to marry.

Grandma picked Winnie up from Ponoka in 1933, but she didn't go to Claresholm until 1953. She spent twenty years at home in between. Bob and Harold had left the house. Bill would have been at work. Winnie may have been in the depths of whatever was her hell.

We found an autograph book at my parents' house. In it, Winnie wrote: "There is so much good in the worst of us and so much bad in the best."

While at the Big Valley Museum, a train whistle blew, and we could see a light farther along the track—a tourist excursion from Stettler. My dad hoped to see the old steam engine. When we walked over, ladies in old-fashioned dresses stood on the platform. People snapped photos. I thought of Winnie holding her boys' hands, and my grandmother teaching at a one-room school nearby. How would things have been different if Winnie had made it to Calgary or if my grandma had come to find her instead?

Winnie was not Joan of Arc. She did not lead an army. I don't know if she heard voices, but for Joan, the voices came regularly. They calmed and emboldened her. Many now think Joan had schizophrenia, but others argue that dismissing the voices as illness or delusion would be as good as removing all meaning from her life.

When we got back to my parents' house, I looked for the photo that made me think of Joan of Arc. In it, Winnie sits straight in the saddle. Regal. Saintlike. She doesn't have bobbed hair though, and she wears a 1920s helmet-shaped toque. I'd combined the bobbed hair from the photo with the Japanese dress, the various horses. In reality, Winnie wore a big wool coat.

Hal doesn't know what was wrong with his mother, but he believes she fell into a deep depression. If she'd had the same troubles fifty years later, she might have been fine.

He and Maxine had been heading to a reunion in Byemoor when they heard that Winnie wasn't doing well. They drove three and a half hours on to Claresholm and found her curled up in bed, comatose and suffering from pneumonia. The nurse told them to keep talking, as hearing is one of the last senses to go. The funeral was small: Hal's brother Bob, his wife Doris, my grandparents, some of the hospital nurses, Maxine, and Hal.

Rest in peace, Winifred Tipper. I'm glad I took the time to get to know you.

31.

Bingo and Black Ice

George K. Ilsley

The Ambulance Driver

One of my brother's jobs was as an on-call ambulance driver. The ambulance was called out to motor vehicle accidents, along with the police and the volunteer fire department, and he'd help use the Jaws of Life to free people from the wreckage.

This frosty early December evening the dispatcher called my brother, wanting the ambulance taken out to a single car accident on the old number one highway. The phone rang a couple of times, but before my brother answered the dispatcher hung up and called another driver.

The dispatcher said later that he didn't know why he decided to call someone else. He could not recall any reason for changing his mind. All he knew was that he was glad he did. Because otherwise, my brother would have driven the ambulance to the scene of the accident where the rescue crews were extracting the lifeless body of our mother from her car.

The Week Before

The week before this I was in Nova Scotia to visit my family. My sister had died "suddenly and unexpectedly" (as they say) in March of the previous year, and I did not go home for her funeral. After any death, following the initial crush of friends and family, casseroles and condolences, mourning becomes more private and lonelier. I visited about a month after the funeral and then as often as I could. My mother was lonely. Her mother had died, and then the next year her daughter. These two women were my mother's bracketing generations. She talked to them almost daily for decades and then, suddenly, they were both gone.

The Grave

Every time I went home, my mother and I visited my sister's grave in the Wolfville cemetery. "No one else wants to go with me," my mother said.

The trees in the cemetery were budding bright green, or were in full leaf, or they were bare. Yellow-trumpeted daffodils nodded in the spring breeze. Marigolds and zinnias defied the summer sun. Cut flowers wilted, dried, and crumbled into dust. My sister's gravestone never changed, and offered no clues.

By this point, I was angry with my sister, although I was unable to express these feelings. I was pissed off that she had done such a horrible thing. I was pissed off that she had done a horrible thing and left me to deal with our mother, who was now even more thoroughly depressed, and confused to the point of heartbreak. I was angry about the whole business. My mother's sadness made me angrier and angrier. Anger was buried deep in my body, and everything I was feeling was filtered through this pervasive bitterness. When my sister killed herself and left an ugly mess, I didn't waste any time with denial or negotiation. I headed straight to anger and got stuck there.

I don't think my mother ever got over her daughter's death. Maybe she would have, in time, but she only had twenty-one months. Twenty-one extra-miserable months until she herself died, still grieving.

The Theories

Every time there is a death by suicide people try to fill in the big blank. You make all sorts of wild guesses, because that is all you can do and you have to do *something*.

There is a paradox at work here. When someone does a crazy thing, you want to believe it was somehow, on some level, logical.

My mother promoted this theory: my sister had a lump in her

breast, went for tests, but then did not wait for the results.

I developed my own theory after seeing a movie several years later. I can't recall the title, but these are the highlights: a young woman, a rural setting in the 1920s or 1930s, and a hysterectomy. I believe the women kills herself, and I remember sitting in the movie theatre with my partner after everyone had left and crying my eyes out. Suddenly, I felt I had some insight into my sister's predicament. My sister had suffered from some kind of growth all over everything inside, a fungus perhaps, and had been scraped a couple of times, but the problem kept coming back. Eventually, when she was about thirty, she had a hysterectomy. This hormonal catastrophe, plus living with chronic pain, must be an emotional bombshell. The bomb exploded. That is my theory.

The problem, of course, is that there is no way to ever know. The ongoing problem, when a family member kills themselves, is getting used to the idea that you will never know.

Here is what I do know. In photographs, my sister is smiling and always looked happy. When I see one of these pictures now, she looks like she is in pain. Her eyes look incredibly sad. The smile has become a grimace, a weak stab at a brave face for the camera. That is now all I can see, the pain and sadness in those glistening eyes, and I cannot fathom how I never saw that before.

The Week Before—Dad

Dad never changes and lives on his own timeless plateau. He talked for hours and hours if Mom was not around, especially about things fifty years ago. He watches two TVs, sound and pictures, at once. He said you just focus on the one you want to watch.

When the police came to tell him his wife had died in an accident, my father said he didn't know whether to laugh or to cry.

The Week Before—Mom

A short round woman, Mom had taken to wearing black because black was slimming. She looked like a black ball punctuated with perky little sag-proof breasts.

We talked of death a fair amount. She was afraid, and I tried to make thoughts of death easier. She told me how as a child I used to cry when she was ill, lying down with her and saying, "Don't die Mommy, don't die."

You might think my mother had some kind of premonition. But no. She had been like that for years—imagining her absence. She was forever saying, "What would you guys do without me?"

That Man

One time when I was a teenager my mother and I were shopping in town. She turned to me and said, "That man is your sister's father."

I already knew at this point my sister was born before my parents were married. I don't remember anything about the man my mother pointed out.

My Mother's Story

Before my mother was born, her mother was a maid for a wealthy family in town. The old man of the family knocked her up, so of course my grandmother was fired. There was no such thing as sexual harassment or sexual assault in the early 1930s. If a wealthy old man wanted something, he just took it. So my grandmother was pregnant and out of a job, and this is where my mother came from. She was the unacknowledged bastard child of one of the town's most prominent and respected families.

Scorned at birth, my mother in turn rejected the hypocrites, dismissing the townspeople as pretentious snobs who "wouldn't say shit if they had a mouthful."

Lucky Trolls

If Dante had lived in small town Nova Scotia in the 1980s, he could have based his vision of Purgatory on smoke-filled bingo halls crowded with doomed souls forever suspended in the state between Winning and Losing.

These doomed souls played every night (Saturday at the Lions Club in Kingston, Sunday at the Fire Hall in Berwick, Monday in Aylesford, and so on) and endlessly talked about almost winning: being "set"—

only needing one more number to win. These women (for they were most often women) each commanded about a half-acre of bingo cards, their territory delineated by rows of big-haired lucky trolls, stuffed toys, framed photos, cigarette lighters, ashtrays, backup daubers, snack food, coffee or pop, and rows of change.

My mother always wanted me to go with her because I was deemed lucky. My mother paid my way, and we split the winnings. She played her half-acre of cards and minded my small patch as well. I often won, but I found the suspense of almost winning so excruciating, I rarely agreed to go.

It was a revelation to see my mother smoking at bingo. Officially, she had quit, and indeed she had—except at bingo. Suddenly, I saw why she was so keen to play every night. It got her out of the house and she could smoke in secret.

She had quit, you see, after the cancer. She had breast cancer, first in one breast and then the other, and eventually had a double mastectomy. She then had annual screenings, which she found very stressful. She had been given the idea that if she could just reach five years cancer free, then she might have good odds of living even longer.

Father Too

In fact, my father also had breast cancer and has a huge concave scar on the right side of his torso. My father had his mastectomy the year I was born and at the time his doctor gave him only a few months to live. More than fifty years later, he is still alive and cancer free.

My mother used to joke about it, declaring that her and my father only had one tit between them. She wore little foam prosthetics, and was not shy about them. In a town where some women hid their dainties in pillowcases before hanging them outside to dry, my mother washed her little foam breasts and pinned them out on the clothesline along with everything else for the whole world to see.

When feeling particularly lighthearted and mischievous, my mother would reach down her top, pull out one of her little foam tits, and throw it at my father. Later, I would fictionalize such a scene by having a character reach for both her falsies at once in a double-barreled onslaught, described as a "surreal cross your heart barrage." I don't recall Mom ever throwing both her tits at once, but if the first did not get enough of a reaction, she would then hurl the second. My mother only threw her tits when she was in a good mood. She mostly flung her tits at my father.

The Railroad

When I left my mother drove me to the train station in our small town. This would be the last place I saw her. It would be the last time for the train as well, since passenger service to the Valley was being cancelled. I had never taken the train from the Annapolis Valley before, but this was the last chance, so that's what I did.

My mother drove me to the soon-to-be-defunct train station and said, "Come home anytime." Little did I know that in less than a week I would return for her funeral.

When I turned to wave goodbye, I had my last glimpse of my mother. She was sitting in the car, in the driver's seat, in the exact spot where she would soon meet her death. Her hand was raised up, and pressed against the glass. She was crying.

Travelling and the Dream

I was living in Montreal. It took about a day to get there on the train. I could not afford a sleeper, so it was an ordeal.

I'd only been in Montreal a couple of days when the police told me the news. I returned to Nova Scotia the next day, this time by plane. I had to borrow money to buy a ticket.

For years, my parents had slept in separate rooms. The bedroom where my mother slept was known as the spare room; however, this was, to my mind, my mother's room.

At that time, I still had my own bedroom in the house, preserved like a time capsule or shrine to permanent adolescence, and this room is where I always slept. I had just slept there the week before.

When I arrived home after my mother's sudden death, I slept in her bed. The pillowcase smelled of Noxzema underscored with the burnt metallic tang of ironed cotton. From the sheets wafted hints of baby powder and Ivory soap. I slept in my mother's bed and breathed it all in.

That night I had a dream. In the dream my mother was standing in the driveway next to her car, a new car. She was all excited because she was going on a trip. She was happy.

I found this dream very satisfying, even though at the same time, it seemed to be rather obvious wish fulfillment, a transparent attempt to put a positive spin on a tragic event. Yet this dream I had when I slept in my dead mother's bed was a great comfort to me.

When I went home for my mother's funeral, I slept in my mother's bed, and neither my father nor my brother said a word to me about it.

The Uncle

While I was home for the funeral, one of my mother's uncles adopted me. It is strange, but now I can't remember who this was. I guess I was in shock. Hanging out with this great-uncle is mostly what I remember from that time. He lived just up the street, with his wife, in a small house they had recently moved to. The fact is, on my mother's side, there were so many aunts and uncles and cousins, and shifting factions of in-laws and out-laws, that I never did know half of them.

The great-uncle who took me under his wing—he was curious, he said. He liked to see things for himself. He drove me all around so we could see things together. He drove me to the scene of the accident—a series of curves through a low-lying stretch of the old highway. My mother's car had flown off the road and struck a hydro pole. The damaged pole was atilt and propped up with temporary struts. The earth was cut and wounded.

Next my great-uncle and I drove to the junkyard. He explained to the man that we were looking for a particular car. My uncle said "the young fella" wanted to see it. The attendant waved us in.

We drove around the junkyard (a cemetery for machines) until we found the dirt-brown Valiant. The car was deemed to be a write-off, although it did not look that bad—until we walked around to the driver's side. The driver's door was crushed inwards. There was blood. On the bent steering wheel, on the jagged crushed door, and everywhere you looked, until you stopped looking.

The uncle, who liked to see things for himself, commented on what had happened, based on what he could divine. "She must've hit the black ice there on the curves through the marsh, and slid off the road ninety degrees into the power pole. The side of the car there, that's what hit. She flew around and hit the pole right there square on. Yes sir. That's what happened. Hit the ice there, flipped around into the pole and that was that."

Then we went back to his house, sat in the kitchen, and drank rye. We had seen for ourselves all there was to see.

The Hydro Pole

The hydro pole that arrested the flight of my mother's car had to be replaced. A few months after her funeral, the power company sent my father a bill. This bill, for replacing the hydro pole damaged in the accident that killed my mother, provoked most of the emotion my father expressed following his wife's death. He was some upset. Oh, he was livid. He could not believe anyone could be so callous. In a huff, he phoned the utility—he was a shareholder, after all, not just a customer—and declared he would not pay their bill. And he did not pay. The power company declined to pursue the matter.

A Recent Dream

The night after writing the section about my mother's uncle, I dream about my mother. We are in the kitchen of our house, near the sink, a location where I have heard many secrets. (For example, this is where we were standing when she told me she had another baby, after my sister, before she met my father. That baby was put out for adoption and remains otherwise unknown.)

In the dream, I want to ask her about the mysterious uncle who reached out to me, but I feel emotions welling up, and I know that if I speak, I will cry.

My mother happens to mention Uncle Lou, who had moved to a small house up the street. "How long did he live there?" I ask. "Four years," my mother says. So it was Uncle Lou, I thought, already starting to write the dream out in my head.

All I know for sure is that I don't ever remember seeing Uncle Lou before the week of my mother's funeral. And I've never seen him since.

The Ashes

My mother's ashes are scattered in the garden, but nowhere near the strawberries because she was allergic.

My father has also asked for his ashes to be scattered in the garden. He wants to be with his wife. I hope that he and my mother will not fight as much as they did when she was alive. However, my father does not remember any quarrels or tears or incessant nagging. He only remembers the good things.

The End of My Mother's Story

All those years worrying about cancer and look how she died: in an instant. In a car accident. On the way home from bingo.

If I happen to mention having a dead mother, people ask, "How did your mother die?" I usually just say, "Bingo."

"What? She died playing bingo?"

"Well," I say, "to be precise, it was a lethal combination of bingo and black ice."

And for twenty-five years, I have been meaning to tell the story.

32.

Shattered

Helen Gowans

She thought it didn't matter, it was so long ago, she was doing fine, it wasn't important, it must have been her fault. The phone rang. Her brother rarely called. Said their niece had disclosed at school years of sexual abuse by her father, their older brother. The news oozed out to only immediate family who gasped. She stood rooted to the spot. A burl rose out of that place where secrets live. Her, then, at the same age—confused. Him standing inside his bedroom motioning her in—an unexpected invitation. A single bed of polished wood, the cover a loose weave of rust and cream stripes. His face beckoning her to lie down, his hand sliding under her knitted yellow sweater, soft muttered words groaning, pleading, his nail-bitten fingers caressing her breast buds.

Down the hall from the kitchen, her mother called "Dinner's ready!"

She leapt up, never again entered his room nor spoke of it to anyone.

Forty-five years later. "I wish we'd had more fun, she seemed hounded by the past" a friend casually mentioned after her visit with her ex-sister-in-law. The burl she'd forgotten she carried sank like a stone in her gut. They had moved on, hadn't they? Made adjustments, created a new, safer life? Erased the trauma? Wrong. The burl demanded she tell her this was not the first time her brother had abused. But how to do it? They had become strangers, had only distant shared memories. A chance trip to her city meant an airport meeting if she desired. At the coffee shop the burl splintered, she told her story. Awkward but they both maintained their composure. Acted as if this was a delayed but ordinary meeting. Made no promises to meet again. A soothing spread, a little justice had been done.

33.

In This Adaptation

Judy LeBlanc

A skinny woman with grey hair that hints at a once bouncy bob meets my sister and me at the door. We're told my father is downstairs with the men watching the game. Since he prefers the company of women and has never been a game watcher, and since I don't recognize a single face, this reunion seems off kilter before I even cross the threshold from the covered porch into the crowded kitchen. A gaggle of middle-aged women, several of my father's hundred or so nieces, are about to identify themselves as my cousins and remind me of their names or assume that I remember them, even though it's been years since I've seen most, if I've ever met them at all. My sister, always better at this than me, quickly removes her shoes and steps into the throng, smiling and greeting people, while I fumble at the door, aware of the skinny cousin's pale eyes following my every move. Without introducing herself and before I remove my coat, she's insisting that she once babysat me. A vague gesture or tone from her reminds me that she'd been blonde and smooth skinned, and around her, I'd felt clumsy, my hair heavy and brown, although mostly I took after my freckled father. She says she's sorry to hear about my mother's death: "Your mother was always so beautiful." The cousin stinks of cigarette smoke, and I suppose at one time, I'd have considered her glamorous with a cigarette between her fingers. She goes on about my mother's physical beauty as if there'd been nothing more to her than skin and hair. "It was that combination, don't you think," she says, "of Dutch and Indian blood."

On June 1, 2015, the Truth and Reconciliation committee released its report on the impact of residential schools and its ninety-four calls to action. Nineteen days later, my mother died. One week to the day before she died, a raven flew through the open doors of my patio into my living room. I feel a little fraudulent writing that—the bit about the raven. What are the chances a bird that big would fly into a house? Likely it was a crow, a dream, a starling, a hallucination, and if it did happen, its timing had to have been mere coincidence, didn't it? In the way I've doubted the raven, I was taught to doubt and deny our Indigenous ancestry. This is exactly what assimilationist policies intended: an unknowing, a forgetting. If there is a heart to this unknowing in my family, a place of origin, the singular body that might be named the source of the family secret—so layered are secrets I don't know if there is a source or if it's findable—let's say for the sake of the story all arteries lead to my great-aunt Stella.

The Secret Garden by Frances Hodgson Burnett was published in 1911, the same year my maternal grandmother was born. This, of course, is another coincidence. I read the novel sometime in the late sixties and recently read it again after watching the 2020 film adaptation. In both the film version and the book, a locked door stands between Mary Lennox and the garden. I know so little about my grandmother that I think of her this way—as a locked door. At the heart of this walled garden is a secret, and as is often the way, at the heart of this secret is a story of grief.

Family history on my mother's side is a patchwork of guesses and estimations. Ancestors hovered like phantasms over my childhood. At a time when Don Ho's "Tiny Bubbles" was big, my mother claimed "Hawaiian" blood to explain her own and her siblings' black hair and brown eyes. There are early vague memories of Saanich cousins and an old uncle from the Tsartlip reserve. It's not that she denied the Saanich connections, only that it wasn't talked about. Genealogical research I've done in the five years since her death confirms that both my maternal great grandparents were of mixed Scottish and Coast Salish heritage. One of my great-great-grandmothers was from the W̱SÁNEĆ and another from the Tsleil-Waututh or possibly Suquamish in what is now Washington State. Both were "country wives" to Scottish blacksmiths.

I've learned in the past few years that the old uncle was Gabriel Bartleman, a respected W̱SÁNEĆ Elder, and that he was my grandmother's cousin. My dad liked him because he was "a hard worker" and had "a nice house" off reserve when we knew him. My dad, who is eighty-five and has taken up watching documentaries about the First Nations, tells me he once said to my grandmother: "There's nothing to be ashamed of." I imagine the raised voices, the insults, and the long period afterwards when we didn't see our grandmother—a white man telling a half breed woman how she should and shouldn't feel.

"Is she Italian, Spanish, Greek?" my second husband asked of my mother when we first started dating. He wasn't the first who made that assumption.

"Why not Coast Salish? We live in Coast Salish territory. Spain's a long way from here," I said.

The Secret Garden had much to enthrall my younger self in Mary—a plain, unloved girl who'd lived in exotic India under the Raj with servants at her beck and call until orphaned after a cholera outbreak. Placed under the guardianship of a widowed hunchback uncle named Mr Craven, she's taken to Misselthwaite, a sprawling estate on a desolate English moor. She's allowed the run of the place except for the locked garden, and at night, she wakes to mysterious cries from one of the mansion's many rooms.

The Secret Garden was written at the beginning of the end of the English empire and reflects colonial attitudes of the time: the hierarchy between the wealthy Craven family and the servant class, the superior haughtiness of Mary and her cousin, and the romanticizing of Martha and her brother Dickon who's depicted as a simple nature boy. How did my child self take this in? Mary is furious at Martha, not because she says about India that "there's such a lot o' blacks there instead o' respectable white people" but because before Mary came to the manor, Martha assumed she was Black. "What!" says Mary. "What! You thought I was a native. You—you daughter of a pig!"

I'm certain I would have thought Mary rude and spoiled while Martha's poverty would have elicited my sympathy, but as if I took it as a given, I don't recall any awareness of the assumption of white superiority. By the end of the book, I wanted to be Mary—self-assured, bold, politer now, and with the world entirely on my side. Why wouldn't my grandmother have leaned in favour of her white side?

I often hear ravens high above the cedar trees surrounding our house, but until the incident before my mother's death, never had anything larger than a junco flown through our wide patio doors. I'm looking for plausibility. Ravens are shapeshifters, messengers. Hadn't it appeared to tell me as the obvious? My mother would die soon. Its argillite feathers and size, as well as its frantic flapping against the glass, frightened me. It was a creature out of place.

At first, I hid, but then I took a broom to it. Well, no, I didn't exactly take a broom to the raven, but I waved it around in an attempt to steer it from where it squawked on the wide sills of our tall living room windows. It leaped about, and I feared it might come for me. I cowered in a room down the hall. Moments later, it flew out the open doors. Its departure left me empty with only a wish that I'd been more fearless. Perhaps my actions were parallel to the stages of grief.

Not long after my mother died, I dug through my papers and retrieved a wrinkled sketch of a family tree I'd received from a distant Saanich cousin a number of years before. I signed up for Ancestry.ca and Newspapers.ca. I emailed another cousin who didn't remember me and discovered another one online who'd done extensive family research. I wish I'd asked my mother more questions. Sometimes when I'm at my computer, I glance at her photo on my desk. She watches me work, spurs me on, freezes me: "Write it faster... Stop, it's nobody's business. What do you think you're doing?"

Eventually a robin led Mary to the key that would unlock the door to the secret garden. My mother claimed a robin followed her around the garden, returning every year and often hopping near where she dug in the earth, chiding her for imagined slights. Her face lit up when she talked about the bird: "He scolds me for not being out there early enough." My sister says when she sees birds, she thinks of my mother, especially robins. A few months after my mother died, a kingfisher followed me along the shore where I paddled my kayak. I imagined it was her, all that scolding that covered up her fears. So much cover.

I barely knew my grandmother, not that she didn't come around now and then or that we didn't visit her in a small house in North Vancouver. She was a cold-hearted woman is the way it's been told to me, no love lost between she and my mother. I recall a gravelly laugh and no particular conversation with her. Since my mother died, I've discovered more about her than I knew when she was alive. William and Rosalee Houston, my great grandparents, had eight children in all. My grandmother (Pearl), born in 1911, was the youngest and Stella, born 1890, was the oldest.

Stella died five years before my grandmother was born. When my grandmother was twenty-five years old, she had my mother and named her Phyliss Stella Rose.

My mother who went by *Rose* lived a lifetime without knowing she carried the name of her grandmother Rosalee and her Aunt Stella.

Why would my grandmother, this unsentimental "cold woman" who would rather forget the past, name her daughter after her own mother and after a sister she never met?

No one knew what Stella died from. Not Ancestry.ca, not a distant cousin from Tacoma.

I recently had a conversation with my father.

"Your mom never thought of herself as First Nations." These days he's careful to use the correct lexicon.

"We knew she was. It's not that we didn't know."

"I always told you kids that you were."

"No, she always told us that we were."

"I told her it was nothing to be ashamed of."

I tell him that my mother's sister told me her husband used to call her a "squaw" when he was mad at her. I want to make a point, as I often do with my father. Regardless of how my mother saw herself, sometimes who she was, what she was, got decided by others. And sometimes her ancestry was used as a weapon against her.

Silence. I wait.

"One time when I was young, angry, you know, stupid, I called her a 'bloody Indian,'" he says, and it has the ring of a confession. My father was raised Catholic, although he despises the church.

Liar, I think but don't say because he's an old man now, and it was a long time ago, and because it's against the family rules to remind him in this way. You didn't call her a "bloody Indian" once. You called her a "squaw" several times, maybe when you had her pinned against the wall or that time you upended the kitchen table in the middle of dinner, the night the neighbours called the cops. My recollection of these events is murky, the way I experienced them at the time: disconnected yet present.

This is the first time he's admitted to this, and for the first time I don't doubt my own memory.

My great-grandfather worked in the infamous San Juan Island lime works, came home covered in white dust, and learned how to pass as a white man. He and Rosalee, my great-grandmother, bought a thirty-acre farm on which they likely raised sheep as did a lot of islanders. All their eight children were born either on the island or in Victoria. It appears they went back and forth between the two places. Before the Canada-US border divided the territory, travel between what is now Saanich and San Juan Island was common with the Coast Salish as were kinship ties on either side of Haro Strait.

Up behind the world-class Roche Harbor resort in a forest of spindly firs in an open area overgrown with thistle, the graves of the lime company's workers and their families cluster in a haphazard arrangement. In October 2019, under an overcast sky, my husband and I wander the Pioneer Cemetery during my first ever visit to San Juan Island. Some graves are fenced in by white pickets tangled in invasive blackberry. Inscriptions are faded and indiscernible. I step carefully to avoid the smaller rectangular slabs scattered on the ground. None are marked. If Stella is buried here, there's no way of knowing.

It's haunting—the low sky, the dead surrounding me, and for a moment I'm not searching for this great-aunt whom only months before I didn't know existed. It's me I'm looking for, or maybe she and I are converging, my own existence as arbitrary as hers.

Mary learns from Martha that the locked garden, once a place of joy for husband and wife of the manor, was tended by Mrs. Craven herself. The film flashes on an image of her on a swing hung from a tree and surrounded by flowers; she's diaphanous and smiling, reminiscent of the eighteenth-century Fragonard painting titled "The Happy Accidents of the Swing," except that Mrs. Craven holds an infant in her arms. We learn that a fall from this tree took her life while sparing that of her son Colin. This tragic event caused her widower to lock the garden and cloister his son away in the belief that he's an invalid. Mary discovers Colin, now ten years old, and draws him in along with Dickon to the restoration of the garden. The garden, once a secret, becomes both a symbol of grief and of renewal.

One late night scrolling through back issues of *The San Juan Islander* on Newspaper.com, the headline "Death of Stella Houston" appears on my screen, dated August 4, 1906.

> Stella Houston, oldest child of Mr. and Mrs. William Houston, died at the home of her parents, Wednesday, July 25th, of consumption, aged sixteen years, five months and eleven days. A year or two ago, Stella went to Chemawa, Oregon, to attend school and it was while there that she contracted the dread disease which terminated her life.

I imagine my grandmother acquiring the 1943 edition of *New Twentieth Century Websters*, a hulk of a book, from a door-to-door salesman. According to an official marriage document, she could read, although my grandfather couldn't. It's one of the few objects that were handed down from my mother's family. It defines consumption as a "wasting or emaciation of the body; specifically (a) pulmonary tuberculosis."

During the nineteenth and early twentieth century, tuberculosis was the leading cause of death in the United States. It is a highly infectious bacterial disease that primarily affects the lungs with symptoms that include a chronic cough, fever, and weight loss. Rosalee would have watched her daughter Stella waste away.

In 2018, The World Health Organization reported there were 1.5 million deaths from tuberculosis worldwide. Statistics from the Centres for Disease Control site show that in 2018, the rate of tuberculosis in American Indians and Alaska Natives was "over eight times higher than the rate of TB in non-Hispanic whites." Nested into the history of the ongoing story of tuberculosis is the story of Stella at Chemawa.

"Chemawa" is not in the 1943 Webster's dictionary, although the book contains many supplementary sections, including abridged biographies, maps, photos, a brief survey of the great books of the world, of famous sculptures, a history of Canada and the United States, as well as a table of weights and measures. Yet when I google "Chemawa," the screen displays a long list of entries containing the words "Chemawa Indian Boarding School."

Chemawa Indian Boarding School, located near Salem, Oregon, founded in the late nineteenth century and run by the Bureau of Indian Affairs is the oldest of four off-reservation schools still operating. A report from Oregon Public Broadcasting (OPB) in 2017, titled "Life and

Death at Chemawa Indian School," outlines an investigative series looking into the recent deaths of three Chemawa students, one on campus and two shortly after being sent home. This, then, is also Stella's story, only Stella died over a hundred years ago, and because time and stories untold can be disorienting, it's as though this is the same story that goes on and on. Another headline from the OPB published in 2017 reads "Behind the Fence: Chemawa's Culture of Secrecy."

Tuberculosis spread in Native American boarding schools and Canadian residential schools during the last half of the nineteenth century and the first half of the twentieth. Great-aunt Stella was roughly one of the one in five children who returned home from an Indian Boarding School with tuberculosis only to die shortly afterwards. She would have attended Chemawa with around six hundred other students; they would have slept in a crowded dorm, shared the same wash water, attended classes, and worked in the laundry and kitchen. Ventilation in the institutional buildings was poor, the food was insufficient, and the healthcare was negligible. The conditions were ideal for the spread of disease.

In the novel, the secret garden is seen as a place of magic—"as if magicians were passing through it, drawing loveliness out of the earth and the boughs with wands." This is far from the more inclusive Indigenous view in which humans are a part of the natural world and nature is not something that can be walled off. Still, the natural world became a place of solace for Mary, and it was passages like these that drove my child self to the field and creek located behind our house.

It must have been the same solace my mother sought in the acreage she transformed in her senior years after she and my father moved to Mesachie Lake near the tiny logging community of Lake Cowichan. When they bought the property, it was choked with alder trees, considered a pioneer species; such trees were among the first to colonize after a devastation, such as a clear cut. My father cut down the alders, and my parents carted in soil, fertilizer, and exotic plants. He built a pond and paths between my mother's beds of flowers and shrubs: pieris japonica bonfire, begonia, chrysanthemum, viburnum, and more.

She was happier there than I'd ever known her—hands deep in the earth, absorbed for hours, cigarette dangling from between her lips, her slight strong body capable of twelve straight hours of physical work. She'd lose track of time and forget to stop for lunch.

Later, in the way that history repeats itself, approaching our own retirement years, my husband and I buy an acre in a rural community. We yank and tear at the masses of black plastic with which the former owners had covered the earth in an effort to smother the unchecked growth that is inevitable on the edge of a temperate rainforest. It takes our first few years to free the trapped and choked roots from beneath the plastic, enabling the return of those plants native to our ecosystem: salal, evergreen huckleberry, and sword fern.

The old gardener in Burnett's book tells Mary that bulbs spread beneath the ground and return year after year. Eventually, however, untended, they choke each other out, their growth becomes stunted. A secret becomes an ugly, starved thing.

It's hard, impossible, to miss a raven in the house. I know what I saw. "Now," I say to my father, "I will tell you what I saw," and although he at first protests, at last he's quiet, which doesn't necessarily indicate listening but is a shift from the way it's been.

In the most recent film adaptation of *The Secret Garden*, the implicit becomes explicit. The magic in the garden manifests in embroidered butterflies coming to life and visual sleights of hand. Martha is mixed race. The ghost becomes visible. In the most recent adaptation of my family history, Stella emerges as does the Truth and Reconciliation Commission; my father watches documentaries about the First Nations, and I have not yet located Stella's gravesite.

34.

Would You Trade This Family?

Kae Solomon

It was one of those summer days. Heather, the twins, and I were hanging around my back yard. We were hot and bored. "C'mon let's go in your house," Christy suggested, her long athletic legs swinging over the edge of the picnic table. "It's too hot out here, and there's nothing to do. At least your house is nice and cool." She swept her long dark blonde curls dramatically off her forehead. A little too cool, as I always had to layer on sweaters and leg warmers, or would shiver uncontrollably. My mom stayed inside almost all the time, due to her allergies, she said. She was strict about keeping the air conditioning at 68 degrees. But that was not the reason I didn't want to invite them.

"Let's run through the sprinkler again." I tried to stall them.

"We did that already." Cathy was insistent. "Let's go in and get some cookies and Kool-aid."

"How about I bring them out here? My mom said she didn't want us coming in today." I thought that excuse might work, as the twins' mom could get pretty annoyed when we showed up at their house too often. They coaxed and cajoled until I ran out of reasons.

"It's just that, it's vacuuming day, and my mom vacuums topless," I sputtered.

They all looked at each other, wide eyed, and incredulous. If I'd hoped for any understanding or nonchalance, that was shattered when they all burst out laughing. Just what I needed—to be the butt of another joke. The list of things they had to make fun of me just grew longer. Thankfully, it was the start of summer holidays, or it would be all over our grade-three classroom the next day.

When they could see I wasn't going to budge, they jumped on their mustang bikes, with banana seats and chopper handlebars, and headed to Heather's house, not inviting me with my shiny green but unfashionable bike. I stormed inside the darkened house; the drapes were closed against the light. I let the screen door bang behind me and made sure the other door was all the way closed. Mom would scream, "You're letting the cool out!" if it were even open a crack.

I was greeted by the whine of the vacuum coming from somewhere down the hall, so to slam into my room, I had to pass by Mom's large breasts.

I took refuge in my record collection, which consisted of a few forty-fives. At $1.25, they were affordable on my allowance of fifty cents per week. The first one I bought was *Dark Lady* by Cher. Some of the girls in my class brought movie magazines to school that featured Sonny and Cher and their toddler Chastity. I wanted to have a perfect life like them.

The only albums I had were my Partridge Family records. A poster of David Cassidy hung right beside my bed. I spread their albums around me on the floor then put one on my portable turntable. I lay on the hard floor with my ear right beside the speaker. The stereo in the living room was much better, but Mom made it clear that I had to play my records in my room. Mom's preference was classical; she blasted the Saturday opera on CBC every week. It seemed to last all day, taking up the whole house, with Mom singing along or conducting.

The Partridge Family was the family I imagined myself in. I was just one year younger than Tracy, so in my head, I was the sixth kid in their family. I made up shows and situations, usually some kind of rescue fantasy involving Keith helping the little girls who had gotten hurt or in some kind of trouble. He was the perfect big brother figure. They were a family who cared about each other. They had fights but always forgave each other, and things turned out all right by the end of each show.

I spent hours lost in the dream world travelling in their brightly coloured tour bus and performing on stage. Keith let me sing duets with him. I threw my heart into singing along with the records and knew all the lyrics. I didn't even have to shut my eyes anymore. The faded pink walls of my bedroom disappeared. I could turn to all these brothers and sisters for love and friendship. In school, when the taunts and teasing got too much, my fantasy world made it bearable.

I had wedged the doorstopper under the door tightly to keep my little brother Keith from barging in. (That he had to have the same name as my teen idol seemed a cruel twist of fate.) My parents let him get away with almost everything. He'd been sickly since he was a baby and had nearly died a few times. He was still really skinny and had all kinds of allergies. He cried about the least little thing and kicked me with his heavy orthopaedic boots, specially designed for his weak ankles, but I was always the one reprimanded by our parents.

Mom tried to shove her way in but could only open the door part way.

"What...? Ow, look what you made me do!" Her voice went up several notches. "Open this door!"

The spell was broken. My real family, the one who mattered, evaporated as Mom yanked the needle off the record then shook her finger at me. "You haven't picked up anything, and you've had all this time! How am I supposed to clean in here?" She hauled the vacuum behind her and poked the wand at my Barbie family, carefully laid out on a blanket on the floor beside the closet. I rushed to scoop them up, knocking them together, a tornado evicting the family.

When they were safe, I gingerly stacked my albums on the bookshelf. The vacuum was louder than ever, shrieking into my head, trying to reach the songs that were still playing in there. I shut my eyes, and there was Laurie, letting me try on her clothes, Danny, Chris and Tracy asking me to play ball, Keith rounding us all up for rehearsal.

It would come true. It had to.

35.

Stiff Upper Lip

Kate Eckland

Carmelo's is a little Italian restaurant nestled in sleepy West Vancouver, filled with warm colours and happy memories. My dad took me there as a child once with my friend who lived just down the street. We wore fancy dresses and drank Shirley Temples with my dad and my stepmom, Trudy, and revelled in this adultlike adventure. Back then, I had been delighted to finally have a reason to wear one of the princess dresses that I always begged for on my birthdays. When I was fifteen years old, in early November, my dad took me there again—just the two of us. I had the same glimmer of excitement; a meal out together always seemed like something special.

I had a strong bond with my dad, as if our minds were connected by a silver string that no one else shared. He had a mischievous nature; he was a spark of bright light that others gravitated towards. We both had a loud laugh that echoed in crowded spaces. My mom and my brother, Baxter, were more reserved, more cautious. My fearlessness worried them—but it thrilled my dad. He always seemed to understand how my mind worked.

I had just switched to a new high school. I was starting to make new friends and was working on securing the cute jock as my boyfriend. I told my dad all about it over dinner at Carmelo's. We also talked about the party that was happening the next day, the one my mom didn't want me to go to. She had found the social media event page for it—The Remembrance Day Rager—and had pleaded with me on the phone not to attend. She was worried about the name and that she had found it online—what if it turned into an enormous party? What if there were drugs and alcohol? But wasn't that the whole point of going, I thought.

My dad agreed with no pause that I could go and nodded his head as I complained about my mother's lack of flexibility and her tendency to jump to conclusions.

After dinner, he asked if we could go to the beach before heading home. We sat in his car as we watched the waves. He cleared his throat "I have something to tell you." My dad was not serious very often; he was infamous for his practical jokes and wicked sense of humour. But he was serious when he told me that he had been sick for two and a half years.

There had been no clues. No foreshadowing. His only slip was a piece of mail from the BC Cancer Agency—I was the one that found it. But he covered his ass, and I thought nothing of it, since Granny donates to them. In truth, he had been diagnosed with prostate cancer and hadn't told a soul other than Trudy. She was the only one who knew and only because she was at the first appointment with him when he was told. "I would never have told her otherwise," he remarked later.

Being raised at a strict British boarding school and by a family intent on keeping secrets and avoiding truth, my dad's stiff upper lip was exemplary. Miscarriages, divorce, family scandals— everything was buried, even the birth of a child, which was kept hidden for forty years. So why would my dad share his diagnosis? So he could have sympathy? Compassion? Help? Nonsense. Better to deal with it himself.

For two and a half years, my dad's cancer had been treated and kept in check. Prostate cancer is typically quite treatable, quite survivable. My dad told Baxter that "prostate cancer is something you die with, not die from." But now his had spread; it was in his lymph nodes and would require chemotherapy to beat it back.

We had always teased our dad that he had been bald since he was an infant. As a baby, he had a high forehead, and as he aged, his hairline receded further and further until as an adult all he had left was a black crown of hair along the sides and back of his head. His shiny, freckled scalp was prone to sunburn as well as to getting cut or bruised if he hit his head while out on his sailboat. Despite our own broad foreheads, Baxter and I teased our dad for his bald head relentlessly. And it was that bald head that gave him away. The chemotherapy was going to take away what little hair he had left—and his secret.

We both cried in the car. We stared at the waves, not able to look at each other, as he explained his illness. He confessed that he had been hiding this from us. He asked me not to tell anyone. Baxter had already been called in England where he was attending university, and together now we would go tell my mom, but to everyone else, it was to remain a secret. My dad didn't want the fuss that would come with sharing—didn't want the pity or the fear. He didn't believe it was worth anyone worrying.

We drove to my mom's townhouse, and we politely ignored the shocked look on her face when my dad asked to come inside. He had never set foot in this house. The three of us sat in the living room, and I stared at the parquet floor as he told my mom what I already knew—that he was sick.

I think I managed to keep the secret for twenty-four hours. The next day, at the Remembrance Day Rager, I drank and danced with my new friends, pretending a bombshell hadn't just dropped on my life. The cops showed up to break up the party, so everyone pooled onto the streets. We roamed the neighbourhood, drunk, and with no real destination. The jock was there, and at some point, I blurted it out, "I just found out that my dad has cancer."

I do not remember much else of that conversation, only his embrace, although I do know I gave him permission to leave. Permission to lose interest in the girl that was now more complicated, more damaged. Thankfully, he decided to stay.

A few weeks later, I confessed to my best friend that my dad was sick. We were now at different schools, and we'd been fighting over something, and so, in my angst, I told her in the worst way possible, that is, through a social media app, anonymously: "Well I just found out my dad has cancer, so maybe you shouldn't be such a bitch."

No one had ever called her this before, and I was the only person she was feuding with, so this anonymous insult was obviously from me. She did not let on that she knew who I was, but she urged me to talk to her in person. When I did, she was supportive and kind, no mention of me calling her a bitch. Her mom had survived breast cancer a few years prior—they had been through all this.

At fifteen, it did not occur to me that there could be another option. Chemotherapy killed cancer, and then you kept living. My dad confirmed it. So I continued on. I lost my virginity to that cute jock, now firmly my boyfriend; I went to parties as often as I could, drinking and dancing late into the night. I returned home one or two minutes, maybe three minutes if I were lucky, before my 1:30 a.m. curfew; each time, I raced to my dad's bedroom and confirmed my return with a "I'm home Daddy!" A few times, I even sneaked out after arriving home to meet my boyfriend. I ignored my dad and Trudy when they asked me to help out around the house—insisting I would mow the lawn or clean the bathroom tomorrow.

My dad started taking naps, and his diet changed, but other than that there was a sense of normalcy in the house. Trudy was a workhorse. Dinner was still cooked every night, and the fridge was still stocked. She kept their struggling businesses afloat, kept their employees. My dad's hair loss explained to them as a "new style decision." We had a house cleaner for the first time, but it was Trudy who mowed the lawn when I failed to after being asked three or four times. Trudy kept everything running.

My dad was still lecturing me on the right way to present myself to the world and was trying to get me to put more effort into my math homework. And was still horrified when he found my newly acquired birth control pills. He allowed a wayward friend of mine to live with us for months after she had been kicked out of her parent's house. I heard no complaints when I asked my dad each weekend for a trip to the liquor store. (After a bad night with a litre of vodka, he insisted that he would rather dole out ciders and beers like a prescription so that he would know what and how much I was drinking.) I had to find my own way to and from parties, but I was always allowed to go.

Our last Christmas with my dad was quiet; a Christmas tree only materialized on Christmas Eve—an outdoor plant that was quickly decorated and brought inside. Trudy's three adult kids, Baxter, who was home for winter break, and my wayward friend also joined us. After Christmas, we went to Vancouver Island to visit the rest of my dad's family, his mum, sister, and grandkids, our last big family dinner.

In May, for his birthday, we went sailing. Baxter was again home from university, so the three of us packed up the car and drove to the tiny marina where we had spent many summer vacation weekends. We had complained our entire childhoods about going sailing; it was so much work, and our boat was small—barely room for all of us. But once we were on the water, we always understood the joy that pushed our dad into the water. This time was the same, although everything was slower. Dad was tired and feeble, but the thrill was still there—the sun and the salt and the joy of the wind pushing you faster than you ever though possible. It was the last time we ever went sailing.

The chemotherapy didn't work; the cancer spread into his bones, affecting his legs and spine. Over the previous months, he had given up many things in hopes of naturally combating the cancer that was coursing through his body. He stopped using mouthwash, stopped eating red meat, and even gave up wine for a while (which we all believe was his biggest sacrifice). He started growing wheat grass and making his own sauerkraut.

After the first round of chemotherapy, they refused to do a second; my dad was too sick. But he wasn't ready to give up. He started an alternative treatment and drank the vials despite their horrific effects. He lay there, tears streaming down his face, and told me that he wasn't in any pain.

What a load of bullshit.

He walked painstakingly slow. I was at an age when everything your parents did was mortifying, and despite the horror of watching my vibrant father wither into an old man, I was still embarrassed. He winced when bending over and would request to sit in different types of chairs in restaurants, trying to find one that wouldn't hurt his cancer-riddled spine. A few times, he sat down with me to give me advice about my life—I wish I had listened.

I still have the drawing that he made in one of these discussions: an apple sliced to expose its core. His talk centred around trying to help me identify what was important, a core value, and what was only skin deep. I scoffed when he wrote "math" inside the apple core and ignored him when he wrote "your boyfriend" (whose name he could never remember) at the edge of the apple skin.

In July, I decided that I had to move in with my mom for a bit. He was declining so fast that I was struggling to witness it. It was becoming obvious that things were not getting better. I needed a break from this reality, and just as I was packing my bags, my dad told me that he would be checking himself into the hospital. He assured me it would be temporary and that I had nothing to worry about because he had another five to ten years at least.

He was adamant that we should not visit him. His voice became so hoarse that I couldn't hear him on the phone when I tried to convince him that I should see him. It was so hoarse that he was unable to tell the transportation team that they had the wrong person as they mistakenly wheeled him out of his ward at St. Paul's Hospital thinking he was someone else. Somehow, he found his way back to his shared room, where I visited a few times against his wishes. Once while watching a movie with my dad, I tried to ignore the brown cloudy liquid in the clear plastic urinal next to his bed. My brother visited against his wishes, too; he brought my dad a laptop so that he could continue running his business from his hospital bed.

My dad had to undergo a liver biopsy to confirm if the cancer had spread there. With the biopsy came risk, so everyone went to visit him the night before. But it was the same night my boyfriend and I had planned to celebrate my birthday. I chose not to go see my dad because I needed a break—a small sliver of enjoyment in this dark time.

They performed the biopsy laparoscopically, threading a tiny tube through his body, but his body was so weak that it looked like the tube had destroyed his torso.

And yes, the cancer had spread to his liver.

Within a week, he was transferred to palliative care at Lions Gate Hospital, the same hospital where I was born sixteen years before. I didn't even know what palliative care was until I was told that he had fought with the doctors about this placement—insisting that he didn't belong there.

The last time I ever saw my dad, I was with my mom and my brother. His body had shrunk, while some parts of him had swelled. Two days later, I woke up with my brother in my room. It was early, way too early; and I instantly knew what he was there to say: "He's gone." We woke our mother; she knew in the same way that I had.

Trudy was downstairs waiting, the first time she had ever been in any of the houses we lived in with our mom. Even then it occurred to me how strange it was to have the woman that ended my parent's tumultuous marriage in my mother's kitchen.

I was given the opportunity to say goodbye to my dead father.

I said no.

My dad had told me that he had five to ten years left, but he died in less than three weeks. Just short of ten months after telling us that he was sick. My entire world became uprooted and changed in less than a year. I was now bereft of a father with whom I held a fierce kinship. At least he told us. Trudy had to call his best friend of more than thirty years to tell him of his death. That he had died of cancer and that no it was not sudden. It had, in fact, been going on for more than three years. That best friend was furious and probably still is. My dad's secrets prevented any goodbyes and put Trudy in the position of telling people of his death.

I am part thankful and part angry that my dad lied. His secrecy allowed me to enjoy my adolescence a little longer, when I was too busy being a teenager to look up and realize all that I was losing.

36.

Secrets Breed Questions

Carole Harmon

I've been living with our family secret since I was a girl, and it has only become more convoluted: Each answer spawns new questions. In 1942, Dad is training in Quebec to be a navigator with the Royal Canadian Air Force. He receives a chatty letter from his father about life in Banff during the war, which fails to mention his failing health. My grandfather, Byron Harmon, died July 10, 1942. Dad was denied leave and flew into the teeth of war believing he was parentless.

Wartime. Night. A navigator from the Canadian Rockies, lost in a storm, guides an emergency landing in the Pennines, in Yorkshire.

Wellington HE553 on Fremington Edge, Reeth

On 29th May 1943 the crew of this aircraft took off from base at Skipton on Swale near Thirsk at 22.40 hrs tasked with bombing Wuppertal. On their return to Yorkshire they became lost when flying in cloud and over-flew their base. While letting down through cloud to try and work out their position the aircraft crashed onto high ground on the side of Swaledale at Fremington Edge, near Reeth, at 04.40hrs on 30th May 1943. Sadly two of the crew were killed in the crash and the other four on board were injured, some seriously. The navigator is recorded in the squadron records as being able to telephone base to inform them of what had happened.... Both he and also Sgt Leadley returned to operation flying with 432 Squadron and Harmon was involved in a number of further tricky situations. On 3rd January 1944 he was flying in Lancaster DS830 when the throttle to one engine jammed on the return to East Moor, the aircraft swung on landing and was slightly damaged. The following night he and his crew were back on Ops to Berlin and their aircraft was badly damaged, his pilot was awarded the DFC for returning them safely to the UK.[1]

A photograph of the crash site shows a flat dale bordered by a drystone wall, which guards the precipitous edge of a limestone escarpment; Fremington Edge drops steeply into the valley. Dad's plane crashes through the wall and stops with its nose over the edge. Four survivors help each other down the steep slope, clambering over stone fences sliding down scree slopes to safety. All are hospitalized, Dad with a broken arm.

In Canada, a letter, freed from my grandfather's censorship, flies through the Atlantic Theatre avoiding bombs, torpedoes, and depth charges. It's written to Dad by his mother, who he'd been told was dead.

What did Dad feel when he received this letter? Who sent it? "It was a bolt out of the blue," Dad said. Did the letter arrive when Dad was in hospital or when he was on active duty between bombing runs? Who sent it?

My parents meet at a tea dance in Edinburgh while Dad is on leave. Dancing—in pavilions with sprung wood floors, aircraft hangars, gymnasiums, industrial sites, air raid shelters, and sometimes the streets—buoys spirits during the war. Jazz and swing are passions of the day. Mom cuts a tiny glamorous figure: Her strawberry blond hair curls on her shoulders and rolls on her forehead in two fat sausages, and she wears heels and a fitted skirt with pinch waist and wide twirling hem.

Dad isn't just looking for a dance partner. They sit in the back of the hall while Dad tells Mom about the family secret that had been kept from him since he was a child.

When Mom and Dad return to Banff, after the war, they visit Rosehaven, the long-term care facility connected to Panoka Mental Hospital, where my grandmother has been living since Dad was a young boy. They are told that Maude Harmon's diagnosis is paranoid schizophrenia; she is normal much of the time but has violent psychotic episodes. Visitors would upset her.

Byron Harmon and Elizabeth Maude Moore, my grandparents, marry in 1907. My grandfather emigrated from the United States and is fast becoming a well-known wilderness photographer of the Canadian Rockies. They expand Byron's photographic business to include a movie theatre and gift shop in a new building on Banff Avenue. The Canadian

Rockies are wild and only partially mapped. There are no roads. Travel is by horse or foot. Byron is sometimes away for weeks photographing in the mountains, leaving my grandmother to oversee their business and growing family. Aileen is born in 1912, Lloyd in 1914, and Don, my father, in 1917.

War rages in Europe, business is slow. The night Dad is born, January 9, 1917, Harmony Theatre burns to the ground leaving only the river stone pillars and some negatives stored in a metal safe.

My grandfather rebuilds in record time, but the slow wartime economy forces him to search for wider markets for his photography, in Eastern Canada and the United States. Now, he is away on business trips in winter as well as photography excursions in summer. Winter in Banff is eight months of snow from October to May. My grandmother's mental health deteriorates. Attempts at treatment in several facilities in Ontario, Vancouver, Oregon, and California fail. Eventually, Byron signs the papers committing her to Panoka Mental Hospital, the Alberta hospital for the insane.

My grandfather then invents her fictional death, at least within the family. Dad was always told his mother had died; being the youngest he believed this. It's hard to believe that Aileen, the oldest didn't know the truth—possibly Lloyd as well.

At this time, when mental illness is little understood and considered a social stigma, such a deception is not unknown. Ever since *Jane Eyre* the story of a secret mad wife locked in the tower has horrified readers.

What is extraordinary to me is the success with which this deception was maintained. Who knew Maude was alive? Banff was a small town; many people must have agreed to keep silent. Grandma herself knew, of course—a realization that shivers me. She was from a large family. They knew.

Grandma Harmon never forgets my birthday when I'm a girl. She sends me her poems and homemade divinity fudge every year. The summer I turn thirteen I ride my bike to Lake Minnewanka to open her present. It's a hot July day, long past my birthday, which was in March. The box is blue with flowers on the lid, crushed at the corners. Inside, crumbs and chunks of brick-hard fudge are wrapped in wrinkled wax paper. Maybe she made the fudge in March. I eat the fondant stuffed dates because she has gone to so much trouble. Mom and Dad make me write a thank you note to her. I worry about this all the way to the lake.

What should I write? What would it be like to be sick in your mind? Her letters only ever talk about her poems. Some are too sweet, like her fudge, but others make me feel so sad.

One dark winter day in 1967, as Dad drives me home from university for Christmas vacation, he tells me more about his mother. I ask him, "Do you remember her?" "Only the haziest impressions," he replies. "I remember coming home one day when I was three or four and seeing a head shaped hole in an upstairs window." I stare at him. He takes his eyes from the salty slush to glance at me. Snow bombards our windshield. "What happened, Dad?" He sighs, "I don't know." We're on the scary section of highway between Red Deer and Calgary, where corners want to push us off the road. "Why did Grandpa tell you she was dead?" "I don't know Carole, you know Dad died before I found out." "Who else knew?" I insist. "I really don't know." Passing headlights look like glowing animal eyes as snow beats against the windshield. "Aileen was engaged at university," he resumes. "I think she broke it off for fear of passing on mental illness if she had children." "She must not have known, Dad," I burst. "Grandpa must have told her at that time." "I really don't know, Carole," he says. "Please don't tell her I told you."

I'm the only child in my generation. My aunt never married, and my uncle married an older woman after the war. I think about this as each passing car buries us in grey slush. "You and Mom had me anyways," I say. "Yes, we did."

I have a vague memory of driving to Portland to visit Grandma's favourite brother, Uncle Jim, and his wife, Aunt Elizabeth, when I was three. Mom and Dad were on a pilgrimage to find out what happened to Grandma. Uncle Jim told them that Grandpa took his wife all over North America looking for help: Vancouver, Ontario, California. Sometimes she was treated as an outpatient and sometimes in a sanitarium, which promised new therapies and cures. Nothing succeeded.

"It was a tragedy, no one to blame," Uncle Jim told Dad. "Your father was heartbroken."

I cling to this version of events.

Dad instigated his chat about Grandma because the rules at Rosehaven were about to change. In 1969, the "no visitation" rule is dropped. There are new treatments, Dad's told, and new policies. Patients are encouraged to reunite with their families. I thought the former "no visitation" rule, followed by the "no correspondence" rule, only applied to Grandma. It must have been an institutional policy.

Dad and Aunt Aileen visit Grandma. I'm busy rehearsing a play and don't join them, a choice I regret to this day. Dad reports, in his understated way, that it was a wonderful reunion.

Aunt Aileen goes a second time, on her own, and it's a different story. She won't tell Dad exactly what happened but says she's never going back. As it turns out, none of us visit her. Grandma dies in 1977 at age ninety-three. She has spent over fifty years of her life in a mental hospital.

In 1928, Grandpa obtained a Mexican divorce and married Pearl Rebecca Shearer—divorce from the mentally impaired was illegal in Canada. I knew her as Mrs. Harmon but seldom saw her. As a stepmother, she was loathed and later avoided by both Dad and Uncle Lloyd. She treated both my parents badly after the war, telling Mom she had tried to have all three children disinherited. In my eyes, she was the classic wicked stepmother. She was buried in Banff Cemetery.

My aunt asks me to go with her to the cemetery. I've never been in Banff Cemetery, and the mountain shaped headstone of red rock towering over my grandfather's grave is a shock. At the foot of his plot is a small brass plaque for Pearl Harmon. Grandma is buried in Camrose. "This is not a happy grave site," I think.

My aunt and I walk up Wolverine Street to her house for tea. I ask questions about Mrs. Harmon, but my aunt has her mouth zippered, as usual. After tea, she brings out a cardboard box overflowing with shabby black binders and bundles of handwritten and typed pages pinned together with straight pins. "These are Mother's journals," she says. "The hospital gave them to Don and me after she died. I can't bear to keep them, but I can't bring myself to destroy them. You take them, Carole. Do with them what you will." She refuses to answer my questions.

I sit on the couch and weep. These are accounts of Grandma's incarceration, thinly disguised as fiction. Rage howls from the pages. The journals follow her from institution to institution. There are poems as well, reams of them. She never sees herself as ill. She sees herself as innocent, as wronged. Her journals are a plea for justice, a command to be heard. She blames my grandfather, but also the system she's trapped in. She refers to the spoiler, a malevolent spirit who ruins all good things.

"Beware, Beware"—E. M. Harmon

...Giving its warning, telling you true

>To beware of the precipice sheer

The spoiler is here waiting always

>So beware, so beware, beware...[2]

I long to understand Maude's illness. Having read as much of the journals as I can bear, I am on fire to learn more. I research paranoid schizophrenia—its diagnosis and treatment in my grandmother's time and my own. I contact Rosehaven, hoping to get her medical records, but am told they have been destroyed. Dead ends everywhere. I berate myself for never visiting her. For putting her out of my mind and relegating her to a cramped closet in the back of my heart.

When I become pregnant, I worry, like my aunt must have, will my children inherit her mental illness?

When my parents die, in 1997, I inherit the other half of Maude's journals, which I hadn't known existed. Again, I sit on the couch and weep. These journals include earlier chapters from her life before she was committed. She writes of her suspicions about my grandfather. He's having an affair. He has abandoned his family (when he travels on business). She's being followed around town by Mounties; she has seen them in her backyard. People are whispering about her behind her back. Her husband and doctor are plotting to get rid of her. People accuse her of having her babies too quickly.

I seize on this last repeated comment, which she sees as an accusation, and do another research dive. Postpartum psychosis affects one to two out of every thousand new mothers. It's brought on by hormone imbalance, stress, and sleeplessness and manifests as confusion and paranoid delusions. It is often blamed for suicides in new mothers and is rarely recognized or treated.

In one of Grandma's journals there is a disjointed account of the night Dad is born. Grandma sees flames reflected on her hospital window, but no one will tell her what is burning. Towards dawn her husband arrives and tells her. Was this the tipping point for a mind already overburdened?

Grandma's journals baffle me. There are sections I think are delusional, but others are insightful accounts of events. I'm mystified by her accounts of attempts to escape from the sanitarium in Ontario, then her success in escaping, only to search for someone in authority to support her claim of false incarceration. She describes being released or receiving offers to release her, provided she never return home. Did these events happen, or are her journals, which she refers to as a novel, part fiction?

In 1998, I consult a psychiatrist for help with understanding Maude's journals. I want to know whether her committal was warranted. She asks me to bring a single page to our meeting, I select one at random. She points out that the account begins rationally, is well written with a distinctive style, but then deteriorates to a rant by the bottom of the page. I have noticed this pattern. She explains the dividing line between neurosis and psychosis, the ability to sustain a consistent experience of reality over time. This page shows her inability to do so. She also tells me that, in her opinion, paranoia is the most difficult mental illness to treat because it is always based on some kernel of truth.

In seeking treatment for his wife, and in trying to reason with her and educate her, my grandfather reinforced her fears and forced her to defend herself. It's a bleak realization. Her journals are peppered with statements like this one: "For years she had fought, yes fought it alone, her intellect battling their craft, as it were, and the outdoing of the wiley."

In 2012, I contract Lyme's disease on a camping trip. In searching for treatments, I am diagnosed with pyroluria, a common genetic blood condition, which causes the body to excrete zinc and B vitamins, especially in times of stress, causing deficiencies. It's been linked to mental illness and some chronic physical conditions. It's treatable with supplements.

Could my grandmother have been cured with vitamin pills and minerals? A better diet?

Grandma wrote poems about the First and Second World Wars and the Great Depression. She never lost her love for her children and followed their progress through life. Who kept her informed about their progress?

It feels to me as though a vast web of individuals and beliefs has been supporting our family secret all these years. When my parents died, I talked the Town of Banff into allowing a memorial stone for

Maude to be added to the family plot along with headstones for my parents.

I believe I've come to understand the spoiler. Grandma taught me this. When I contemplate the warped versions of reality as well as the mass beliefs, conspiracy theories, ancient thirst for revenge, and uncontrolled and uncontrollable hate speech I see in modern life, I think of the spoiler. What else is unbridled paranoia?

I wonder whether it is best to say, as my aunt did, and as Maude's brother Jim did, that "it was a tragedy" and leave it at that. Another question I don't have the answer to.

Endnotes

1. McGinnis, Woody. "Pyroluria: Hidden Cause of Schizophrenia, Bipolar, Depression, and Anxiety Symptoms." Direct Healthcare Access, 2004, www.alternativementalhealth.com/pyroluria-hidden-cause-of-schizophrenia-bipolar-depression-and-anxiety-symptoms-4/. Accessed 28 Aug. 2022.
2. An extract from a poem written by my grandmother under the pen name E.M. Harmon.

37.

The Boyfriend

Liana Cusmano

My grandmother is tiny and old and Italian, and she knows just enough English to ask me: "So, you have boyfriend?" For my grandmother, the Italian word for "boyfriend" is the same as the Italian word for "fiancé." And so the best way for my grandmother to strike out along a linguistic path littered with landmines is to use English words that are as unfamiliar to her as the concept of being with someone when you have no intention of marrying them. Every time my grandmother and I have a conversation about a boyfriend, I know that each of us will be reminded of just how much we don't understand. We are as close as two people can be when they are part of one family that is split between two worlds, like two different types of pasta sauce, like members of two different generations.

My grandmother doesn't understand why I can't just do things the way she did and the way her mother did and the way my mother did, as if we were all objects on an assembly line instead of items crafted by hand. When I say to my grandmother that I have something important to tell her, she asks me if I'm pregnant. When I tell her that I'm bisexual, when I tell her about how much love I have to give, she says that she would have preferred it if I'd been pregnant.

When I tell my grandmother that I am dating someone small, gorgeous, and female, she groans like she can see the faraway specter of her great-grandchildren rapidly disappearing into nothingness. My grandmother doesn't see the simple elegance of my own devastation when she says, "Wouldn't it be better for each of you if you had a man instead of one another? Wouldn't it be better for this girl if she had a man instead of having you?" And the words in my mouth are like stones in my pockets when I say "Neither one of us wants a man right now, if we have chosen one another over every other man, woman, person, haven't we already proved that each of us is enough? Doesn't that prove that I am enough just as I am?"

My grandmother has always made me feel like I will always be more than enough. It's only when we broach the topic of the boyfriend that I start to believe that maybe there are exceptions. It's only when we discuss the concept of the boyfriend that I understand that I will have to pick and choose which of my grandmother's words I will allow to affect me because the alternative is to be fractured and splintered by her opinion on something she can't and doesn't and will never understand.

My grandmother tells me that my queerness is the worst thing that has ever happened to her. She is boldly and nakedly truthful about how, to her, family is the most important thing, pairings that bring pregnancy are the most important thing, and my womanhood manifesting itself in a child is the most important thing. On a Tuesday evening, years later, my grandmother phones me and takes back every thumbtack that has been lodged in my throat since that conversation. Her apology is an admission that even the things we don't understand deserve to be accepted when we trust the word of the people we love.

My grandmother has told me that she loves me always, forever, without exception, with or without a boyfriend. And that distinction—between *you are not enough* and *I love you anyway*—is a double-edged reassurance that I would not accept from anybody else, and that is changing over time. My grandmother is tiny and old and Italian, and she loves me, and she is mine. And this is all that matters, that love is all that matters, and that love is a bridge that can be crossed even in translation. That love is what I pick and choose to remember, when there is still so much we both have yet to understand.

38.

A Real Doozie

Pat Buckna

The day before my sixth birthday, a new boy named Gerry arrives. He's come to stay with us. The new boy's much older—nearly fourteen—and much taller than me. Mom carries his suitcase into my bedroom. She sets his suitcase on my bed, undoes the old leather belt that holds it closed and says I have to share my room and even my bed with the new boy. She puts everything into the drawer of my dresser that she had emptied earlier in the day. Before then, I never had to share anything with another kid.

The next morning, Gerry and I both wake up at the same time and come out of my bedroom for breakfast.

"Happy birthday," says Mom.

"Thanks," we both answer.

"But it's my birthday," I say.

"No, it's mine," says Gerry.

"Don't argue, boys. You're both right, it is your birthday. You were born on the same day, nine years apart."

Perfect, now I have to share that with him, too.

Gerry's much taller than me and has a goofy smile. His top teeth stick out a bit, like Mom's. One morning, I take him down the hallway on the main floor of the apartment to suite five—Mrs. Dingman's. I want him to see the ship she has in her apartment. An entire ship—with sails—on a table in a bottle. Gerry likes it. I knew he would.

"Wait a minute, boys."

She opens her closet and brings out two golf clubs that are really old, like her; the shafts are made of wood and wrapped with leather, with heavy metal ends attached to the bottom.

"All golf clubs were like this in the old days," she says. "You boys have fun but be careful."

Mom doesn't think it's safe for us to use these old clubs, but Gerry says he'd make sure I'm well out of the way when he hit the ball.

We take turns. Gerry goes first.

"Stand back. Watch. I'll whack it over the clothesline."

He winds up and takes a big swing. I hear a crack. The ball flies up towards the laundry platform. That's when I see the stars.

Gerry comes running.

"Are you okay?"

The stars are so bright I have to sit down on the grass.

"Mom. Mom, come quick!" yells Gerry.

I tell Gerry about the shooting stars and how bright they are, about the different colours, how fast they're spinning and twirling around me.

"You should see this one, with the huge tail!"

But then Mom's there and pushes Gerry out of the way.

"I'm sorry, Mom. It was an accident," says Gerry.

Mom picks me up and runs inside. We're in the bathroom. Mom fills the sink with water. I try to tell her about the stars. Gerry's crying. She presses a cold cloth over my eyes; the stars are even brighter now.

We're in a car. Mom holds me so tight I can't see a thing, except the stars, and I can barely breathe. The car bounces as we swing around a corner. I nearly slide off the seat.

The stars still swirl all around me but not as fast as before. The colours have faded. I lift the corner of the cloth. We're in the back seat of a stranger's car. Mom's on one side of me, Gerry on the other. Mom's friend, Gail, the tenant in suite four, leans back over the front seat. She looks scared.

"Don't worry, Mary. He'll be fine."

I am fine. What's she talking about?

"Where are we going?" I ask.

"To the hospital. Just sit quiet."

Mom presses the cloth over my eyes again. The car bounces and shudders; my hands are sticky and taste like salt.

When Gerry came to stay with us, it excited me to have someone to play with. Everyone in the Birkett Manor—the three-story red-brick apartment where we lived—was old. I would wave to a couple of kids across the street, and they waved back, but I'm not allowed to cross Seventeenth Avenue because of the traffic.

"How could you do something like this?" Mom says to Gerry.

"It was an accident. The club broke. It wasn't my fault."

"You could have killed him. It is your fault."

"But I didn't—"

"Don't talk back."

The car stops.

"Get out."

"I'm sorry. Mom, I'm sorry."

"You could have killed him, you little bastard, you know that, don't you? Get out."

"Where did Gerry go Mom?"

"I don't know."

"How come he left?"

"Things weren't working out."

"When's he coming back?"

"I don't know."

"Will he stay with us again?"

"Who knows? Stranger things have happened."

"Did he take the train?"

"I don't know."

"Did he take the bus?"

"I don't know."

"A taxi?"

"I DON'T KNOW."

I go to my room and open the dresser drawer. Empty. I look in the mirror. All I see is my face. The bruise and the stars are all gone. I miss them.

One afternoon, years later, I'm sorting through Mom's papers and find her will. She's made two specific bequests—one to Gerry, and one to someone named Christine.

The nurse leaves the room.

"Mom, who's Christine?"

Nothing.

"Christine. Do you know someone named Christine?"

Mom's eyes unfocused, dull. Her colour isn't good today. She's said nothing all week. The nurse comes in with her meds and helps her with the straw. Mom drifts off again, and her jaw is slack. She has a rasp in her throat.

Later, she stirs. I try again.

Who's Christine?"

She opens her eyes and stares past me.

"What is it, Mom?"

Her voice raw but unmistakable.

"The ghosts, they're all in the closet."

"Mom, are you alright?"

She closes her eyes.

"Hi, Christine?"

"Yes."

"This may sound strange, but I'm your half-brother, Pat. I called to tell you that Mom died."

"Maria. She died? Today?"

"Three days ago. Brain cancer. I would have called sooner, but I didn't know who you were or how to reach you. I only found out yesterday from Mom's brother Bill. Apparently, she made everyone promise not to tell me or Gerry about you until after she died."

"Who's Gerry?"

"Gerry? Our half-brother. He lives near Edmonton. He stayed with us when I was small, but I haven't seen him in close to forty years."

"How old is he?"

"Nine years older than me—to the day. April 15, 1942. He has two kids, married, and works on a ranch."

"Did he come to the funeral?"

"No, he wasn't there. I'm not sure why. I figured Bill would have called him and you. Perhaps he just didn't want to come."

"Bill, you mean Wilhelm, Maria's brother."

"Yes."

"I heard the name but never met him. How did you get my number?"

"From Bill. I don't know how he got your number. I saw your name in Mom's will but had no idea who you were. I tried to ask Mom, before she died, but she wouldn't say anything. I guess you were a family secret. Bill told me about you the day after Mom died. She left you a bequest. I wanted to make sure you got it."

"I met her. Did she tell you?"

"No. When?"

"Three years ago. It took me years to find out who she was and how to contact her. When I phoned, she agreed to meet me, so I flew out, but she wanted nothing to do with me, so I left. She wouldn't tell me a thing."

"She never said a thing, but that doesn't surprise me now. She was the same with Gerry. I just don't get it. Did she say anything about your father?"

"Nothing. All my birth certificate says is 'father unknown.'"

"Mom never told Gerry the truth about his father either. Bill mentioned a Russian boy from the farm next door. Did Mom say anything about him?"

"No."

I didn't tell Christine, but Uncle Bill said the Russian boy from the farm next door raped Mom. Her parents wanted to prosecute, but the boy's parents shipped him off to the United States and nothing ever came of it. He wouldn't say more. Mom was only fifteen or sixteen when it happened. She kept the baby; her folks raised her for a time and then adopted her out before Gerry came along. Mom made Bill and the whole family promise not to say anything.

"The whole thing just makes me mad. I don't know why she agreed to see me if she didn't want to get to know me."

"Of course, Christine, I'd be mad too. And disappointed. I can't imagine. Listen, about the bequest, it isn't a lot, but she wanted you to have it. I just need an address, and I'll send it off right away."

"Sure. Do you have Gerry's number? I should call him."

"I'll send it and his address. And a picture. Perhaps someday we could all get together."

"Perhaps."

"Okay. Bye Christine."

This was the only time we spoke. Christine and Gerry talked to one another and got together twice, but Gerry said they'd had an argument and lost touch. When I tried Christine's number again, it had been disconnected.

I drive to Gerry's ranch in Alberta, curious to know what having a brother is like.

"You know Gerry, the last time I saw you I was six. That was over forty years ago. You were working on that ranch."

"Oh, you mean the egg farm in Okotoks, right after Mom booted me out. Remember the big rock? You and I walked out there and climbed it."

"I remember we drove out to buy milk, but I don't remember climbing the rock."

"We sure had a good time."

"Mom kicked you out after you hit me in the eye with the golf club."

"That wasn't me."

"What do you mean?"

Gerry tells me he never hit any golf clubs with me, I must be mixing him up with someone else. As he says it, I remember it wasn't him; it was Dad's nephew, Marvin, not Gerry. Everything else—Mom's anger, the trip to the hospital, kicking Gerry out of the car—was false, a memory my mind fabricated and connected to Gerry's departure.

"But she made you leave, right?"

"Twice."

"You lived with us twice?"

"The first time, about three months, longer, the second time."

I only remembered Gerry being there once, for what seemed like only a few days.

"The first time we drove back together after Grandma's funeral in Saskatchewan. When she died, there was no one to look after me on the farm, so Uncle Bill drove us back to Calgary. It was a long cold trip."

"I don't remember."

"You were only four, not surprising. I went to Mount Royal School same as you did later, except Mom wouldn't let me come home at lunch, so I hid out in a fellow's garage a block down the hill from the school. One day he saw me, invited me inside. After that, I ate lunch with him and his wife nearly every day."

"How could Mom treat you like that?"

"Beats me," said Gerry, shaking his head, "but she did. Not long after, she shipped me up north to La Crete to live with her sister and family. I was fourteen. Man, I hated it there. So I ran away and hitched down to Edmonton to Uncle Bill's."

"That's awful, Gerry. What did you do?"

"I showed up at Bill's, said I wasn't going back. Uncle Bill called Uncle Jerry, and the two of them drove me to your place in Calgary. Bill told Mom I was her kid and her responsibility; it was up to her to look after me. They dropped me off and left. I was there for nearly a year before she got mad and kicked me out. One night during the Stampede, I came home late after the fireworks. She tore a strip off of me, told me I had no right to be there, and asked who the hell I thought I was, coming and going as I pleased. Told me to get out, just like that. What the hell did I know. I was just a kid. So next morning, I went to the employment office, saw an ad for a ranch hand, and that egg farmer picked me up that same afternoon. Johnny, your dad, he tried to stop her, but she'd have none of it. He was a good man, your dad. Treated me real good. Even gave me some money."

I can't figure out why Mom treated Gerry so badly—it was completely out of character. Overprotective and smothering with me, cold and horrible to Gerry. And now Gerry's still trying to find out who his father was, clinging to some faint hope that someone still alive can tell him. No one in the family will say anything. I wonder if Mom ever told Dad. If she did, he never let on. Maybe he got the same story as Gerry and me.

"You know Mom says your father was a pilot who went missing during the war? I think that's just a story she made up—a story you tell people when you don't want the truth to come out."

"Oh, I wouldn't know anything about that," said Gerry. "All I'm looking for is a name."

Poor Gerry, still willing to give Mom the benefit of the doubt. Not me. Not now, not after that business with Christine. I'm sure it was traumatic for Mom, but what good does it do to take a secret like that to your grave and not let anyone in the family know about it?

One evening, Gerry calls.

"Hey little brother. How's life in Lotus Land?"

"Good. Any luck in tracking down your father?"

"Well, not so much."

"I hope you find out."

"Me too, but that's not why I called."

"I went to the doctor. He sent me to Edmonton for a pile of tests. It's not good news."

"What is it, your heart?"

"ALS."

"Oh no, Gerry, that's awful."

When he had visited the coast, Gerry mentioned the problems he was having with his legs. He would lose sensation and increasingly had trouble walking.

"I guess the older you are when they catch it, the less time you have. I'm already walking with a cane, and soon they say I won't be able to walk at all."

At the funeral chapel, just before the service, Gerry's wife asks me to take his ashes back to the coast. "He wouldn't even talk about what we should do, but that time we came out to visit, you took him up to see his Mom's grave. That meant a lot to him, so maybe that's what he would have wanted."

I did not know they would inter someone's ashes in another person's grave. In some ways, it's fitting. Mom wouldn't have Gerry near her when they were alive. Now, at least, there's nothing she can do about it. I tell Gerry's wife that it won't be a problem.

Many of Mom's relatives—nieces, nephews, first and second cousins—travelled in a group to be here for Gerry and his family. We're all booked in the same motel. I'd met one or two at Mom's funeral years ago in Calgary. Several have the same protruding teeth, receding hairline, and dark-ringed eyes as Gerry and Mom, features I now recognize I share.

The relatives hold an impromptu reception in one of the reception rooms. Most bring their own food, set out in plastic trays, Tupperware containers and paper plates. They invite me to join them. I do, even though I'm sure we have little in common. I see gestures and hear phrases I've known all my life. I know I'll likely never see any of them again but exchange phone numbers with a couple.

I wonder if other families only come together like this when someone marries or dies. Is this kinship? Family? Must be. Aside from the brief time I spent with Gerry, I never knew what being or having a sibling felt like. I never knew what being a grandchild was. And that's okay. The short time I had with Gerry was enough to get to know and like him. I certainly didn't come to his funeral expecting to be taking him back with me.

I sit there, watch these familiar strangers visit and tell stories about Gerry and other relatives I've never met, and think about my grandmother's wake. A different group of relatives—my father's family—who sat and told stories, not about my grandmother but about my Dad and his childhood. I learned more about my father that afternoon than he'd ever told me. I found out his ex-wife got custody of his other kids—Bobby and Sharon—through a shady transaction in a Vancouver doorway that involved them and Dad and money changing hands and how both were adopted into different families. Two more siblings I never got to know.

I also recall the day after Mom died when Uncle Bill rushed up, relieved to share the secret about my sister, Christine—how he handed me her phone number and said, "Now it's up to you." Had Mom really been raped? Or was she in love with the Russian boy next door? Was Christine the result of a teenage pregnancy. Did Mom's parents keep her and the Russian boy apart? Why hadn't there been a trial? Was the Russian boy Gerry's and Christine's father? I want answers but not enough to go digging. Like Mom would say, "Let sleeping dogs lie." All I know is Mom had wanted no one to know about Christine until after her death, and Gerry never learned who his father was.

One of the distant cousins at the reception—an older woman in her seventies or eighties I'd only met that evening—waves me over and clasps my arm in hers.

"There's something you need to know," she whispers, "about your mother."

I want to stop her but let her continue. A "real doozie," Mom would have said—completely unexpected. She tells me about my grandfather, how attractive my mother was as a young girl.

"She was the prettiest, and the youngest."

She adds something else I didn't want to hear, won't repeat to anyone. Was it true? I hope not. I should have stopped her but didn't. I wish she hadn't said anything. Not about Mom, not now at Gerry's funeral. But once she told me—even if it wasn't true—everything fell into place about Christine and Gerry: why they had been raised by Mom's parents, why she refused to welcome them into our lives, why we never visited Saskatchewan, and why she would never talk about her childhood. It all added up. Mom's overprotectiveness now made perfect sense. All the resentment I felt towards her and had carried with me for much of my life dissolved.

Finally, I understand.

The Real Truth

Susan Braley

She told him
his seafood allergy was a fluke,
his long thighs from the men on her side,
the freckles strewn across the tops of his hands
a trick of the August heat.

She told him
his gift for checkers was thanks to his grandmother,
she taught him before he moved here.
Didn't he remember?

She told him
she couldn't find the photos of him
in his first two years. That carton got lost.

She told him
when he was a toddler, his father
crooned Springsteen, danced him to sleep
in the dark.

She told him
don't race into romances—girls can be provocative,
their dance-floor moves.

The day she screamed, seeing him
pin the dog down on the family room carpet,
she told him
gentlemen never play rough.

She told him
she thought his real father was too much for him to know.

40.

The Doll

Laurel M. Ross

My mother surprised me with the news one morning that I was going on a trip that very day. I would travel with Dad, she said, on a train from Youngstown, where our family lived, to Columbus, where he would take a state exam to certify him as a civil engineer. This was presented as a special treat. My younger brother, John, was told that we were going to the dentist so he would not make a fuss. My parents were poor at concocting plausible lies, and I am not sure if John believed them. Maybe he even relished the opportunity to have Mom to himself, but I gave it little thought. My sympathy for John was as yet undeveloped.

In reality, most of the trip was not much of an adventure. The train hours were slow. We slept in a hotel with two double beds. I was delighted to learn in the morning that someone else would tidy up after us though slightly embarrassed that I had not known that until Dad explained it to me.

I spent the long day while he was being tested amusing myself by exploring the elevators and hallways of the downtown hotel and aimlessly wandering the nearby blocks. The most striking thing I remember was watching people feed pigeons in a public garden. It is unimaginable to me today that a child of nine or ten would be expected to navigate a strange city with no adult help, but at the time, it seemed just fine.

At the end of the day, Dad told me that we would be visiting a friend of his. This was astonishing to me. My parents didn't really have any social friends. I also gathered that this was a friend from a distant past, a past that I knew almost nothing about. He did not explain much, and

I knew not to ask, but I was on high alert.

Sixty years have passed, and I have forgotten much about that evening, but I remember clearly that the woman seemed glamorous. Her home was beautiful. She gave us a little tour, upstairs and down. We probably ate and drank something, and I remember that she gave me a doll. I was a little too old for a doll, even in the conservative fifties. But this wasn't a baby doll. It was something I had never even imagined before—an African doll made of rough black fabric, an adult doll with a hard body. She wore a colourful dress and held a basket filled with tiny bananas and other unfamiliar fruits. I didn't love this doll exactly, but I instantly knew it was a treasure that I would never have had access to except through this woman.

I was exploring the details of my exotic new plaything as we sat in her fancy living room when I overheard the woman casually ask dad about his marriage.

I was riveted. "It was a big mistake, a really bad decision," he said unequivocally.

Well. This was new information. Or maybe a new way to see my parents. They had lots of fights, and they didn't seem to like each other particularly. I had never even asked myself if they were happy. I had no idea what was normal or average or okay in a family. I had only just begun my investigation into the reality of the outside world by reading fiction from our local library.

But now I knew this thing. My parents didn't love each other. Their marriage was a big mistake.

On the train ride home, I dozed and puzzled and held my new doll close.

41.

Fractal

Adrienne Gruber

There are glass boxes separating butterflies, fossils, and leaves at the fractal exhibit at Science World. My daughter Quintana and I examine the complexity of wings, noting the unique dimensions as the veins subdivide. The butterfly wing pattern is a complex lattice of processes, timing, and genetics, and each element blends together—pigmentation, pattern size and shape, position—after the caterpillar enters its pupal stage. Quintana holds a magnifying glass up to her eye but doesn't know to bend down. She's instantly enraged that the butterfly wing seems so far away. Her hair falls in blond wisps around her small fuming face.

Mesmerized by the never-ending patterns, we twist knobs and dials on a display case, and then the trees grow, and branches grow from the trees, and twigs grow from the branches. This keeps going until we reverse the knobs and dials, and all this growth disintegrates.

Chaos explores the transitions that exist between order and disorder, which often occur in surprising ways.

Quintana comes home from kindergarten and points out fractals. In the laminate flooring and her stripy socks. In the succulents on the windowsill. In her sister's tangled hair. Daily, she thrashes her limbs at me, and I can't retract my own violence. Fists clench. My voice threatens. I sit on my hands to keep from smacking her. She beats her wings, and there's a 6.4 earthquake in California. She appears random. I can't tolerate this much uncertainty.

Anger erupts from my daughter with ease. She spews it, volcanically, in every direction.

"I'll laugh when you're dead. I'll cut you. I'll push you off the balcony. You'll be sad when I kill you." Can a dead mother be sad?

My husband, fresh from the shower, sits on the floor in his underwear and holds Quintana while she thrashes against his large damp body. It's 8:55 a.m. We're in a state of disorder. We're late for school again.

Chaotic systems are predictable for a while and then appear to become random.

My husband and I sit in the windowless room of Janine, our daughter's psychologist. Neither of us says it, but we both fear the session isn't worth the two hundred dollars we shelled out—that we'll leave with nothing to show for it. After answering dozens of questions about the interactions between us and our daughter, between our daughter and her friends, her sister, her extended family, after revealing our lack of parenting strategies and complaining bitterly that our home life is just fucking hard and basically poor us, Janine agrees that we could use some help.

Transitions are fractals. Kindergarten begins in September. Kindergarten ends in June. Grade one begins in September.

"Most of us live at about here," Janine says, raising a hand and holding it flat in front of her chest. "And it sounds like Quintana lives right about here," she raises her other hand several inches above the first, until it's hovering in the air at eye level. "At this higher frequency, a flurry of activity and noises can overwhelm her."

My mom has five sisters. When they're together, their personalities magnify; they become larger than life. They cackle and sing and dance. They cry intricate tributaries of their mother. Each one has been incapacitated from panic. Each one has been swallowed in denial. I hear about these lapses through my mom's fragmented telling. Through the secret emails of cousins, the daughters. Through confessional Christmas letters from aunts.

I use my own therapy as an excuse to abandon my daughter. I schedule appointments during her peak rage times and make sure the clinic is an hour away by bike. I cycle to save the environment, I tell myself. Afterwards, I stay late at the Lonsdale Quay, order maki rolls. and dip them into wasabi paste; the fever in my mouth is a purification.

Some days, Quintana launches herself naked at me. Her movements are quick and agile. Spastic. She's out for the kill.

Fractals are most commonly found in nature: trees, rivers, coastlines, mountains, "dumb mum," clouds, seashells, fiddleheads, geckos' feet, lightening bolt, romanesco broccoli, "you're just a dumb mum," Queen Anne's lace, peacocks, snowflakes, pineapples, systems of blood vessels, "you're dumb and stupid," crystals, sea urchins, stalagmites, stalactites, hurricanes, "you stupid dumb mum." Daughters.

We tell Janine about the tics—the eye blinking, the coughing between each word, the licking her lower lip until it scabs. How, when we speak at the same time, she covers her ears with her hands and screams, unable to absorb anything we say, although we've had her hearing checked twice, and both times she tested perfectly. How we had to buy seventy-five-dollar Hunter rain boots because they have a special flexible rubber that allows her to curl her toes like snails. "You bring that up a lot," my husband says to me after the session. "Well, it's a fuck ton of money to spend on kids' rain boots," I say.

At night, Quintana begs to sleep with me. In the king-sized bed, she folds her limbs around mine and clings to me in the dark. Her tiny feet imprint crystals between my calves. We exist as information for a new study.

The brain is organized fractally. It branches inwards; thousands of pyramidal neurons are clustered in its forest, like a cosmic tree. Dendrites stretching and connecting. Synapses transmitting and receiving. Branch in, branch out. Loop back.

Just like that a switch is flicked, and she is perfect, or as close to perfect as we could order. Goofy. A lopsided bottom-toothless grin. She flops her head around with a brand new haircut, a bob requested after two years of dedicated Rapunzel length. Her eyes are velvet, her touch soft, and I don't dare make any false moves.

We practice breathing at home, and even that is a fractal. I search abstracts with titles like "Possible Fractal" and/or "Chaotic Breathing Patterns in Resting Humans," which question if patterns of breathing are consistent with the properties of fractal or chaotic systems. I come across the fractal model of human bronchi, play the YouTube video, and watch the branching blood vessels and arteries feather out and pulse. I tell Quintana to fill her tummy with air until it looks like a balloon and then slowly let the air out of the balloon. It's a game we can do together. She breathes in and out, slowly at first, her rhythm matching mine, then faster and faster until her eyes dilate and she's panting and sweating. Then she hits me, a swift blow to my arm. She'd rather stay in chaos. Her anger and anxiety split from each other like two neighbouring water molecules that end up in different parts of the ocean. But even with great distance, fluids cannot be unmixed.

My daughter is a butterfly with crystalline translucent wings. The veins in her arms subdivide, and her wings are a formation of iridescent scales—her grandmother, her great aunts, her mother, all nesting together, take flight. She dances around the glass display cases, flapping her arms.

42.

The Ribbon Tree

Shelley A. Leedahl

It's just a few kilometres from my parents' condo in Watrous, Saskatchewan to the wooden sign that reads "Welcome to Manitou Beach, The Carlsbad of Canada," and depending on the weather and my mood, I either run or walk the distance. Usually, like today, I run. I leave town via the Rotary Trail my Rotarian father's particularly proud of, and I always cut through the cemetery. Good places, cemeteries. Generally clean and almost certainly quiet. I like reading the names on headstones and guessing the residents' countries of origin. Imagining their stories. This morning I'm greeted by a white-haired man tending the graves with a rake. We agree it may soon rain.

I say farewell to the spirits and join the highway: I know the shoulders well. This is full-on prairie. There's too much summer traffic for my excursion to be truly enjoyable, but this bald stretch of land between canola fields and impromptu ponds—so much water this year—fires a deep nostalgia in me: it deserves a moment.

What's happening in the present is never the whole story, of course. I recall driving with my children to Manitou Beach years ago, when my parents lived in that lakeside community rather than in neighbouring Watrous. It was winter, and we hit black ice. We spun around rather impressively and slammed—thankfully upright—into the ditch's saving snow. One of the kids yelled, "This is cool!" as we were doing 360s. In a blizzard. On the highway. The minivan was firmly wedged in white—until a farmer pulled us out with his tractor. A few Thanksgivings back, I was on this same section of highway with a former partner who's also an avid runner. It was so terrifically windy we made a show of standing with our arms out and trying to fall forwards, but the prairie wind would not allow it.

Curiously, articles of clothing are often left in these ditches, and sometimes the contents of an entire suitcase are dumped, and the suitcase is left, too. Today I spy not only the ubiquitous beer cans, empty chip bags and cigarette packages, but also shingles, and a woven belt I briefly consider snagging. No snakes, which surprises me. Swallows and a feisty red-winged blackbird divebomb me. The drivers of these passing holiday trailers must wonder at this woman, laughing to herself as defensive birds attack and she tries to snap photos of their wings and the leaning, weather-stripped outbuildings beyond them.

Three bold colours predominate the July landscape: canola yellow, blue (water and sky) and green (grass, occasional trees, cattails, and unripened crops). It's striking: the prairie makes its own flag.

Manitou Beach boasts one of the few remaining drive-in theatres in Saskatchewan. It's old fashioned, like barbed-wire fences, like the province itself. I called Tourism Saskatchewan and was told that the others are in Kyle, my birth town, and Wolseley. On Sundays there's a flea market in this vacuous drive-in space. I'm a thrifter to the core and will be here Sunday looking for treasures, although there's room for nothing in the luggage that will come back with me to British Columbia.

I had meant to turn around here and make my route a neat ten kilometres, but the campground calls. Louder than cemeteries but equally interesting: I've always been drawn to exploring campgrounds, too. I'm easily amused. There's something in examining the ways in which people set up temporary homes. What is necessary? What defines vacation? Family? Fun?

Saskatchewan Roughriders' carpets blanket the ground beneath trailer canopies. There are Roughrider towels and tissue boxes and beer cozies and card decks and whole generations of families wearing green and white garb beneath the broad cottonwoods. My parents and sisters are big Roughrider supporters too; I never got football. I think only my Cree brother Ron—who joined our family when he was five—was with me on that one.

I stop to check the bulletin board at the campground's entrance. Again, this curiosity: what's going on? The Eldorado Band is offering a rockin' country good time on July 8 and 9. I know that on the other side of this campground I'll hit a thin prairie trail. It's high country—high for here, that is—and offers a panoramic view of Little Manitou Lake: a long, valley lake that made this place a growing concern back at the beginning of the twentieth century. The lake was also a balm for Indigenous peoples during the smallpox epidemic in 1837. The popular spa, Manitou Springs, draws its minerals from these waters—denser than the Dead Sea—and tourists from around the world still flock here for its healing properties.

Another major attraction is Danceland, the colossal, arch-roofed hall with its horsehair floor—six to ten inches of horsehair thick—ideal for putting a spring in one's dance step.

I pass the gravel pit where my kids played as adolescents and where my son saved his sister's best friend's life (and received a commendation from the town's mayor) after she was buried in a sandy landslide. I've been here with my beloved Lab-shepherd, Alex Trebek, and the heart's pull to get another large dog is constant and strong. I've written here. Cried here. Loved here. I pick a few plump saskatoons and eat them straightaway. I see a rusty overturned car and think about what and who we abandon. Canada thistle grows as high as me, and I watch not to stumble into one of the many gopher holes that punctuate the landscape.

I stand on a hilltop and see how high the lake is this year; berms have been built to protect the village road, Danceland, and the cabins directly across from the beach. The gazebo where I've listened to musicians perform on long ago Canada Days is up to its hips in water; I'd be nervous if I owned the Burger Buoy (today's special: Loaded Bison Burger Combo w\fries and gravy, canned pop or twelve-ounce slushy, ten dollars).

I skid down the gravelly hillside to Wellington Park, which seems of another time and a fabled place. The brook indeed babbles, and there's the cottonwood I climbed a few years ago with my daughter, because we still and always will do things like this. And there's the tree my brother Ron buried his wedding ring under after his divorce. He tied ribbons around the tree—red, yellow, and a longer green—about six feet from the ground, then lit a ceremonial pipe, and shared it with Mom and me. And this is what else I have to tell you about that tree and about Ron.

In the spring of 2015, I was touring in Saskatchewan and Alberta with my essay collection *I Wasn't Always Like This*. Seventeen events over fifteen days. My publisher had helped me with funding, so I was able to fly out to the Prairies from my new home on Vancouver Island and would take the train between Watrous and my next set of readings in Edmonton. Coincidentally, Ron was also visiting our parents at this time; he and his second wife had just split in Montreal, and he was struggling with the messy business of mending. It was wonderful to see him—it was always a treat to spend time with Ronnie. A fascinating human who gave everyone his full attention. He'd led a peripatetic and undeniably interesting life. He'd performed as an actor, dancer, musician, and storyteller and taught drum making in an Ontario prison. He was known across Canada, in Germany, Switzerland, the United States, and South America for his Aboriginal wisdom, creativity, and leadership. Ron was an Elder. I am thinking now about the scars on his chest after he completed a Sun Dance in North Dakota. Mom was there, holding Ron's baby daughter on the sidelines with all the other kokums. Ron's wife, who was menstruating, wasn't allowed at the Ceremony.

This first wife was Swiss, and I adored visiting their little family of three in their cute, immaculate village in northern Switzerland, where strangers greeted me with "Grüetzi." Ron's second wife was from Latvia, but they had lived in metropolises, including Vancouver, Toronto, and Paris, where Ron and this multilingual wife lived a block from Notre Dame. Together we three—dressed in scruffy clothes and carrying flashlights—illegally snuck through a manhole and down an interminably long ladder in central Paris, well after midnight, and got lost in the maze of catacombs beneath the City of Light. Unable to find our way out again after too many hours, Ron and I thought we might die down there.

I'm friends with both of these ex-wives and as such have been privy to some of the struggles they've encountered with my brother. As Ron's sister since almost forever (I'm one year older), I'm also cognizant of the horrors he experienced within his biological family before he came to live with ours. Those early years. The dark closet. The smoking ashes. His biological mother's body was found beneath a bridge. He told me his own brother raped him.

Ron and I artistically collaborated on that spring trip to Saskatchewan. While I read excerpts from *I Wasn't Always Like This* to a small crowd at the Watrous Branch Library, he coaxed atmospheric tones from his hand-carved flute, almost two feet long and about an inch and a half wide, with leather fringes near the top. He closed his eyes and exhaled the wind from his lips. He emulated a hard rain with his homemade hand drum during the pauses. We didn't rehearse this. Didn't need to. Ron's music was intuitive, melancholic, and seemed almost too intimate for this world. He cut a smart figure in his black turtleneck, black pants, black boots, and neatly styled, thick black hair. I can't remember now, but I'm hoping that we shared the pay-what-you-can donations from that evening. I hope I was that kind of sister.

Another of my readings on that Saskatchewan tour was at the Moose Jaw Public Library, and because my host was putting me up at that city's Temple Gardens Hotel & Spa, I invited Mom to join me on the overnight trip, so we could both enjoy the posh room and mineral, indoor-outdoor spa. Upon returning to Watrous the following afternoon, I experienced a visceral sense of foreboding at my parents' condo.

"Dad, where's Ron?"

"He said he was going to walk to Manitou Beach." A long walk, even longer for someone not given to physical fitness, like Ron.

This was out of character, for sure.

"When did he leave?"

"A few hours ago, I think."

Shivers.

"Dad, can I borrow your car? I want to go find him."

I sped off, and it wasn't far past the cemetery—where I'd had that long-ago black ice scare—that I saw a figure stumbling down the shoulder of the highway like a half-drugged bear. I pulled up beside him, opened the door. Ron got in.

"It broke," he said, and passed me a leather belt. He yanked his coat collar down to reveal the bruising and then tossed me a crumpled paper—his suicide note—written on the back of a draft of one of my poems. He'd hung himself from the ribbon tree and was already one foot into the next world—seeing himself from outside of himself—when the branch gave way.

"It's okay, Ron. I'm taking you to the hospital. We're all going to take care of you. Everything will be okay." Calm, calm. It comes when most required.

One never imagines she will walk into a medical centre with a steadying arm around her barely-conscious sibling and tell the first person she sees that this shattered brother needs immediate help. She never imagines phoning her parents and explaining that their son is being ambulanced to the Leslie Dubé Centre at Royal University Hospital—Saskatoon's mental health facility—because he has tried to end his life. She never fathomed answering a doctor's questions—yes, he's tried before, many times—or watching her incoherent little brother tremble so much it would be a victory if he didn't fall off the gurney.

And less than an hour after the ambulance left, I was on a train to Edmonton with my suitcase full of shiny new books.

Our lives are movie reels, and some days, I rewind, hit pause, and, in retrospect, I recognize how one frame segues into another. As I run again towards Manitou Beach, scenes splice together as easily or as uncomfortably as one merges memory and dream. People appear and disappear like ghosts and breezes. The establishing shots, the close ups, the sequences. Over and again, we photograph dilapidated barns and outbuildings, gold-bright crops, mushrooms, cathedrals, bridges, sunsets, birthday cakes, five siblings in a row from shortest to tallest, and we are still excited about the results, like they're not clichés.

Another scene from my movie. December 12, 2016, Ladysmith, British Columbia. I was awoken in my bedroom by a woman singing, operatically. An aria. What the hell. Was someone inside my home in the middle of the night? I threw back my blankets.

Two weeks earlier, Ron had contacted me via Facebook Messenger. He had asked me to tell Mom that he had admitted himself into the hospital again, and I was to tell her not to worry. He would be fine. He had been in and out of the Leslie Dubé Centre several times since his first admission in 2015. The last time I'd seen him—July 2016 in Saskatoon—he was on a good track: living with his cats in a house in the Riversdale area, eating nutritious foods, busking with his flute in front of the Delta Bessborough Hotel, and enjoying healthy friendships. He seemed to favour bright yellow shirts, and I love the photo I snapped of him beaming at the camera beside Mom—gold Celtic-knot earrings dangling from his ears, his arm around this blonde, smiling woman he loved so much, and who loved him as deeply as any of the three children she'd given birth to as well as her daughter Crystal, whom she and Dad had adopted in 1968.

I stumbled downstairs towards the beautiful music. I have a small radio in my kitchen above my microwave. I never use the radio. The voice was coming from the radio. How strange. I turned the radio off and returned to a restless sleep. A few hours later, I looked at my cellphone—the ringer always on silent during the night—and saw that I had missed two middle-of-the-night calls from Mom. I immediately called her.

"Your brother's finally been successful at his attempts to end his life, Shelley. Staff found him in his room at the hospital a few hours ago. He hanged himself with a belt."

Sometimes all I need do is inhale and I am back in Venezuela with my former husband and our children and the fragrance of tropical flowers, having the best day of my life. English Ivy reminds me of the month I spent writing at Hawthornden Castle, south of Edinburgh. Hiking along the cliffs on Hornby Island, the ocean's particular hue transported me to an all-day hike with a stranger in Portugal's Algarve. How hot that day had been, walking to the end of the world. The wind was a lion. I listen to a man playing sax in Ladysmith's Maya Norte restaurant and I could be in Montreal. Hell, I could be in Chicago, and I've never even been there. Show me Christmas tree lights and I'm back on a carpet in Wilkie or Meadow Lake, Saskatchewan, playing Monopoly or Clue with Ronnie, our brother Kirby, and sisters Crystal and Heather.

Everything is everything. I run across the prairie in 1994, 2000, 2013, and now, as a visitor, on these old but still well-muscled legs. Sage always smells exactly the same. I've loved the woods since my beginning. Pipe smoke drifts towards the ribbon tree's leaves beside the creek in Wellington Park. This is the reel of my life. Cabbage butterflies and train whistles and my beloved ghosts follow me. My brother let me know he was on the other side through a small radio in my kitchen, and it was something to sing about.

43.

life examined through frames

Joan Conway

in a rusty tin   I discover black and white portraits
where our family pose
as we squint into the viewfinder

      i.
      my sister and I sit on father's knee.
      our blond heads halo his white shirt
      wash into stucco walls that streak the backdrop
      he carries his head high
      as though he is the sole begetter of four small children
      at seventy-two

      ii.
      mother's thick hair
      swoops back into a luxuriant knot
      gives testimony that she is thirty years his junior
      father's head floats above her
      his creamy shirt fades into cracked walls

      iii.
      a lost moment easily discarded
      father turns his back to the camera
      sunlight glints   exposes a metal flask
      protruding out of his pocket.
      medicine we were forbidden to touch

cousins whisper
>   *some winters he stayed at our home to get well*

sepia prints lie at the bottom of the tin
reveal father as a young man

> i.
> gloved hands lean over the fencepost
> suspenders hold up the too big work pants
> straw hat shades an alluring grin

> ii.
> stands on top of an open-sided wagon piled
> high with loose hay
> straight back a conduit
> holds the reins of two horses shiny with sweat
> pitchfork dug into a day's labour

> iii.
> this hillside embellished with flaming maples
> details the family farm he inherited
>> *where I too might have opened my mouth to the summer rain*
> when he worked the land and then let it go

amber liquid confined from sight
>   *I feel as though I am betraying him*

>   did it
>>   dissolve his acreage
>>   explain our crumbled house

father planted every inch of our stamp-size yard
>   bean plants spindly in the dirt
a declaration to new beginnings
until he ran out of time

mother   cared for him as her fifth child
she remained
>   silent
as memories   buried in hay

44.

My Three Fathers

Patricia Preston

My search for family—a mother and a father—takes four decades. At sixteen months, I am adopted by a middle-class couple, both teachers, and am finally able to leave behind the children's hospital, the infants' boarding home, and foster homes where I'd been living. This is the moment the first father I knew enters my life.

My new father is gentle and unassuming. Average height and clean shaven. Slightly overweight, he always dresses casually, save for the white dress shirt he wears with loose fitting pants held securely around his waist with a brown leather belt.

He loves our small 1940s bungalow on a quiet street among others of the same design and size in a Toronto suburb. His wife runs the home and any social life they have; my father is content to let her take charge. After he retires, he spends his days happily alone while my mother teaches at an upscale girls' school in Rosedale. Her close association with the socially elite fuels her need to ensure all three of us keep up appearances. No hanging of clothes with tears or rips on the backyard clothesline. No kissing a boyfriend good night on the front porch. And if I dare, the on and off flicking of porch lights interrupts us. She always worries about what others might think and constantly reminds me whenever I break a rule. And my adoption? Definitely a secret never to be discussed outside or inside the home.

But keeping secrets is rarely easy. I notice I neither look like my parents nor have any of the same gestures, aptitudes, and interests. I ask questions, which are deflected. Then in my early teens, I find a glossy booklet hidden in a seldom-used closet. It contains the history of my mother's family beginning with her Scottish great-grandparents. The family tree shows all generations, and there, towards the bottom of the page, I locate my parents.

But there is no mention of me. I don't exist. Bewildered and betrayed, I begin to ask questions, hoping to get answers. After years of unresponsiveness, do my parents feel embarrassment or shame about their infertility? Why are they so secretive?

About three years after finding the booklet, I am called to the dining room. The three of us sit around the dining room table, usually reserved for guests, and my mother quietly says, "We chose you." This is the Children's Aid standard explanation given to adoptive parents when their children raise questions about their birth. My father nods and stares down at the table, silent. Nothing more is said. We go our separate ways. In my bedroom, I ponder what it means to be chosen. Mostly, I feel twice rejected—by my natural mother who didn't keep me and then by my adoptive parents who couldn't have their own child. Being chosen begins to feel second best.

Ours is a quiet home with only occasional laughter. Both my parents grew up under harsh conditions, without love. My grandmother abandoned the family and the farm when my mother was a teenager, leaving her to look after her two younger siblings. My father's parents sent him, aged eleven, by ship from England to Canada in 1909. He toiled as a worker on farm in St. Catharines, Ontario, and never saw his family again. Neither of my adoptive parents had any experience of expressing joy, showing affection, or creating a warm, accepting home.

"What will the neighbours think?" My mother's need to keep up appearances is drummed into me and still intrudes in my life. Even today, I can still feel the sting of her fly swatter on my legs.

"You are going to drive me to the nuthouse," she says after accusing me of bad behaviour. She uses her voice to keep my father's behaviour to her liking. On Friday nights, he likes to relax with a beer but has to drink it in the kitchen with the door closed. And none of my friends are allowed in.

But he and I develop our own rituals, ruefully accepted by my mother. My favourite childhood memory of my father is setting off every other Saturday morning for the butcher's shop, leaving my mother shaking her head in mild annoyance as we say goodbye before shutting the aluminum screen door.

It's a two-block walk to the row of shops we call "the strip." The Family Friendly dry cleaners. The Drive Grill where I hang out after school with friends to share apple pie à la mode and cherry coke. The bank you have to enter and deal with a teller for all your banking needs. A gas station on one corner and a hardware store on the other.

As we enter the butcher's shop, I always breathe in deeply to savour the smell of freshly cut meat mixed with the sawdust covering the floor. I slide back and forth through the powdery particles of wood as my father greets the butcher and says, "The same, Frank." Frank owns the store and knows when we will be coming.

"They're ready, Fred, and I picked the best for you and the girl," Frank replies. "They're warm, just open them up as soon as you get home." Frank teaches me about pork hocks, explaining that although they both come from the rear legs of pigs where the foot is attached, those we eat are really ham hocks because they are cured.

I carry them home, my hands warm from the meat inside, and place our purchase on the table. I carefully undo the peach-coloured, butcher wrap and put the two hocks on plates, one in front of each of our chairs at either end of the table. I wait for my father to sit across from me at our made-in-Montreal, grey-flecked Arborite table. I remember a sweet, smoky smell filling the tiny kitchen.

"Come on Dad," I say impatiently. "Sit down, so we can eat." He pulls out his chair, sits, and we begin. My mother leaves us on our own but not before shaking her head dismissively, saying, "I'll be back to clean up the mess you two always leave."

Neither of us responds. My father always says little, preferring not to spar with her. We are quiet as we chew our way around the bone and gristle to the sweet taste of ham. I feel close to my father as I grapple with the hock. I look over and see him wiping his mouth on a towel meant for drying dishes. We both smile, knowing the reaction this will evoke later in the day.

I can't recall being hugged, kissed, or told I was loved. And I never saw my adoptive parents show any affection toward each other. As long as I can remember, they slept in different rooms. Today, it seems to me, their lives were quite separate.

I begin fantasizing about my real family and my real parents. Surely, they will provide more fun, more love, and a lot more intimacy.

Finding my birth father, after my adopted father dies, is challenging.

It's been several years since I read the files from Children's Aid, but this time, I pay attention to an unusual Italian name. I am busy as a media advisor to a federal cabinet minister in Ottawa with little time to devote to finding the man behind the name. My search is on hold.

About six years later, when a new job means I relocate to Toronto, my teenage stepdaughter says she's going to a party at a friend's. When she says the name of her friend, I inhale deeply then blow the air out loudly. It's the unusual Italian name found in my adoption papers. My husband contacts the friend's father at his law office. He agrees to meet.

We meet him, a cousin, at a popular restaurant on Bloor Street. Lots of noise and young people greeting each other with obligatory yet perfunctory kisses on both cheeks. I see him arrive wearing a designer jacket for those who seek the cool and edgy look. He scans the room and decides we older folk must be whom he's meeting. His black jeans and pink shirt suggest to me a legal career that's flourishing. The gold chain around his neck confirms it.

"Here's a photo of your father," he says as he pushes a manila envelope across the table. He neither removes his jacket nor orders anything. We dispense with small talk, but as the envelope nears me, he reveals the family came from southern Italy and my father had two sisters and a brother. He tells me that both my father, who was a pilot, and his brother were killed in WWII.

"I had it touched up with some colour," he says with pride. I thank him as he stands up. "You can have the photo," he adds, " but on one condition: Do not contact any other members of the family." He leaves quickly with no explanation. I am puzzled but grateful to have the photo. I open it and see a dark-haired man in his late twenties wearing a Canadian Air Force uniform. Later, I learn my father died just after my birth, when the plane he was piloting was shot down over Burma. I feel cheated. I will never meet him. I am sad, but the framed photo of him, handsome in his uniform, reminds me of him daily.

No father's name appears on my birth certificate, but a court judgment requires the Italian to provide financial support for my mother. The three-dollars-a-week support would be crucial for her, since her family abandons her when they learn of her pregnancy. She's alone, looking for work, and, I believe, depressed after my birth and her decision to put me up for adoption.

Decades later, now retired and living in British Columbia, I tell my story to a friend who offers that she knows a person with the same unusual Italian name. My promise, made so long ago to the Toronto lawyer, now seems irrelevant so I contact my friend's acquaintance. It is the same family, and she, a cousin, is welcoming. We exchange visits and later, when I visit Toronto, I meet more of the family, who also greet me warmly, and I begin to feel like one of them.

About a year later, I come across the box of files dating back to the beginning of my search. Some pages are discoloured, but those from Children's Aid are as I'd seen them almost forty years ago. I begin rereading them and am reminded that my Italian birth father consistently denied paternity. Shocked, I wonder what to do.

It's now 2017, and DNA testing is widely available. I order a kit, spit in a test tube, return it, and wait for the results. What comes back is another shock: no Italian ancestry, but I am 50 per cent Ashkenazi! Unwilling to accept the result, I repeat the test with another company. Same results: 50 per cent Jewish. I must now say goodbye to the Italian family who accepted me as one of theirs. I am sad to leave them, but I know I must move on.

I contact relatives whose names I glean from the DNA results. The first, a cousin, is wary. He's a criminal lawyer in Toronto, so perhaps that's to be expected. He researches DNA, learns how results are formulated and matches made. And then sends me an extraordinary email.

"Welcome to the family," his note says. Shivers slide down my body as I read this. I smile and share the news with my husband. He hugs me. His love and support have brought me to this happy place. We agree we'll meet this new cousin on our next trip to Toronto.

In his email, my Jewish cousin explains that my birth father, born in Poland in 1910, was one of six brothers and worked as a furrier in the family business close to the area where my birth mother was attending business school in a secretarial program. He was already married with a young son when he met my mother. How that meeting occurred remains a mystery. No one is alive to explain. And to my dismay and disappointment, my true biological father died in 1979 while I still believed my birth father was Italian.

My cousin describes him as "a good uncle who was lots of fun." He sends me a rare photo taken when my father is almost twenty. I see I inherited his rather large ears. A more recent photo of my birth father now replaces the handsome pilot I looked at and admired for twenty years.

I meet some of my new family on a Toronto visit a few months after receiving my cousin's welcoming email. They greet me joyously, and one agrees to drive me to my birth father's grave. With some trepidation, I agree and visit his tombstone in a Toronto Jewish cemetery. Rows of headstones stand in harsh contrast to the surrounding green grass.

The front of his headstone reads "In Memory of a Dearly Beloved Father and Grandfather." I weep. "You were my father, I think. Secrets kept us apart." I walk behind and see, in Hebrew, an inscription, which the cousin translates: "Here lies a dear man and beloved father." I wipe my eyes and long for the father I'd never met.

Only a few graves have flowers, and they're wilted and dying. Others, like his, exemplify the Jewish tradition of the placing of stones. None of my relatives know why, other than it's tradition, and they lay stones.

I stand alone beside my birth father's grave for quite a while before speaking. Maybe I was hoping for a spark to bring him close. I am certain he will hear me.

"Max," I say. "I'm your daughter but we never met, and I doubt you even knew about me—I was a secret."

45.

What's New, Wild Child?

Joy Thierry Llewellyn

I don't remember much about the beatings, just hints of sounds: his steel-toed work boots stomping up the stairs as he got closer and closer to my door or the soft whoosh of his leather belt being pulled through his belt loops. Until I was five or six and moaned when I gingerly sat down on the toilet, and my mother, standing at the bathroom sink, turned to see what was wrong.

And went still.

Or did I invent her response? Did she really look at my black and blue body and say, "This stops now!" and quickly leave the room?

Or was I so well trained by then that the beatings stopped because I followed the rules, did what I was told, and learned to become invisible when anger reigned.

Was that why I was attracted—love at first sight just like in romantic comedy movies—to a violent man? Did the child inside my twenty-three-year-old woman's body recognize something familiar, something I thought a man should be?

My father now relies on his belt to hold up pants that no longer fit his shrinking body. My mother's death and his strokes and dementia have him getting lost in a town he's lived in for thirty-five years. He wants me to take care of things—to help him fight his boredom and loneliness and fear. So he phones me five or six times a day, asking, "What's new in your house?"

What's new? A calmer second husband who makes me laugh even after thirty-three years together.

What's new? My thoughts about those childhood days, the stories I write to give them a page to stomp on.

What's new? I'm still well-trained and follow rules with embarrassing ease and consistency. But maybe, if I write enough words, I'll reach that dancing wild child my mother once said I was.

What's new, Dad? I'm digging, digging deep, and ready to dance.

46.

Děda

Claire Sicherman

In the spring of 1981, you haven't yet turned four years old when your grandfather, your Děda, takes his life. You remember him through photos that your parents keep in the basement, albums stuffed full, the plastic stuck, pages peeling.

> Here is what you remember:
> His bald head
> His sad eyes
> His houndstooth cap
> His quiet
> His swivel chair in Babi's living room
> Brown age spots on his head

You grow up believing the stories your parents spin for you about the way your Děda died. "Heart attack," they whisper, bodies hunched, faces pressed close to yours, as if they're telling you a secret.

The story goes like this. Your grandmother, your Babi, phones your parents and when your father answers, she tells him that Děda is dead. You picture your mother somewhere in the house, maybe sitting on the couch reading you a book or taking a nap. She's three weeks shy of giving birth to your sister; her body is swollen. You imagine your father wrapping the phone cord around his fingers, twisting tighter until they're red with blood.

When you're in your mid-thirties and a mother yourself, you learn the truth. Your mother mentions it at the end of a conversation about something else. As an addendum. A "by the way I forgot to tell you something." A "you might want to know this but it's no big deal."

In Judaism, suicide is prohibited. Your understanding of this law is about harming the body, which belongs to the divine. Jews who take their own lives are not allowed to be buried using traditional practices of mourning. Often those who take their lives are not buried in a Jewish cemetery; if they are, they are put in a special section, sometimes even outside of the gates.

Did you expect your family to live without secrets?

If suicide is not permitted, how could your Babi live without shame?

Your mother tells you she wishes she could have done something to help her father. She knew he was on antidepressants but didn't grasp the severity of his depression. When you tell your mother that you believe his depression is linked to the Holocaust, she disagrees. "No," she says. "He was depressed. That is all."

You tell your mother that trauma lodges itself into the body and transmits generationally. That epigenetic changes are present in her body, too. You and your mother agree to disagree, but you find this difficult. You want her to believe you.

Maybe it's denial. The closer one is to the trauma, the harder it is to see.

You learn that secrets kept in families carry more power than stories that are known.

When you stop drinking coffee in your forties because you notice it's hurting your stomach, you switch to chicory, the drink that your Děda was forced to swallow in the concentration camps. It has a sweet burnt smell, like candy-coated popcorn that has been sitting on the stove too long and is slowly turning into tar. "Black mud," your Děda called it, in one of the two pages he wrote about the Holocaust. At first, it makes you feel strange sipping this drink that was forced upon prisoners. At the same time, it makes you feel closer to your grandfather. And this is what you want. To feel closer to him. Connected.

You know this may sound radical, but you think it's time for Jewish laws around suicide to change.

In the concentration camps, your Děda fell ill with tuberculosis, from which he never fully recovered. Your grandparents were worried they wouldn't be let into Canada as refugees based on the x-ray of your Děda's scarred lungs.

You wish people would stop saying that trauma is something to "get over," like if someone snapped their fingers, the wounds would disappear like magic. You know it doesn't work like this. That healing takes a long time, often a lifetime, and sometimes it doesn't happen at all.

You don't find it strange that your grandmother never spoke about your grandfather. You know it was probably too painful. It was the same reason your Babi didn't speak of the Holocaust. As a child, you knew not to ask questions.

You remember your grandmother sitting at the head of her kitchen table, facing west, staring out the window, to the ocean and the sunset, the same direction in which your Děda jumped.

You remember your grandmother's silence. The way her hand would cover her mouth and rub the lines on her forehead. She didn't like to be around people. She stayed in her apartment, listened to opera, and walked to the library. As long as your mother called her every evening and you visited every week, that was enough.

You wonder how much the other suicides factored into your grandfather taking his own life. Your mother tells you that your Děda's father, Bedřich, died by suicide in 1943 in the Theresienstadt concentration camp ghetto. Years after, your mother reveals your Děda's suicide; she tells you his cousin's wife jumped out of the apartment window a year before he did. The same one your grandfather jumped out of. You have heard of this before: copycat suicide.

Your mother tells you like it's no big deal, like it's common knowledge: "You know the story about how G. jumped a year before Děda?"

Sometimes when secrets come out, there is no big reveal. They are simply stated as fact, and one is simply to keep moving and digest.

But if there is no space given for the secrets to metabolize, what happens to the body?

Depression is never spoken about in your family. Anger is the most common emotion expressed. Somewhere in your childhood, you stop crying, and your heart hardens. It feels safer this way. You can protect yourself.

The prolonged periods of sadness start in your twenties, a few months where everything goes heavy and grey. You think there's something wrong with you, that you are broken. When it feels like you've been stuck in the dark forever, suddenly the fog lifts, and the sky turns blue again. You never tell anyone about this. You don't have the language. You are used to feeling alone.

You're not angry at your grandfather for taking his life, but you do have questions. You imagine sitting next to him on your Babi's couch, his arm wrapped around your shoulders. You snuggle into the space where his shoulder meets his chest. You drink tea together and talk, look out into the dark forest of the North Shore mountains. But mostly you're quiet, listening to the thrum of his heartbeat.

You don't talk about your Děda; no one in your family does. Sometimes your mother will remind you of his birthday or the anniversary of his death, which you put into your phone so you can remember. You also know the dates he was deported to Theresienstadt, to Auschwitz, and to other concentration camps. You don't need to put those dates into your phone because you have memorized them.

Your mother tells you she was shocked by his death, that she couldn't understand how the world hadn't stopped. She says she feels bad that she wasn't able to do more to help him—to save him. You don't remember your mother's sadness after your Děda died. She said she was focused on her kids, the birth of another daughter. You are not sure if she ever grieved.

Here is one reason families keep secrets—because it feels too painful to face the trauma. "It's better to keep it a secret," the family says. "For their protection, for their own good." What people don't realize is that secrets are often more destructive than touching the pain of the trauma. It's what is not talked about that hurts the most.

You don't keep secrets from your son, but sometimes you think you veer in the opposite direction by telling him too much. You worry about him, about his mental health. He tells you he is happy. You smile at him, and you bring him in for a hug, even though at age fourteen, he towers over you. You press your cheek into his chest. "Hello small one," he says, laughing.

Your grandmother never sits in the swivel chair by the window where your grandfather sat. She prefers the end of the couch, far away from the chair. When you are younger and your dad visits, he sits in the chair. When he isn't there, you and your sister take turns spinning. Sometimes the chair flips, and your Babi gets angry and yells. Mostly the chair sits empty. After you are married, your husband sits there. Later, your son plays in it too. "Spin me," he says.

> Here is what your mother remembers:
>
> His old beat-up purple Ford Cortina, which he drives as a courier in Vancouver
>
> His love of classical music, especially Dvořák's Symphony No. 9 in E minor
>
> His love of the outdoors, of hiking and skiing in the Czech mountains
>
> His interest in politics
>
> The way he defends her when your Babi gets angry and yells
>
> His sensitivity

When anger shows up, sometimes you forget that what lies underneath is grief. Often, you're angry for a long time before the grief comes. When it does, a few tears roll down your cheeks, but mostly it feels stuck in your body, and you don't know how to move it out.

At first, your mother doesn't tell you how he did it. She says that you don't need to know this information. You begin imagining ways he did it anyways and picture him in the bathtub with his wrists slit or a gun to his head or an empty bottle of pills beside him. It isn't until you begin to write about your family a handful of years later, unearthing what has been buried, that your mother finally tells you the way that your Děda died.

After your mother tells you, you picture him mid-leap, soaring from the bedroom window on the sixth floor. You can see your Babi walking back from the store, bags of groceries in her hands, the flashing lights, the paramedics, the crowds gathering. She keeps walking. She already knows he is dead.

You will probably never know the full story of G. jumping out of the window a year before your Děda does. Just like you'll never know the entire story of your grandfather's suicide. Or your great-grandfather's. These stories remain buried.

You peel a photo out of an album in your parent's basement. You are forty-three and sitting alone on the floor, a short orangey brown carpet.

It's a photo of your Děda holding you. You don't know how old you are. You guess maybe three months, but it doesn't matter. Because when you look at the photo, you can see your Děda smiling at you. In just over three years, he will take his life. But for now, he holds your gaze, eyes steady, as you smile back at him.

47.

Little Bird

Cornelia Hoogland

Family Secret: Sex

Bathroom to bedroom in her slip, Mom in a spritz of steam
and smelling of *Eau De Cologne.* My friend Linda,
the Salvation Army Captain's daughter, slides a pointed finger
into another, circle-shaped finger; shows me what
naked people do. In bed. Over supper dishes my sister sends-up
her girlfriends who—*can you believe it*—chase boys.
Well, that sister's now holding hands with one. I walk behind
their twined, pressed-together palms. And about
the elder at church who reads pregnancy in a woman's eyes—
man I avoid like the sniffer dog at the airport.

I wring the shame from these images. A towel twisted
in two directions—like that. The stain on the floor
where water's dripped takes years
to fade. Takes one who loves me; the same
who sculpts figures that stand
on one leg. The secret
is the years it took to say I'm loved. To know.

Pudding (Proof)

The way you tell it, I crushed you on Twelfth Night, Epiphany. I say you were muddled on plum pudding: two litres of Madeira into the mix, also rum, macerated suet, three different kinds of raisins, currents, lemon, fruit peel.

My first sighting of you? Wonderland on the Thames. Sunday afternoon concert, the skeleton trees on the riverbank, three deer at the top of the ridge. You wore a Sherlock Holmes cape, carried a cello;

I meant to type a period after *cello*; a semi colon inserted itself and look what happened. It charged up the riverbank, ricocheted off the deer grazing the shrubbery, glanced the musician carrying his instrument, the cook cooling the pudding that bubbled into whatever it was that pressed the man—who, today, end of October, in what we call the upstairs north bedroom, puts up storm windows;

Family Secret on My Mother's Side

I was born half-wolf on my mother's side.
Bare-wrist, back alley, stripped hide.
My bag-of-hammers body forgot the wolf part.

The street's jagged bottle, rough-sleeping nights snapped
in two, in twelve. Each bent weapon.
Took up the tool of my body, gave chase.

Howled up the sun,
tracked its path east to west.
Governed by rain, heat
and cold, wind and wildfire,
plant and animal. I read scat,
prints in the sand, snow.

At dusk, cold air creeps under day's
still-warm air, carries sound.

I answer dove with raptor,
purple finch with my under-brow stare.

I was born for meat. My body a mouth.

Sister Life

Flight delayed. Beside me, the empty seat of the woman
who failed to show, her luggage pulled from the hold.
She's not flying to the coast after all. A choice un–made.
Maybe she returned to the Black Swan on Danforth
to watch the bluesman bend over his instrument.
A last note. Now raising his eyes, now catching.

As the plane lifts from the tarmac of the Toronto airport
my blue house recedes at 494 miles per hour. Even when
I can no longer see, it's there, the life I leave behind.
Tranströmer called it his sister life. In mine, a woman
paints the concrete floor in a laundry. What colour says diverge,
says don't be afraid? We cut through cloud, my arms interrupt
something veering toward me. Shadow crosses my cupped hands,
the pads of my wrists, my face—like contrails, thin then thinner.

Weighted Stone Has Brilliant Feathers

Saturday morning. Dad's new heart is one day old. It started beating
as soon as they hooked it inside his chest. We're crying, it's raining.

In the newspaper there's a photo of a scientist clutching a bird
small as a human heart, also in rain.
It's the white–ruffed manakin. They've included the Latin name,
corapipo altera, but the modest bird
looks like the knob of the umbrella the scientist holds.
The bird wonders: should I stay or should I go?
Snow in a snow globe constantly shaken.

My brother phones to say he's shrinking.

Remember the time Dad unhooked the fish, lowered
it into the Salish Sea? The fish flicked its muscle
and was gone. You see how much the heart wants?

My brother says: Your shirt with the flowers—give it away.

Tavern-Days with the Blind Cat and the Lame Fox

A son I've never met drops in, fills a chaise lounge I don't own. And the setting: a house beside a graveyard, tombstones for effect. My real–life son acts the elder brother, offers the newcomer a beer, asks "How are you?" Catches up. I'm sitting opposite trying to remember giving birth to him, a name, *something*. Talk about awkward. There's family resemblance, his bruised–cloud eyes, that bag of tricks. Other–son seems okay, as if he never expected to be held as a baby, swimming lessons, his seventh birthday passing without cake.

Have I stumbled into my tavern-days with the blind cat and the lame fox? Their scheming ways: the precious thing I carried? Leonard Cohen returning from Hydra to winter-Montreal? Or the dwarf at the door, smirking and saying, "Remember me?" Calling in his marker.

Douglas-firs on the periphery of the tableau offer pine siskins shelter from the gathering cloud. Ah, the forecast: rain, cold and rainy. But right now it's happy hour. No mosquitoes, nobody shouting or crying, and Death doesn't seem eager to be off with any of us. Wearing the pink evening sky, he drinks us under the table.

Little Bird

My daughter
my six-year-old
my tiny human
did not
go to bed
as the babysitter instructed but
waited
at the front door
until
I came home with a man not my husband. Showed me
a rash like a message
on her thigh.

48.

A True Story

Anonymous

My mother died when I was three and a half. She was twenty-seven years old. My sister was twenty months, not even two, at the time. Apparently, my mother had a brain aneurysm that killed her while she was in bed with the baby. The baby fell out of bed onto the floor. She had a concussion. My father, who was twenty-nine years old, came home from work and found his wife dead in their bed and the baby unconscious on the floor beside her. What could he do? He rushed the baby to the hospital, where he told the doctors there about my mother. They saved my sister.

I can't imagine it. What that must have been like for him.

We never talked about it, and now we can't. He's dead, too.

Growing up, I suffered from headaches. I would sometimes worry that maybe I had an aneurysm, too. That could kill me without warning. But I never told my dad about my fear.

I wasn't home when my mother died. I was at my grandmother's—her mother—who lived in another city, an eight-hour drive away. One of my earliest memories is lying in the back seat of a car, covered in a coat. We are driving. It is dark. I ask, "Is Mummy coming?" And my dad replies, "Not now. Go to sleep." So I guess I did.

We moved in with my father's sister. She was wonderful to us; her two kids, both older than me, accepted us I guess. My grandfather, my dad and my aunt's father, lived with her too, so it must have been hard for her. That I can imagine.

We never talked about it, and now we can't. She's dead, too.

I don't have many memories of those years. Vignettes, here and there. Being sick, lying on the couch in the morning, and my little sister crying bitterly because they were making her go to nursery school without me. We were inseparable at that time. Helping my dad wash his car. This was our special time, just him and me. A meal where there were doughnuts for dessert and my older cousin (he was two years older than me) saying he would eat the doughnut, and I could have the hole. I started to cry, and everyone laughed. True story.

I remember being at my grandmother's, with my uncle, my mother's brother. I guess he lived with her. My grandfather had passed away years before. I think my dad took us there for weekends or something. I don't remember that he was with us, although there are photos where the three of us are together, my sister and my dad and me, and we are laughing, dressed up sometimes, happy. But what I actually remember is traumatic. Playing outside and having to pee and waiting too long. Rushing into the bathroom and peeing on the floor before I could sit on the toilet. I cried and cried, and my grandmother said, "It's all right. It's all right," but I was crying from humiliation. I remember that sense of shame very, very strongly. Another time in the bath, when suddenly my eye started stinging, and I screamed and screamed with the pain of it. They took me to the hospital, and the doctor couldn't see anything; he told the adults that perhaps some soap had caused the pain. They put a patch on my eye. I don't remember how long I wore that patch. My uncle said I looked like a cute pirate. And then there was the day he invited me to go the store with him to return milk bottles. I asked if I could carry one, and he agreed. I felt so grown up! Then I tripped, and the bottle sliced my left hand open in the centre of the palm. I still have the scar and can count the stitches (ten). My uncle ran home carrying me in his arms. To comfort me on the way to the doctor, they offered me a marzipan candy; it was dyed blue. It was horrible. It actually nauseated me. True story. I still hate marzipan.

All this happened over a period of about two years because my dad married my mother about two and half years after my biological mother died.

My mother was divorced, with two small boys, my brothers. One was thirteen months older than me; the other was seven months older than my sister. I mention these numbers because they were used to support our story as we grew. My mother was engaged at seventeen and married at nineteen to a man her father and older brother pushed on her, despite knowing he was a drinker and a philanderer. She had doubts about the wedding, but her father forbade her to back out because the commitment was public, the engagement announcements were sent, and the wedding date was set. He told her it would kill her mother if she didn't get married as planned. Her mother had a weak heart and in fact died when my mother was pregnant with my younger brother. She was twenty-two at the time. She told me this once when I asked her why she married her first husband. Then I asked why she left him. "He wasn't faithful to me. Women would call him in the middle of the night," she said. "But when he put the baby outside in the snow one evening because he dirtied a diaper I had just changed, then I knew I couldn't stay."

It was the 1950s. Women didn't get divorced so easily then as now. I can't imagine what that must have been like for her. We never talked about it after that.

My sister and I met our new mother before she and my father got married. I remember how beautiful she was. How warm to us. How good it felt, all six of us together. That week when I was helping wash the car I said, "You should marry her, Daddy. Why don't you?" In my heart, I like to think that's why he did.

When my parents got engaged, my sister and I moved in with her and the boys. My dad came every night after work but did not stay over; he still lived with his sister. This was remarkable behaviour—for my mother to have agreed to do that! (I mentioned it was the 1950s, right?) For my sister and me, it was heaven. I remember playing outside and running into the house yelling, "Mummy! Mummy!" and when she responded, I didn't have anything to say. I just wanted to hear her answer when I called "Mummy!" I would hug her knees. My sister asked me, "Can we really call her Mummy?" I was five, and my sister was almost three. My mother later told me that it broke her heart when my sister asked that.

My parents married. We were a family, not only in space but also in the eyes of the law. They both adopted all four of us. The adoption laws required that we all become wards of the state until the adoption was finalized, and although our living arrangements did not change, for a period of time, we were all legal orphans. Then my mother changed the boys' last name legally to ours, and we were a family!

One day after this, on the way home from school, some kid yelled at my older brother, as he was riding past him on his bike, "Your name's not Y, it's X!" (his biological father's last name). This devastated him. He ran home sobbing and cried and cried and cried. "I'm not X, right? I'm Y, aren't I Mummy?"

My baby sister was born when I was seven; my father changed jobs, and we moved to a different state where no one knew our past. The age differences between the four of us were just believable enough for others to accept the story that we were all biological siblings. Blended families were rare in those days. We celebrated our parents' anniversary, counting from one number larger than my oldest brother's age. We never spoke about this. It just happened. I don't remember now who started it. Much later, my sister told me she and my younger brother were snooping though a filing cabinet my parents had and found the adoption papers. When they asked my mother about it, she told them the facts, and warned them not to discuss it with me or my older brother because it would upset us.

So we never talked about it.

We moved back to our home city, and blood relatives came into our lives. The boys' grandparents ignored my sister and me, bringing gifts for them but not us. Once when we were all away at summer camp, they sent the boys a huge care package of goodies. My brother was so angry he wanted to throw the whole box in the lake. I suggested he share it with all of us instead. And he did. But he chose not to eat his share, and he wouldn't let us, either.

My grandmother and uncle were more generous towards the boys when they came to visit. Everyone got gifts, although my sister and I were left alone with them to visit. One evening after they had left—I was about ten years old at the time—I went into the kitchen, where my mother was washing dishes. I put my arms around her from behind and burst into tears. "What's wrong sweetie?" she asked, drying her hands and turning around to hug me back. "You're my only mother," I sobbed, over and over. "You're my only mother!"

My parents had terribly difficult decisions to make. My older brother and I were full of anxiety and anger. We demanded the de facto erasure of our pasts. We were old enough to remember, and we didn't want to. My parents did what they thought was best for our mental health. They wrote to the boys' grandparents and to my grandmother and uncle, explaining that their visits were traumatizing for us and requesting they break off contact.

They never visited again.

My father was a typical absent-minded-professor type—a brilliant man but somewhat disconnected from his feelings, although he had a marvelous sense of humor and took an interest in our activities. As a teen, I felt that emotional distance and began to imagine that I looked like my biological mother and that was why it was so hard for him to be close to me. I never saw any pictures of her so how could I know? When I did finally see photos, as an adult, it turned out I didn't look like her at all, at least not that I could see. My sister did.

As I mentioned, I suffered from headaches during my teen years that caused me to worry that I, too, would develop an aneurysm—or maybe I already had one lurking in wait?—and it would kill me, like it had killed my other mother. I was so scared I could barely eat, and I was afraid to fall asleep and walked around with my stomach aching from anxious fear. Finally, when I was around sixteen years old, I shared these fears with my mother. Then she told me.

My biological mother had committed suicide. She had planned to kill my baby sister, too, but hadn't given her enough of the pills that killed her. My father came home from work and found his wife dead in their bed, and the baby unconscious beside her. What could he do? He rushed the baby to the hospital, where he told the doctors there about my mother. They saved my sister. True story.

"So you see," my mother told me. "You don't have to worry about aneurysms."

I tried to process this new information. I couldn't imagine what my other mother must have felt to bring her to that act. And why did she save me? Because she didn't care enough to take me with her, as much as she cared for my baby sister? Who she must have thought couldn't live without her? Or because she did care about me? Or did she save me? Maybe she just took advantage of the fact that I was visiting my grandmother?

No one ever talked about this. And some secrets will never be revealed. Anyone who might just know something is dead now, too.

According to Jewish tradition, in the past, suicides were not buried within the walls of the cemetery, or had to be buried in a specially designated place in the cemetery, and this is because in Judaism, preserving human life is among the highest duties of the religion, and suicide is seen as counter to this fundamental value. Apparently, the story of the aneurysm was created to avoid such a shameful end for my birth mother. She was buried within the cemetery walls, with proper mourning rituals. I never knew anything about her gravesite until my grandfather's (my mother's father) funeral. Then my older brother asked me if I wanted to see her grave. Of course I did! How did he even know where it was? I still don't know, but on that day, I learned her name for the first time as well as the dates she was born and died. I was already married with children by that time. Without knowing her name, I gave my oldest son a name that reflects hers. My sister, too, used the first initial of her name when naming her oldest daughter. Our mother was wounded by these name choices, but it was years before she said anything about it, and when she did, it was in a moment of anger, during an argument we were having. I was bewildered by her response—how could I have hurt her feelings when I didn't know my other mother's name? I did not feel guilty about that, and I certainly didn't apologize. But I do wonder. What deeply buried memory and desire to honour my birth mother expressed itself in my choice of name for my son? Today, I believe something like that guided me.

I had moved to another country, where I raised my family. My sister moved across the country to raise hers. Were we running away from our mother? My oldest brother once told me that he thought so.

My sister and I do sometimes talk a little about these things but not often and not much. My brothers and I don't. With my youngest sister, the so-called real child of our parents, I don't remember ever finding a time that seemed appropriate to discuss it. For years, I lived my life perpetuating the make-believe story of our family. It never seemed like something I needed to tell people. My husband's family doesn't know. However, when my children reached the seventh grade, they each had family genealogy projects assigned, and I used this opportunity to tell them the true story. It never shocked them the way I feared it might. I never told them, "This is a secret." I never said, "Don't tell." They never really questioned me further. Maybe I'm a little disappointed about that, but they were just kids, and I simply shared the story as my biography. Perhaps, I unconsciously conveyed that I wouldn't welcome further inquiry. At any rate, we don't talk about it. Old habits die hard.

We did all notice during visits we occasionally made to my parents' home that there were pictures everywhere of their grandchildren from my youngest sister—but not of them or my sister's kids. The kids, my husband, and I made jokes about our second-class status. I did once ask my mother about it, and she said that the displayed photos came framed, whereas the photos my other sister and I sent weren't. Well, we had to mail them, so framing wasn't practical. In my heart I thought, "That's pretty lame. She's your real daughter and we aren't." Something, by the way, my mother always denied. In truth, my thoughts shocked me. I didn't know I felt that way. I didn't allow myself to know.

I don't blame my parents for the choices they made. They did the best they could under the circumstances and certainly what they believed was best for my older brother and me. As I write, I am filled with sadness for the lost family relationships, for the conversations I missed out on, for the pain I inadvertently caused my grandmother and uncle, and for the distance between my father and me when I was growing up.

When my mother was dying, I came to visit. She was willing to talk more about the past. She confessed that she had been jealous of my other mother because my father had loved her first. "Oh that's so sad," I said. We hugged. I can only imagine what was going through her mind. We didn't talk about it. Then she told me that my birth mother's mother and brother wanted to take custody of my sister and me when our mother died. My father refused. "These are my girls," he said. "They stay with me."

I did not know that story. We never talked about it. And now it's too late for me to tell him how grateful I am.

49.

Family Still Life

Kathleen Vance

My little brother had gone missing. Funny what comes up in your mind when something like that happens. So while looking for my little brother, I was thinking about a lot of things. Like about how Pam Lawson who used to live up the street had once made up a new game. In fact, it became the only game she wanted to play anymore. We were scouts, like in the westerns, and we had to sneak around her house, starting at the woods behind it, running from tree to tree, and then approaching the house on our stomachs pulling ourselves forwards under the shrubs with our arms, keeping a sharp lookout for the bad guys. We kept circling the house, until I would have to go home for supper, and Pam's mother would be calling her.

Then one day, Pam was gone, and only a for-sale sign stood watch over the empty house. My mother came to my sister's and my room and told us that Mr. James down the street had done something bad to Pam while he had been doing work at the Lawsons's house and that Mrs. James had begged Mrs. Lawson not to go to the police because Mr. James had already been caught with a little girl in his car, and if she called the police, Mr. James would go to prison and the family would lose their house and probably starve. That was why the Lawsons moved away.

My mother said Mrs. Lawson was wrong not to go to the police and told us we must never go into the James's house or even their yard and never ever go near Mr. James because if he touched us, we would have a baby. At that time, my little brother had just been born, so my sister and I knew what babies were like, and neither of us wanted to have one. I was confused by the touching bit, but my mother was crying so I decided it was better just to swear to God to do what she said.

I kept looking for my little brother, and I tried not to think any more about Pam, but then I remembered Mrs. Thompson, the school bus driver, who one day had come towards the end of her winter afternoon route when she was shot to death on a country road near our house. When my mother heard about it on the radio, she called all of us into the house, and we all came in except my older brother. So that time, it was my older brother who was missing. Then my mother saw a light moving in the woods behind our house. She wanted to get my father's rifle, but I was pretty sure it was my older brother out there. I ran out of the house to the edge of the woods in the dark all the while pleading, "Please God, let it be my brother and not some killer." My mother was no killer, well except for the goldfish that one time. When she was very mad, she would reach out to hit you, but we all quickly learned to run away, so she would break our things instead, until the anger was gone. Later, she would go shopping and replace at least some of what she broke. My older brother and I always ran to the woods. I climbed my favourite tree as high as I could, my legs on either side of a branch, holding on to the trunk as tight as I could, rocking back and forth in the wind. My crazy sister hid in the closet. Only a crazy person would want to sit in the dark under a bunch of clothes while listening to someone smashing your things. That one time my mother threw my brother's goldfish bowl out the window, my sister and I ran to the rescue, but one fish was pinned to the ground with a sharp piece of glass, and we could only save the other one, hiding it in a can of water in the cellar, until my mother repented, and we were able to sneak it back into the new goldfish bowl with the new fish.

So the time when Mrs. Thompson was shot, I yelled into the dark to my older brother, "You have to come out. Mommy's going to get the gun, and you know she doesn't know what she's doing. Please come back to the house." Except for my father, only my older brother knew how to use the gun. I wanted to learn, but my father wouldn't teach me on account of my being a girl. My brother came down out of the woods and walked into the house, head down, ignoring my mother shouting at him: "You idiot. I could have killed you. Don't you know there's a murderer out there?"

What funny things go through your head. Mrs. Thompson was shot in the winter. It was almost summer when my younger brother had gone missing. We needed to find him. My sister and I helped, but my older brother stayed in his room with the door closed. I searched the woods, looking up in all the trees, and my sister looked through all the closets. Then my mother said I was to come in the car with her while she drove round the neighbourhood. She was crying a lot, so I had to go with her.

Suddenly she stopped and pointed way out into the field beside the country road. There was our golden lab sitting upright, the highest point in the whole field. "Go get that fool dog," she told me. I started to run across the field, but then I caught something out of the corner of my eye, and my stomach turned over and slowed down my feet. "Keep your eyes on the dog. Don't look at anything else," I told myself, "Or you'll never get there." I got there. And there was that dog standing guard over my little brother, who was curled up fast asleep in the late afternoon sun.

50.

Wilted Valentine/ Green Shame

Christine Smart

Wilted Valentine

Fold laundry   make the bed
do anything   but think
                         of that fetus
like a wilted valentine
in a metal tray
in a sterile clinic room
              every December forever.

Fold towels   sheets   pillowslips
do anything   but accept
a red tulip in bud
always ready
to bloom   fecund and full
but never unfurling.

Fold sheets   kneel down
straighten and tuck loose corners
do anything   to forgive
let go   tear sheets   sew strips
              a white flag billows through tears.

Green Shame

You know what it means
to have no money for a new dress
for the school play. You know
about hand-me-downs. A sacklike
plaid dress with a white lace collar.
The green colour clashes with your
personality.
                   You know
what it's like to get
the black strap, turned upside
down on your mother's lap
bare skin sting of leather. You know
shame
                   but you don't know
why you're punished. You know
you laughed and jumped
on the bed with your brother and sister
and your doll's plastic bottle filled
with water squirted. Your sister
and brother watch as your skin
blotches and you know
you will never wear green,
your mother's favourite color.

51.

If It Weren't For You Kids

Leslee Silverman

I ran away from home for the first time when I was six. No one told me that I was from a dysfunctional family, or I would have left sooner.

"If it weren't for you kids, I would have left him a long time ago." The bedroom door slams and my mother is wailing behind it. My father has retreated to his workshop in the basement, and I am on the floor above in the deserted kitchen.

I see that little girl. She is braiding the fringe of the plastic tablecloth while maniacally pumping her knees up and down. There is no adult there to yell: "Stop that right now!" And she is left alone to kick all she likes and to decipher "if it weren't for you kids."

She goes to the fridge and looks at the pictures held in place by her dad's industrial-strength CNR magnets. Her mom looks so happy in all the pictures with just her father and big sister, before the little girl was born. "It must be me," the little girl reasons. "Mom is saying: 'if it weren't for you kids' because it was good when there was a kid but not so good when there were kid-z."

She hears the evening train whistle. The familiar sound suggests a plan: She will leave and then her mom won't have to because she will only have one kid again, not "kid-z."

That settled, she opens the fridge and takes a little red box of raisins with the sun maiden on the front and goes to get her stuff from the bedroom. Her sister and her sister's friend Alexis are lying on her sister's bed. They ignore her, as usual, as she collects her pajamas, *The Blue Book of Fairy Tales*, and Peter Penguin, her stuffed animal for sleeping.

"What are you doing?" her big sister asks disdainfully when she sees her filling the little suitcase that's for her dolls who live under the bed.

Alexis shrugs, not interested. She has two dumb sisters of her own at her house.

"Get out of here," says her big sister.

"I am. I am getting out of here," she tells her, neither of them appreciating then that each will repeat those words many times over in their lives to come.

Her winter boots are easy-peasy to get from the floor in the hall closet, but she has to tug and yank to get her winter jacket off the hanger. Happily, her mitts are waiting for her in the pockets. She empties the raisins from the little red box into her mitts like her sister taught her so that she can pour them straight into her mouth without freezing her fingers off. And she leaves, out the back door into a Winnipeg winter's night.

No one stops her. No one calls out. It will become apparent as the years progress that no one, particularly the significant others, will ever try to stop her when she leaves.

What a clever little thing! She goes to the side door of the stucco garage with the blue paint that matches the wood trim on the house. And luckily, the beach pail and the shovel are next to the barbecue briquette bag in the summer-stuff pile on the floor. She takes ten steps to the back gate, lifts the metal latch with two hands, checks for big dogs in the lane, and—shh!—is as quiet as a mouse when she shuts the gate.

The light from their kitchen window pours out moon coloured onto the snow. She looks up to see if anyone is watching. Years later, the girl will dream about the faces she often sees in the kitchen windows she walks past during her childhood: Mrs. Atkinson, Mrs. Lenowski, Kayla, the nice crabapple tree lady, and the priest's wife. All the mothers, all in their kitchen windows, singing Frank Sinatra songs as they wash the dishes and gaze out unguardedly, looking so different than their front-yard faces. But the little girl sees no mothers in the windows tonight.

Crunch, crunch—the sound of her boots on the hard-packed snow in the back lane imprints on her memory. It is as eerie as the inside of a candlelit church.

Crunch, crunch—the sound is like a prayer that asks God to notice: "I exist, I exist."

The little girl is not frightened. She is headed to the ditch next to the railway track crossing, her secret place. She goes there in the spring to catch tadpoles and collect pussy willows for her mom's pink vase that lives on the piano.

Her nose is running, and her cheeks are beginning to tingle from the clingy frost that makes her scarf wet when she breathes out. The railway crossing is clear because a man with a big shovel comes to keep it clean. She knows this and the other kids don't because her father works on the trains. He has a blue-striped cap that she got to wear to kindergarten last year on parents day.

She looks both ways for trains as she is supposed to do before she stands right in the middle. Nope. No train coming yet. "But when it does," she thinks, "I will flag it down like a school patrol." She drops her suitcase and pail to practice the arm waving to stop the train, but, oops, she has to eat the raisins first before they all run out of her mitt.

The little girl sits on her suitcase and pours the raisins into her mouth. They are frozen and need way more chews than the unfrozen kind. She has time to think of what to tell the caboose man when the train stops: "I will tell him I only need to go to Toronto, where my Aunty Ada lives. Uncle Morris is a little scary, though. He has joined-up eyebrows. He probably just goes to work and listens to hockey, like all the dads." She gets up to look as far down the track as she can but still no train. Then she takes off her mitten and puts the few remaining raisins on the tracks to see how flat they will be after the train squashes them.

In the future, the little girl will bring both her grief and fatigue from living and the racket from the skeletons in the closet to the sanctuary of this place and to other railways in other places. She will smoke cigarettes and drink bourbon out of bottles by train tracks, hear the saddest stories in the world, and be dumbstruck by fresh love near a railway crossing at night. But not this night.

This night she knows that she should dig a snow fort, but her fingers are burning, even when she sits on them. What if she gets there and her Aunty wants a boy, not a girl? What if her toes freeze and fall right off into her boots?

She knows, even at six, all she has to do is get up and go home. But she can't.

She abandons herself to the pain and the aloneness. That way, it can't eat her up.

That way, it is she who has chosen to leave, not they who have abandoned her.

Eventually, the little girl's father comes.

It might have been an hour, or it might have been three. She hears him calling her name. She hesitates but in the end answers. She does it for him because she doesn't want him to fail her mother again by not finding her, like all the other things her mother says he hasn't done or should have.

"I'm here Daddy, waiting for the train. Right here!" And she raises her patrol-crossing arms high in the air so he can find her.

He picks the little girl up and holds her close. He says nothing. He isn't the talking kind of father. But he makes sounds, like aches from the inside coming out.

He carries the little girl home, just him and her, and there is the crunch of his big boots on the snow and the smoke of his breath in the air, trailing behind his head. She hears the gate opening.

She sees the light from the kitchen window on the snow in her backyard.

That is the end of the story of the little girl in a prairie town one winter's night.

Another night in the future, she and her mother will be in a hospital room as her father is dying. She will remember him lying there, breathing away chunks of himself as the heart machine beeps and beeps like a warning signal at a train crossing.

"Please, Please," he will say to her, his eyes suddenly open and impossibly wide.

"Please, Please" will be his last words ever. She knows he is asking for her to remember him as the one who lifted her up from the darkness and the cold and carried her home.

52.

A Risk Worth Concealing

Christine K. Anzur

A transgression, a one-night stand, a momentary lapse in judgement, can be kept to oneself—unless you are unlucky. Unless your secret, quite literally, takes on a life of its own.

I enlarge the picture as much as I can until it becomes blurry, and I pore over it. The sunglasses frustrate me; I want to see his eyes. I focus on what I can see. Maybe the shape of the jaw, maybe the mouth. Definitely not the nose. These damn sunglasses. I move to the two sons, and I find what I'm looking for. For the first time in my life, I see my features on another person. On two people. My younger half-brothers.

My adoption itself was never a secret; we were a family with two adopted children, and the subject was raised frequently enough. But as one of the last closed adoptions of the early 1990s, my history is shrouded in secrecy in a way that my sister's is not. My own past has been hidden from me, and the people responsible for my existence were, until recently, mysteries known to me only as "birth mother" and "birth father." As a child, I accepted this; as my sister learned the names of her birth parents, learned the circumstances of her adoption, and made contact with her biological family, I was content to accept that my situation was simply different. I was content to accept that perhaps my adoptive parents knew nothing; as it became evident that this was not the case, I grew annoyed. I perceived information about my birth parents as my information. I had a right to it, and I did not appreciate their secrets.

I managed to extract a few details over time, usually through carefully engineered conversations. When I was in college, I learned that my birth father had been in the military. Several years later, I learned that he had been, in my mother's words, "dragged back here" from Florida for my adoption hearing. When I was in my late twenties, my mother let slip that I was the product of my birth mother's affair. By the time my birth mother knew she was pregnant, she had initiated divorce proceedings, but she feared that evidence of the affair would threaten her ability to gain custody of her other children. She hid me under baggy sweatshirts, drove herself to the hospital, and signed the papers without ever meeting the people who would raise her child. I was a secret before I was even born.

My story is a stark contrast to my sister's—the result of a careless teen romance. She was surrendered for adoption by two birth parents who made a difficult decision, the decision they felt was best for her. They spoke of her often and kept in contact with my parents. When she turned eighteen, they were waiting for her. Hers was a story of love, care, and sacrifice; mine of betrayal, shame, and secrecy. For my parents, who loved us deeply, the thought of sharing what they knew of my origin may have been unbearable. Best to pretend to know nothing.

I felt entitled to own my story, but my parents were neither able nor entirely willing to give it. I gave up; I was tired of trying to manoeuvre conversations in that direction, to ask questions with exactly the right tone of distant, false disinterest. My birth parents had so carefully covered their tracks that I would need the help of a lawyer to unearth them; their names are not even on my birth certificate. The only information I had was that I'd been the product of a transgression. It seemed that was all I would ever know. I learned to joke about it and to laugh about the mystery of myself. The sticking point, the thing that I could not get over, was my lack of family medical history. That terrified me.

After years of lamenting about this lack of medical information, my husband bought me a DNA kit. The kit sat on my nightstand for weeks as my internal debate raged, and I may never have used it if my husband had not asked about it, fearful that he'd offended me with the gift. He hadn't; his intentions had been kind, and I did want my medical history. I opened the box, but as I completed the registration, I left the option for DNA relatives unchecked. This was not the point, I reminded myself.

A month later, I received my results and learned more about myself in an hour than I had in twenty-eight years. I am of Irish descent. I am not a carrier for the cystic fibrosis gene. I am likely to be bitten by mosquitos more frequently than others. I spent hours poring over these reports. Something that people in biologically related families take for granted is the ability to trace their attitudes and traits, but I had never thought about whether I was predisposed to like cilantro or to have a specific finger-length ratio. I was entranced, and as I read more about myself, I began to experience a feeling I hadn't had in a long time. The desire to know, which I thought I'd long since buried, was back, and this time I had an option. The "family and friends" tab was right there. I could check that box whenever I wanted.

I made it about a week before I gave in. One night, while my husband was away for work, I poured myself a glass of wine and sat down at the computer. I opened up the site and navigated to the "family and friends" tab. I hovered over the "see relatives" button. I hesitated. I graded some papers. I went back to the tab. I poured another glass. I clicked.

I stayed on the page long enough to notice that I had a cousin—a first cousin, someone who shared biological grandparents with me. It was overwhelming. This was the closest I'd ever been to finding genetic relatives, but it felt wrong. I felt like I was betraying my birth parents, who had so clearly done what they could to distance themselves from me. What right did I have to intrude on their lives? Yet at the same time, I felt I had every right; their history was my history. Their decision to keep me secret—to keep themselves secret from me—was denying me information that I perceived to be rightfully mine. It was too much to process; I closed the page and left the computer.

I don't remember exactly when it occurred to me that I'd never returned my privacy settings to hidden, but eventually it did. After this realization, I made a conscious decision to leave myself available. I found this to be an acceptable compromise; I would not intrude on them, but if they wanted to reach out, I would be easy to find. I should have seen the flaws in this compromise, but I did not. My own family experiences were so shrouded in uncertainty that it never occurred to me that someone would notice a stranger in the mix. Having grown up with no biological ties, I had never considered the possibility that someone might take an interest in mapping their family's genealogy—that the presence of an unknown would be obvious.

Months after I'd clicked that button, I received an email from the site. It was two weeks before I could bring myself to open the message and another three before I could respond. Sandy[1] was the unofficial kin keeper of her family, the one who collected the family stories and maintained the extensive family tree that went back generations to family's origins in Ireland. Her email was an innocent inquiry. She wanted to know where I fit in the 23andme family tree. She was tactful, but her confusion was evident: I should not have been in her family tree. I was an anomaly, unaccounted for, a puzzle piece that had never been missing. Suddenly, Sandy found herself as the unwitting co-owner of a family member's decades-long buried secret.

Despite her surprise, Sandy was kind; she reiterated that she was not only the family historian but an amateur genealogist, and without pushing, she made it clear that she would happily share as much information as I was interested in knowing. At the end of the message, she provided her email address; she would not bother me, but if I were interested, I could reach out to her. She emphasized that it was fully my decision and that she would tell me as much or as little as I wanted. Once again, I felt the flare of possessiveness—this was my history, too. Did I not have a right to know? I debated for several days, but finally, I sent the email.

Sandy was able to determine that I was the biological child of one person in a group of eight siblings—her cousins. She speculated it was likely one of the men, as she thought she'd have remembered a pregnancy. She did not know my age or birth location, and she apologized for not being able to be more specific. She hypothesized that it was likely one of three men, and she included a few short sentences on each. I read through them carefully until I reached Carl. Carl, she wrote, lived in my home state, to which he had moved after his military stint in Florida. I had expected this woman to send me a general family background—maybe some information on when they'd emigrated from Ireland, some family traits, perhaps an indication of any health issues that ran in the family. Instead, she'd found my birth father.

To this point, I had given Sandy no information about myself. She didn't know what "military" or "Florida" meant to me. She'd included just as much information on the other two. I ignored them. For the first time, I had my birth father's name. I reread what she'd written about him. Carl had two sons. In my head, I used the word "siblings" in a way I never had when thinking about my birth mother and her children. I had siblings. Half-brothers. I spent that entire day googling his name and found his birth date and anniversary, which confirmed that it had been an affair on both sides.

After hours of web searching, I wrote back to Sandy. I told her what I'd learned, and she sent me the only picture of Carl that she had. There he was: a tall man, wearing sunglasses, smiling with his two boys. I ignored the sons and focused on Carl, annoyed to find that he did not look much like me. There was nothing about him to mark him as my birth father, no obvious similarities between us. I'd been expecting that I would see his face and feel a connection, but I didn't. I was just looking at a picture of a man and his sons.

The euphoria of the day began to wane, and I closed the photo and returned to Sandy's email. In addition to the photo, she'd written a bit more about Carl and his family. She closed her email by offering to send any more information that I might be interested in knowing and reassured me that she would keep my secret. As I read that line, my heart sank. My secret. My crusade to uncover family secrets had led me to expose his affair and his illegitimate daughter to his cousin. I had made her responsible for this secret. In my excitement, I had also blurred the lines between my own information and Carl's. He had not wanted me in his life, had not wanted to know me. Yet here I was, announcing my presence to a member of his family and viewing a photo of one of his private family moments. It was not until I saw the faces of my half-brothers that I understood what Carl might have stood to lose.

I am still struggling to unpack what I have learned. I argue back and forth with myself: I have the right to know. It doesn't matter. The arguments circle, and the secret wins.

I return to the photo on the screen. Carl is still a mystery, still hidden behind sunglasses, a physical manifestation of the barriers he's constructed since he learned about me. My gaze slides to his sons. I feel the weight of my own secret: I have half-brothers. Half-brothers whom I would love to know. Half-brothers who may share my sense of humor, laugh the way I do, enjoy cilantro, too. But our story ends here; this is as far as we go. On the other side of the country, their secret half-sister closes their photo for the last time. Deletes the image and the email, destroying the evidence, just as our father did thirty years ago. I will keep his secret; it is a risk worth intentionally concealing.

1. All names are pseudonyms.

53.

The State of Our Father

Ingrid Rose

Imagine a large grey-brick block of flats in St John's Wood, a leafy, wealthy neighbourhood in London, England. Neo-Georgian elegance in a six-storey building gracing the corner of two streets. Two separate entrances from both streets, each manned by uniformed porters. It's the early sixties, our parents have rented the top floor flat, number sixty-two South Lodge on the Circus Road side, since before we were born.

Light enters into my brother's bedroom and into mine from the east. We share a wall. Our parents' bedroom is lit from south and east. Through large sash windows, from south and west, the drawing room and dining room, Nanny's room and kitchen glow red when clouds don't hide the setting sun.

Dad needs light. He has a terror of dark dwellings like the one Ma's sister Aunty Gerty lives in, on the first floor, looking onto a grubby courtyard. But her husband is only an employee in a mattress company while she is a social worker; both Dad and Ma are directors of separate companies manufacturing womenswear. We can afford a classier address.

Considering Dad's radical politics, what he doesn't need is the class divide implicit in our block of flat's 1930s design. Running under our side of South Lodge and the Grove End Road side where his two brothers live is a warren of dim corridors.

It is Tim, my twin, who first goes down our back staircase, unclad metal steps clanging behind the back door in the kitchen, leading to the tradesman's entrance. Later he shows me the way through the basement to our Uncle Phil and Uncle Harry's side.

On one occasion down there, where you can hear the constant rumble of two huge boilers that almost entirely fill one of the large underground rooms and provide us with heat and hot water, we discover a row of cubbyhole bedrooms hidden away for the domestic help. Now I wonder if Daisy, the young hotel maid who came back with us from a family holiday abroad, didn't live down there when she wasn't cleaning upstairs. Sometimes I dare go down alone when fearful of a test at school, lean my forehead against the side of a boiler, close enough to raise my temperature and not get burned.

Dad says, "Darling, you're a worrier like me."

The class divide doesn't only exist underneath our building but runs through the whole design like a fractal, showing up in our flat, too. It has to do with the division of labour, something I know all about from a young age listening attentively at Dad's side as he walks Tim and me through London parks and will be, he assures us with a conspiratorial wink, resolved by revolution. "The nature and paradox of capitalism," he says. "The inherent contradictions between capital and labour bear the seeds of its own demise."

Tim's not listening as he dribbles a stone between his feet. At home when Grandma comes, we play cricket down the red-carpeted corridor we call "the hall." She stands in front of the glass-paned door of the drawing room, her thick-stockinged legs serving as wicket. Does anyone else realize the corridor wall the ball sometimes ricochets off divides our flat in two?

On one side of this wall are the kitchen and pantry, off which Nanny lives in a tiny bedroom suite, where on nights my parents go out with friends to the theatre or a restaurant, Tim and I also eat with her. A dinner prepared by our cook who willingly lets us help in the kitchen to wash the salad or push lightly-cooked chicken livers through the grinder to make pâté, until Nanny's voice calls out, "Leaf cook alown to get on with herr werrk!"

Nanny doesn't like the way we weaken the divide by being friendly with the cook. Being in her room doesn't count. She's employed to look after us and so has more than currency on our side of the wall. But then she's a conservative and monarchist, so her politics are polar opposite to ours. Dad's always teasing her: "Nanny when will you rise up against your exploitation?" To which she replies, "Ooh Mr. Roose, I'm not one for politics, you know. Would you like another cuppa tea?"

On our side of the wall, the more luxurious side, Dad's state is hidden.

Too nervous to ever have driven, Dad has a chauffeur, Mr. North, who ferries him during the week to his dress shops in and out of London or up to his factory near Northhampton. Sometimes during the week if it's raining, I plead, "Northy, please give me a lift to school?" Dad says, "Mister North to you! He's here for my use, not yours." But he lets him drive me if not in a hurry. I make sure Northy drops me off a street away from school.

On Sunday mornings, Ma's only chance of some peace and quiet, Dad takes Tim and me out walking. "Walk?" Ma scoffs. "Your father doesn't walk; he speeds like a train!"

Nervousness trills his fine frame and restless hands and propels his rapid speech and our legs as we rush to keep up. He only talks politics. Finger raised while hurtling along, "You have to understand, the working class creates the wealth. All we capitalists do is accrue capital to make more wealth without lifting a finger!" Tim's barely listening in his search for another stone to kick. I skip to keep up with Dad: "But what if we shared the wealth?" "Darling, if only it were that simple!" You have to take into account the contradictions of capitalism!"

It's these contradictions that make his legs cover miles of London pavement to get away from the present; to remake a world he doesn't feel ashamed of. But there's no getting away from it, as factory owner and communist, he's pitted against the very people—he and the dozen or so of his Jewish intellectual friends, employers like him—are politically aligned with. "We're a secret cadre," he tells us. "Wouldn't be good for workers to know their bosses are party members!"

He takes Tim and me to lunch with his bespoke suited comrades in a private upstairs room of an exclusive fish restaurant in Soho. I watch his slender hands flail, his cheeks redden as white linen serviettes are flung across remains of dover sole, traces of poached salmon, empty oyster shells, voices in high debate: "Sometimes it's strategic to vote for Labour!" "Not on your life!" "Traitors of the working class!" Only way forward is the Communist Party!" We need enough seats to legislate socialism!"

Dad, steaming at the zenith of his pressure-cooker temperament, always first to show the way. Out comes the chequebook, slim Shaeffer gold nib sparking. With illegible squiggles, he signs away thousands of pounds to the Communist Party, the USSR, for Chile, for the miners' strike.

Sitting in the drawing room with our parents, Tim asks, "Are we rich?" Before Dad has time to put his paper down, Ma says, "We would be darling, if your father didn't give it all away!"

His nervous energy, a part of who he is, is why he feels others' pain acutely. Uncomfortable talking about his own past, stories come out in snippets. Ma's version fills in some bits.

Long before our parents met, he'd been diagnosed with anxiety nervosa, but the first time Ma was faced with him unable to get out of bed was on their honeymoon, a year before we were born. Until then, she'd only witnessed his enthusiasm and persuasiveness that open everyone's hearts and pockets to causes he champions, including his own, defeating two other suitors, both doctors, by convincing Ma to marry him.

She tries to tone him down. But on top of the world, his optimism and confidence know no bounds. Once, he tells us, before they married, he'd gone with a couple of friends to Acapulco—"A wealthy playboys' paradise," said with wry smile. There he'd convinced a complete stranger to lend him money to buy the gold and silver globe clock he came home with, a surprise for his beautiful fiancée. "The days," Ma says, "when I thought your father was rich!"

The clock sits on the mantelpiece in pride of place. Dad, so kind and honest a man, even a stranger trusted him. The elegant figure he must have cut in hand-made shoes and bespoke shirts must have also been reassuring. On his return, of course he immediately paid back the loan.

I don't remember when the clock stopped working.

We never think of his state as a mental illness, what his youngest brother, Uncle Harry, suffers from, the reason our two uncles, Phil and Harry, live together with a housekeeper in the same block of flats as we do, but round the corner where we never visit them, and they are never invited to our side for dinner.

Occasionally on a weekend afternoon, Dad reading his *Morning Star* in his corner of the drawing room Ma reading a book in hers, Uncle Harry appears out of the blue. Either the cook or Nanny has let him in. Without being told, I run into the kitchen to make a cup of Nescafé, hurrying back not to miss any of the odd conversation between the brothers. Ma stays but doesn't join in.

Uncle Harry holds the cup in his fine, nicotine-stained fingers, a saucer in the other hand, one thin leg crossed over the other, bare ankle emerging from a suede shoe. Even in winter, he doesn't sport socks. "Don't get cold you know," his nasal voice declares. Dad asks, "How's Phil?" Harry drawing in air through his pinched nostrils, drawls, "You know how he is Morry! A little business here, a little there. Now he's decided we shouldn't cut our hair!" Abruptly, he sets down his cup and saucer apart, precariously close to the side table's edge. I feel Ma fret and quickly slip close to him, nudge them to safety. Uncle Harry snorts, "Worried they'd break? Not on this bourgeois carpet!" rubbing the tip of his shoe into its thick pile. As he flicks his fingers through the back of his long, greasy hair, his thin lips stretch into a smile. He looks at me, hand suspended behind his head, says, "Yes Ingrid, your Uncle Phil thinks it makes us look like artists."

A thwack from Dad's paper as he smacks the centre fold to close it. Uncle Harry, eyes narrowed, looks at him: "It's alright, Morry. Phil tries to keep us abreast of the times." He smirks as he lifts his cup, ostentatiously sweeping the saucer under it and eyeing my mother, sips noisily. Ma lights a cigarette while Dad makes another attempt: "What've you been up to this past week?" "Oh you know Morry," Harry flutters his long thin fingers in the air: "I go to the club every day. Phil likes me to be home by six for dinner. Maddie always has it on the table by six fifteen." He snickers, "Phil's very punctual that way."

Years later, in my mid-teens on a walk with Dad, he tells how Harry was once an able trade union lawyer. If a worker sustained an injury at a factory, losing fingers or even an arm to a machine, "*They'd be asking for fifty quid compensation,*" But Harry would say, "A thousand or nothing!" He sounds heroic. Dad's voice slows: "Problem was, Harry thought he was god. Wrote letters to the queen, the prime minister, all kinds of important people, telling them what to do. One day the club's president called me in. There had to have been twenty or more sacksful of letters Harry'd written on club stationery to well-placed people in England, lining the walls of his office." He pauses for breath: "Harry wasn't al-lowed to be a member any longer."

Probably, it was at that point Harry was diagnosed with megalomania. It whispers through the flat. Later, named, schizophrenia.

What strikes me as the hardest part was Dad having to be the one to commit him to an asylum. Imagine his own brother! It must have been fairly soon after that Phil got Harry out, on condition he live with him for the rest of his life. Seemed to suit Phil who'd wanted to stay in the army but, as Dad chuckles, "The army wouldn't keep him because he was a vegetarian!"

Even though Dad lets slip these slivers of personal information, his typical response to direct questions about family history is "Whaddya want to know for? Personal history means what?"

He's a Stalinist, and I'm a Trotskyist. I'm reading pamphlets by Rosa Luxembourg: "Bourgeois class domination is undoubtedly an historical necessity, but, so too, the rising of the working class against it. Capital is an historical necessity, but, so too, its grave digger, the socialist proletariat."

Rosa, one of my heroes. Along with the proletariat.

I'm also reading Engels's *The Origin of the Family, Private Property, and the State*. I always suspected the nuclear family wasn't a part of natural evolution but a tool of capitalism to prevent most humans from fully realising their true selves.

That's why I also can't put down R.D. Laing's *The Divided Self*. The wildly brilliant Scottish psychiatrist has a completely different take from the medical establishment on what madness is. Psychosis, he says, isn't so much a mental illness as a conflict between an inner authentic identity and a self we are forced to present to the outer world to be considered sane.

Dad of course is sane but suffers from an illness we know not to talk about, either at home or at school.

Laing says schizophrenia is a kind of suffering from a form of personal alienation. No wonder Harry, as a trade union lawyer, was worried sick. Marx's theory of alienation has a similar take but from an economic perspective. Under capitalism, the worker forced to sell their labour is alienated from what they produce, from themselves, and from the society they live in. No wonder Dad suffers too the contradictions between his lifestyle and belief—untenable.

Suffering comes like a rogue wave, snatching away his words, dragging him under.

Ma has already left for the office. Nanny's clearing the breakfast table. Tim's set out for his school. I knock at the bedroom door, go in. From under the covers weighting him down, he stammers, "Stay with me Ingrid!"

These waves that knock Dad off his feet come in cyclic pattern. One day anything is possible; the next he can't get out of bed. Several painful weeks follow—an eerie hush at home, Ma takes him to hospital.

Although electric shock treatment can make you lose parts of your memory, Dad's fortunate in responding relatively quickly. But it still takes weeks for his words to find their flow again, his smile and teasing to reappear and reinforce them.

He doesn't forget what he believes in, confident one day revolution will come.

No wonder both Dad and Uncle Harry despair when they can't make life better for others.

On a family summer holiday in Italy, my parents make friends with a working-class couple from Manchester, Bill and Iris. I still have the small photo, taken no doubt by another holidaymaker with my Kodak Brownie, of us at the beach—Bill, small and wiry with close-cropped white hair, Iris, a dyed blond wearing sunglasses with glitter on their frames, Ma, tanned and voluptuous in her bikini, while Dad, barely visible, crouches behind them, a mischievous grin on his face. Tim and I are at the front, tanned and bare chested, with Nanny wearing a blouse and skirt, sitting on the towel beside us.

After a fortnight on the Lido, Dad treats us all—Bill, Iris, and Nanny too—to a night's stay at the five-star, palatial Hotel Danieli in Venice. Steps away from the lagoon and close to the Bridge of Sighs. Ma's smile pinned to her face. How do Bill and Iris feel under the glittering chandeliers and the perspicacious eyes of the gold-braided doormen?

What can't be addressed at all is the unconscious fear like the underground rooms of our block of flats, through our childhood. What's admitted is Dad's family is peculiar. Neither of his brothers has married. Ma's fervent hope: Tim and I would take after her family, down to earth and stable. But it's not looking promising. When either of us are feeling low, our chatty selves disappear. Tim bangs a tennis ball harder and more frequently against our shared wall. On evenings when our parents go out and we eat with Nanny I slip chocolate digestive biscuits out of the tins in the pantry, stuff them down. and throw up in the bathroom toilet. Although Ma always keeps her inventory up to date, she doesn't say anything about the disappearing packets.

In our teenage years, when Tim and I come home from a rare party after midnight, Dad's beside himself with worry. Ma berates us: "Don't you ever do that again! Look at the state of your father!"

The state of our father.

At the end of my first year away at university, Ma phones, desperate to have a break from her high-as-a-kite husband. By now, they have downsized and live in their new flat on George Street, close to London's West End. While Ma goes for a week to a clinic in the country to lose weight and find peace and quiet, Dad and I are left to our own devices.

Without her there, we're a pair of wild horses uncorralled. Why temper him, keep him on the right side of the line? A fine line.

He doesn't want me to slave for him, so we go out to eat, walking through London; dusty in sunlight. He doesn't slow down for red lights or traffic, slicing corners at sharp angles as we race across Gt. Cumberland Place, pigeons rising, a trail of crumbs clotting the gravel, the two of us talking.

"Talk!" Ma's eyes blaze. "Your father doesn't talk. He screams!"

He says it's the noise of machines in the factory he has to shout over. Excited, spit sprays out his mouth, hangs to his bottom lip. He pulls out his handkerchief, wipes, and tucks it back into grey flannel trousers; crease breaking as he zips through eddies of traffic choking Speaker's Corner. Still talking. Under huge elms, two soapbox men harangue the crowd. "Freedom of speech!" Dad scorns. "No such thing!" Steers me clear into the park, the constant burr of engines shrinks into a surrounding hum, oxygen exhaled by trees standing guard on the edges of the park makes us light-headed, black painted letters on cream white board blare out—"These gates will be closed at sundown."

Where will the homeless bed down? Hyde Park, property of the Queen, how royal to let commoners stroll in its green shade, not too common, not beyond the pale, stakes fixing the territory, marking you out or in.

Ma returns refreshed, but although I've cleaned the flat and put everything back in its proper place, she's furious, "A fat lot of help you've been! Look what a state your father's in!"

Once, on a visit to my parents, while I was living in West London and working in North London, after Dad and I'd been for a walk through the park, I get on my bike to head out into the traffic flowing round Hyde Park Corner. He stops me with his hand on my shoulder: "Wait Ingrid, let me walk away first. I don't know which is worse, seeing you on your bike in all that traffic or thinking about it."

Much later, I come to know the body's chemistry responds almost as strongly to imagined actions as it does to actual ones.

I've been living in Belgium for over a year with my Flemish partner. I'm pregnant and visiting London with a group of women studying English with me. Tim has already been living on the west coast of Canada for several years, working as Ma says as "a Jack of all trades!" None of these facts are easy for Ma to digest. She's been haranguing me by letter and phone about having an illegitimate child. Even Dad's perplexed. He has always felt his wife a radical when it comes to sex.

Recently he's been put on lithium, a combination of minerals to address what is now referred to openly as bipolar disorder.

After dinner in an Italian restaurant in their neighbourhood, he takes me aside and says, "Go easy on your mother. She's not been having an easy time with me. The new medication stops me from becoming depressed."

His warm brown eyes look sad. "Trouble is—it makes everything grey."

Years later, after both our parents are dead and our own children have grown up, moved away to different cities, found partners, and had offspring, I will begin to sift through family history. Washed of shame, I glimpse recognizable traits running through my being.

Trouble is when Tim and I can't look each other in the eye, but mostly we agree—it takes the time it takes.

54.

Family Secrets

Susan Scruton

"Do we have any family secrets that I don't know yet?" I ask my eighty-year-old mother. She lives with her four dogs in a fishing village in Ecuador. I live thousands of miles north, in the suburbs of Canada. We're talking via Facebook while the pandemic swirls around us both.

"Family secrets?" she replies. "No, just my grandmother's illegitimate child, my mom's backstreet abortion, and my illegal but much safer abortions."

I figured if anybody would have been aborted, it would have been Debbie, since my mother was only sixteen when she got pregnant with her. And if Debbie had been aborted, my parents wouldn't have been together long enough to conceive me.

My parents didn't actually have any say in how that first pregnancy ended. There were only two options on the table: Get married and keep the baby or give it up for adoption. Their fathers made the decision, and they went along with it.

It was a predictably short and shitty shotgun marriage. Debbie and I were Irish twins with less than a year between us. We were two squalling babies in cloth diapers, with two teenaged parents steeped in poverty and resentment. They split up while they were still teenagers, and we were still babies.

Between my mother's first and second marriages, she had a secret sex life. This was back when sex outside of marriage was considered immoral. Divorcees were already on thin moral ice by virtue of their lack of virtue. She says she didn't have the luxury of choosing her lovers because she was poor and chained to her responsibilities. She took what she could get, which was usually older married men.

She kept her relationships hidden from us, and sometimes she kept us hidden from them.

My mother had her abortions when she was twenty-one, twenty-two, and twenty-four years old. Two of them were conceived with Meurig, a high school principal eighteen years older than her. The third one was with her boss, also a school principal, who was also much older and married with three children.

On their first date, Meurig got my mother drunk and raped her while she was passed out. Back then, it wasn't considered rape because they were on a date, and he hadn't violently overcome her resistance. He'd just denied her any choice in whether to have sex with him or not. She blamed herself for drinking too much and went out with him for a year or so. "Meurig was a jerk," she said. "But at least he paid for the abortions."

Another time, at her friend's house party, he demanded anal sex on the bathroom floor. Coerced, she complied.

"He was terrible in bed," my mother said. "He didn't make love. He fucked."

Meurig drove a white Impala, and he talked of taking it back to Wales to show everybody back home how well he'd done for himself. He let her spend her breaks in his white Impala. He didn't even get angry when she took it for a spin, unlicensed and without permission, and scraped its side. That's how much he liked young girls.

I google him. A few years after my mother's abortions, he married an even younger pregnant woman. They had two children: a son who lives in my town and a daughter who is a writer and lives in the UK. I read her books; I love her poetry. There's a poem about Meurig in the war, shipwrecked, drifting in a lifeboat, singing to drown out the cries of misery all around him.

On her Facebook page, there's an old picture of her parents in a restaurant in Antigua. I send it to my mother. She recognizes Meurig's jacket.

I can only describe Meurig as nondescript. He could be any man in his forties in the 1960s. But Lana—Lana is lovely. She looks a lot like my mother at that age. She looks too young to have a nondescript old husband.

I feel a vague familial connection to Meurig's son and daughter. Those aborted babies would have been our shared half-siblings. I reach out to his daughter and tell her I'm doing research on family secrets and her father's name came up. She's open and warm, and she asks about my research.

I don't want to just blurt out that her father raped my mother.

"Are you sure you want to know?" I reply. "It's kind of sordid."

I know she'll say yes. She's a writer and writers always say yes. She assures me that she and her brother have no illusions about their father. They've long suspected he had secrets. He's dead now—suicide—and he and Lana split up in the seventies, so nobody will be hurt by his secrets.

So I tell her about the rape and the abortions. I leave out the coercive anal sex on the bathroom floor because, weirdly, it feels like something you shouldn't discuss in polite company. She and her brother are both appalled but not surprised that their father raped my mother.

We correspond for a while. In the ensuing weeks, Meurig's son takes a DNA test and discovers his father appears to have left a trail of young pregnant women in his wake.

I feel like I've opened up another family's can of worms. I can just walk away, but can they?

I wonder how I will remember Meurig, this man I never knew, this man who might've been my stepfather if not for those illegal abortions. Will he be the man who raped my mother and paid for the abortions or the man who sang in a lifeboat to drown out the cries of misery all around him? Or maybe it's all the same thing. One night I dream of a singing man raping a crying woman in a lifeboat.

Meurig's son tells me my family dodged a bullet. "Meurig was a monster," he says.

I tell him we might have dodged that particular bullet, but we didn't get off scot-free. My mother went on to marry a different monster.

We never talk about that, my mother and I. It's easier to talk about the near misses and the close calls—the family secrets that haven't been marinating for decades in our own shame.

55.

Eulogy

Jim Nason

My hands are small.

My feet are dainty strong; one foot
smaller than the other.

My eyes are my strongest feature,

it has always been this way.
My ears have lobs attached to the flesh of my voice.

My belly has been heart.

My belly has been soul.
My gut is where words come from.

My teeth are good.

Each cavity, filling,
every crown and root canal a story.

Gluteus maximus hold up my spine.

My back has its share of secrets.

My ass has been the object of desire.
My ass is not a sex organ.
My ass is a sex organ.

My ass is gluteus maximus.

I have misplaced my lighter, the long red one

I bought at the Dollar Store.

I have searched the drawers and under the mattress.
I've fingered the banana peels and coffee grinds

of the under-the-sink trash.

I have lifted the grey folds of my memory.
My fingers have been in my nose and ears.

My hands are small.
I have searched the ripples and floorboards.
My mother swallowed four handfuls of sleeping pills—

that didn't work so well. She drank until her skin turned yellow

then orange just before she died. My mother's belly
carried seven children. She and I have the same eyes

and smile. It has always been this way.

My mother wore a Dollar Store diamond
that glistened with warm suds

Sunlight, Tide, and *Dawn.*

My mother's voice was a canyon
of laughter and echoes.

My mother cried every night.

She and I had the same desire to die.
I survive her.
My smile consists of sadness and fragmented joy.

The red lighter rolled under the dresser.
The candles remain silent.

My nose smells burning toast.
My nose is not my best feature.

My hands are small.
My body is more than the sum of its parts.

My mother hid under my bed at night.

She is reaching out in death—wiser,
still hurting, educated now

in the art of speaking with eyes

in the dark. My body came of hers.
My body is made of earth.

She is salt. My mother was the salt of the earth.

56.

Shame

Barbara Barry

She began her life in 1917 during the First World War and the Spanish Flu epidemic and survived. She had an idyllic childhood growing up on the shore of the St. Lawrence River in the small village of Dorval outside Montreal. The youngest in a family of four boys, she helped her mother with the numerous household chores, enjoyed the company of her brothers and friends, and excelled at school.

I don't know when or how the word "secret" entered her vocabulary, but the clandestine whispering must have been troubling. What would have gone through her mind overhearing these words: "Are you going to tell her?" Why didn't she ask or demand, "Tell me what?" When did she first see her baptismal certificate that stated she was adopted only by her father—not her mother—five months after she was born, indicating a private adoption? I will never understand her reluctance to know her story, but this was Quebec in the early twentieth century. Heavily influenced by the Catholic Church, words like "adoption," "illegitimacy," and "unwed mother" carried a devastating stigma. She might have feared a scandal. Best to ignore this secret.

Once aware of a secret, how did she live with this festering sore that she couldn't heal? Her life became one of atonement and low self-esteem, constantly attempting to counteract the facts of her birth. She lived an exemplary life to prove she was a good and deserving person. And she did. She was an avid church attendee and volunteer. She quit school before finishing her senior year to help her family financially. Her teachers were shocked and sent a letter home stating she had the ability to progress so much further. Later, she told my father he shouldn't marry her because he didn't know where she came from or who she really was. As a rather carefree and uncomplicated man, he told her he didn't care about the past. My father was a close friend of her brothers, and I always wondered whether he knew the secret.

She was a faithful and devoted wife. She became a busy, fifties, stay-at-home mother. There were many rules. She was a stern disciplinarian and anxious and insecure. She would always worry about what people thought—a philosophy my sister and I absorbed as well. To this day, we joke fondly about her pursed lips, frown, and head shake whenever we were in adult company and not behaving perfectly. With her pressure and interest, we excelled at our schoolwork, as there did not appear to be another option. Due to her love, pride and financial acumen, my sister and I graduated from university, a first on her side of the family.

There was no mention of the secret while we were growing up until the night my grandmother died, when my mother sat on my bed and told me that the woman I called Granny was not her biological mother. I did know this, as at some point I had seen my mother's baptismal certificate. However, being an immature and a self-absorbed teenager my response was not memorable. Now, I regret not opening a dialogue and encouraging her to find the answer to who her birth mother was.

Once my own children were born, I thought it important to know my family history. I tried to get information from aunts and uncles but with no results. They assured me there were no other records. My older cousins believed her adoptive father was in fact her biological father because she looked like him and the family. They thought or had heard her real mother was a relative. Busy with my own family and concerns, I decided to live with that.

My mother died at the age of ninety-three from the debilitating effects of dementia. As the disease progressed, she seemed to be free of worries, happier, and in her mind was back on the lakeshore in Dorval with no secrets to concern her. But I was with her when she died, holding her hand, expecting a peaceful death like those described in obituaries but hers was agonizing. She gasped for breath for hours, focused on my eyes as if saying she was not ready to go until she knew the secret.

Ever since, I have been determined to find the answer. My quest so far has not been fruitful, and I despair of never finding the answer. The Quebec government told me there is little chance official papers from that long ago still exist and that the only person who could have access to the information is the adoptee.

Grasping for information, I joined ancestry.ca and My Heritage, took a DNA test, and anxiously awaited the results. I am overwhelmingly of English and Scottish ancestry, which was not a surprise. To give me hope, my first two matches were a first cousin and a second cousin on my father's side of the family, whom I did know. However, my next two matches, as second cousins, were names I had never heard before. After some communication with them, neither had been able to find family information going back to 1917.

So I continue to study family trees, hoping to find clues to the secret that kept my mother from living a full and carefree life without the constant fear that her past was tainted and people might find out.

Yes, I am thankful that my mother did not grow up in a Quebec orphanage, and I am relieved that she was treated as family by her parents and siblings. Yes, I am amazed that the secret never came to light in what was, at that time, a small village. I am angry that the secret was not shared with us, her family. And I am sad. Sad for my mother's suffering and shame, sad she might have had half siblings she never knew. I am also frightened because she died from complications of dementia and that might be my future. Above all, I despair because the secret may be one full of love and caring and unselfishness. I may never know.

Who was she?

Who am I?

57.

Knothole

Laurel Sproule

When I was starting grade six, Libby, my cousin, told me I was a "goodie goodie" because I always did what my parents asked. At the time, my hair was the longest it'd ever been. My mother recommended a cut with her stylist. I agreed. Returning to my bedroom, I clutched my braid tied with ribbon. I cried, scrutinizing my new look in the mirror. Top of my class for six years, I longed instead for beauty and popularity, but the haircut—not to mention my oily skin, which was inclined to blemishes, and my shyness—made the fulfillment of my desires doubtful.

I idolized Cousin Libby from Etobicoke. She had pouty lips, long black hair, mysterious green eyes, and was surrounded by boys desperate to win her approval. She spoke easily to them. Tall and handsome young guys wrapped an arm around her shoulder, laughed, and whispered sassy questions. Then, I thought boys' interest in Libby was triggered by charm, which I lacked but desired.

Libby was four years older than I when she and her dad, Uncle Bud, visited us in Pierrefonds, Quebec. My parents let us sleep together in our holiday trailer parked on our driveway. There she read me stories she'd written about her life with boys, mostly Teddy, father to her child I didn't know about then and she didn't write about.

Falling asleep, Libby traced circles on my back with her finger, an intimacy that cemented my admiration.

As I slipped into sleep, she whispered into my ear, "I'm called Liz, now."

My family moved from Quebec to England when I was turning thirteen and in grade six. Dad's promotion meant he'd work at London Heathrow Airport. It also meant uprooting me when I'd started understanding who I was, who I might become.

I attended St. Mary's Girls' School in Gerrard's Cross, Buckinghamshire, where my accent, indistinguishable from American inflection, prompted students' cruel remarks. A few dubbed me "Yank." Every morning, I travelled by train to Gerrard's Cross, walked through the quaint town, and along a rural road thick with hedges concealing the residences beyond.

St. Mary's classes were held in a converted estate. I wandered the hallways without speaking to classmates, nor they to me. A few times, I was summoned to the headmistress's office, once for being spotted in town not wearing my school beret. Students wore navy-blue woolen skirts, knee-high socks, blazer, white shirt, and blue tie. Walking through Gerrard's Cross, I wore a beret most of the year, with a straw boater in summer.

I was also called to the headmistress's office because I'd sported makeup at school. She insisted I wash my face straightaway and remove my rings. Jewelry was a forbidden personal expression. I noticed she wore bright lipstick and rings, which indented her stubby, fat fingers.

At home, after finishing homework, I'd write to Libby. I didn't want to tell my parents what had happened at school. Expecting Libby's letter, I hurried from the train station, skipped the tobacconists and my customary purchase of a Cadbury's Flake Bar, and ran home to check the mail. Finding a letter from Libby, an airmail envelope jammed with handwritten pages, my loneliness lessened, briefly.

I replied instantly, posting my letter next day after school. My parents knew I corresponded with her. They said nothing.

One letter surprised me. Libby announced her plan to visit me in England, asking "Could Uncle Scott pick me up at the airport?"

We'd never discussed her visiting. My parents wouldn't be pleased. Unwillingly, hands behind my back, I approached Dad: "Libby's coming to visit. Could you pick her up at your airport?"

His silence confirmed distrust, doubt.

Dad waited in our Ford Cortina at Heathrow as I fetched Libby.

Together in her room, a spare bedroom in our rented house, she disclosed news she hadn't written. Teddy had forced her to burn all her writing. She described lighting each page in the kitchen sink and watching them burn.

"Why did he want your pages destroyed?" I asked. "Why did you do it?"

"We had a baby girl together," Libby said, amazingly calm, speaking in childish register. "She's been adopted by a nice family. Teddy doesn't want his parents reading what I wrote about us."

Once in Toronto, Libby's dad drove by Teddy's parents' house, an intimidating stone mansion in north Toronto. We stopped. Looked. Drove on.

Possibly my parents knew about Libby's baby. Did they actually believe she'd corrupt me into an unwanted pregnancy? The thought amused me. I was petrified of boys.

Weekends, we wandered footpaths, chatting. Her favourite route funnelled wide among ancient oaks, yew, plane, and chestnut trees she'd discovered when I was at school. There she met Asher, a blonde, chubby American who didn't go to school. His father, an engineer, worked in London.

We met Asher by a large oak. Comfortable together, their conversations excluded me. She spoke in her little girl voice, pouted, and captivated Asher's attention. I rarely spoke but believed somehow Asher was my friend. They communicated through a knothole in the oak, where they left each other intricately folded notes and sometimes chocolate.

Mid-June, Libby left.

Tension at supper lessened.

I still wished to see her tall, lean body, silky dark hair, and eyelashes thickened by mascara. I missed our talks. I questioned why she pouted and spoke in a childlike voice. Asher sometimes ignored her when she acted that way. But he still left her notes and trinkets in the knothole. Why? My enchantment with Libby diminished. She'd morphed into Liz; someone I didn't recognize.

I walked footpaths alone imagining I'd bump into Asher, uncertain what I'd say if I did, or maybe he'd already gone stateside.

June 21st, summer solstice: I strolled from the station in warmth and light, carrying my satchel. In it were my black, prickly wool bloomers, knee socks, and a few t-shirts. The remaining weeks of school, we'd play Rounders in summer frocks.

Deceived by daylight and engrossed in contemplation, I stopped at Beaconsfield library, grabbed Dickens, and read awhile. Realizing it was likely very late, I returned *Great Expectations* and hurried outside, choosing Liz's faster, narrow footpath; holly leaves scratched my arms. Reaching the forest, I spotted the knothole. It was empty. How could I believe Asher might leave me anything?

Almost at forest's end, a hand whacked my mouth shut, someone tugged my hair, pulling my head backwards.

"Don't scream," a muffled, British accented voice commanded; the stocking over his face squished his nose creating a grotesque deviant, who dragged me into shrubberies. I fought. One handed, he restrained me at arm's length. I fought.

"Stand still! Will ya?" He clenched my arm.

In cold fright, I clearly predicted: I'm going to die.

He unzipped his pants, pulled out his penis, and masturbated. "Watch!" he ordered.

Moments interminable, I stared at him. Finally, a white spurt, dripping on grounded branches. Stock-still, what's next? I winced at possibilities.

His grip tightened as he zipped, "Don't tell anyone!" his voice rasped.

I shuddered, nodding my head compliantly.

He released my arm, turned, vanished into trees.

I vaulted home.

At supper, my parents looked up from plates of spaghetti.

"I've been attacked," I bellowed.

They stared at me, speechless.

"He wore a stocking over his face," I said.

My father stood tall. "I'll kill the bastard." He ran towards the front door.

I chased and grabbed his arm. "Dad don't. You won't find him. He's gone."

Mom touched his arm. "Scott, we'll call the police," she whispered.

I sat on my bed in my room when my door opened. My mother led a blonde, uniformed woman inside. The constable perched on the edge of my bed. After tousling papers, with a pen in hand, she blurted, "Why were you so late in coming home from school?" I described solstice light, bringing home my games uniform, and the library.

"Is that how you were dressed?"

I looked down at my jeans and t-shirt. "I changed from my uniform."

"Why stop at the library?"

I stared at her. Her questions frustrated me; blame oozed from everything she said.

"Why walk alone in a forested enclosure?"

I shrugged.

"Is that your usual path?"

"No, I usually take walkways, not footpaths."

"Why change?"

Recalling the empty knothole, nothing I said could explain why I went that way. "I was late," I offered.

"I see," she sighed, wrote something. "Can you describe your attacker?"

I shook my head. "Not really. He wore a stocking over his face." I paused. She jotted something. "He was slightly taller than me."

There, in my space, a woman who could understand my nightmare, did her job well. Nothing I said swayed her suppositions.

"I'll write my report, then." She stood, short, rotund. "We'll let you know if we find him, but you haven't given me much to go on."

I avoided footpaths and open spaces, expecting someone hiding in wait. I hid in my bedroom and did my homework. I finished O (ordinary) level examinations at St. Mary's. Unlike many girls whose schooling ended there, I'd attend sixth form and did A (advanced) levels, which were a prerequisite for university.

A levels required changing schools.

Licensed Victualler's School (LVS), further from home than St. Mary's, required a bus to Old Beaconsfield and a transfer to a double decker to Slough Train Station.

The school grounds were enclosed by high fencing.

Students' parents were engineers, diplomats, and entrepreneurs working away from Britain. Many students, like me, came from somewhere else.

I fit. No more teasing.

For my A levels, I chose two subjects to study, enrolling in English and history, which fulfilled university entrance requirements.

After long bus rides home, I'd walk straight to my room to do homework. Dad, who was away in Europe setting up aircraft maintenance bases, had been my buffer from my mother.

"Why do you question everything?" she yelled. "Just do what I ask," Her voice shrill, I didn't try to exasperate her. She obsessed over housework. I needed her to consider me first, just once.

Most LVS students boarded. At the end of first year sixth form, I asked Dad if I could board. Life at school after class interested me; my fights with my mother had also escalated and the bus rides were time consuming.

He agreed without persuasion.

I moved into the girls' dorm. Wendy, a blonde, attractive girl, blasted "Sweet Baby James" by James Taylor and "Brand New Key" by Melanie. I liked James Taylor and didn't dislike Melanie. But I didn't like how Wendy placed her desires over those of other girls, repeating the same songs, turning up the volume, loud.

I vacated my cubicle to study in stairwells. Sitting on stone stairs was better than being home.

Sixth formers were afforded a lounge with armchairs and a billiards table. When gathered there, I yearned for Georgie, an Italian in my English classes, to acknowledge me.

Instead, I visited with Riaz, who adored me throughout sixth form, while Georgie appeared not to care I existed.

Time with Riaz and his friend Moktar showed me how to talk to boys.

On weekends, students' time was structured so that study time finished before lunch. A group of sixth form boys decided to visit the woodwork shop before lunch. With no interest in woodworking, I tagged along, as I'd wanted to see the shop.

The teacher, students called "Whiskers"—who was short with a thick, black beard—was considered a friend by my classmates. Dinner Bell didn't sound in woodworking. No one mentioned that. After wandering aimlessly in the shop, I realized abruptly that my classmates had left me alone with Whiskers.

I rushed to the door. Whiskers blocked my exit, his hands resting on both sides of a workbench. As he was shorter than me, I could stare into his eyes and smirk at his own grin.

"I need to go to dinner." I insisted.

He stood motionless.

KNOTHOLE

At first, I couldn't understand the motivation for his obstruction but soon had no doubt when he gripped my wrist.

"Let me go!"

He grunted.

"Let me pass!" I surveyed the shop. Definitely alone.

"You don't want to leave." He smirked.

"You're a teacher!" I said, holding his eyes in mine.

His leer dissolved. He released my wrist but still blocked my exit, thrusting his hips as I passed. His erection rubbed against my thigh.

But I escaped. Who should I tell? I envisioned the knothole.

I considered Liz and her boyfriend Teddy, my solstice attacker, who still roamed free, the doubting female constable, Whiskers, the teacher, whose lust destroyed trust, my father, who'd chosen a getaway, and my begrudging, compulsive mother.

I had endured them all.

58.

Bottle Dump

Yaana Dancer

By the time we left the land in Lynn Valley, I was fourteen, and I couldn't wait to get away from the rainforest. It hid things. Cedar stumps ten foot high, rotting slower than time. Racoon skeletons. Squirrel carcasses. The bottle dump.

Brown bottles. Mickeys or twenty-sixers. Canadian Rye Whisky. Enough to fill a bowl-like depression that might once have held roots of a gigantic Douglas fir. Did Mum ever see the bottle dump? She was busy hanging sheets, shoving stews and casseroles and bread in the oven, chopping kindling, and arranging flowers at Livingston Florist.

Dad met Mum when her brothers brought him home from a rugby game, like a trophy. She was smitten with his tweed and singing, piano playing, and dancing. Especially the dancing. And the English accent.

He showed her a weedy lot with a modest shingled house he'd purchase if she'd marry him. They worked flat-out through the 1930s, raising garden beds and chickens and goats and two children. They found a girl to help in return for room and board. That lasted 'til Mum caught Dad mucking about with her and sent her on her way. He was livid, but he reset, sold the place, and moved them to a house he'd finish for a friend.

"All well and good" says Mum. "I was the one managing without running water or electricity, hauling milk bottles up the hill. Seeing your sister off to school on a path down the cliff. Slipped on ice, poor kiddy, cracked a rib."

Mum, in her late eighties, pours tea at her walnut drop leaf table. She describes how Dad bought a small lot on McGuire Avenue, on the flats, where he built their own cottage, but he framed it and moved them in before it was even insulated.

"He ran me ragged, that man," says Mum. "Always wangling this and that. Even in the dirty thirties, he traded eggs or bedding plants for beer or whiskey."

In those days, a baby coming long after the others was often called "an afterthought" or "the little accident." Nine years after my brother, I entered the world, and childbed fever entered Mum. Bloody near carried her off. She shivered and sweated and raved while a mother who'd lost her baby nursed me. Months later, on her fortieth birthday, Mum still had the darkness of death smudging her eyes.

Dad had another reset in mind. In 1946, my sister was twelve, my brother eleven, and I was two when we embarked for England by train and ship, an unthinkable trip during the previous fifteen years, what with the Depression and the War. He sold the fine cottage to fund the grand return to his parents.

Surely he'd seen headlines, heard what a beating the old country took? He added his family to a household already grim with rationing.

Had he forgotten how stern was his father's brow, how steely his eyes? How he'd not have a drop of alcohol in his house? Two years on, Dad was fed up with the old man or the other way round.

We scarcely saw him on the return trip. Mum had her hands full with four-year-old me. My sister and brother roamed ship and the train, catching glimpses of Dad lifting a glass in this bar, that lounge, slipping down a passage, round a corner.

We moved in with Mum's parents, stayed ten years in Lynn Valley, while more and more brown bottles accumulated in the depression in the forest, while Dad cursed and raged until my sister fled and my brother after her, until my grandparents sold the land from under him. Until Mum and I were the last ones standing with targets on our backs. "Nobody wanted you born," he'd tell me.

Mum shuffled people in and out of hospital beds, kept a roof over us, and food in the fridge. By then, I recognized the slurs he spewed fitted him better than us. But slinging them back stung his fury.

Mum and I were the walking dead. Numb. The world was out there, a mile away, beyond brick walls we'd raised. Numbness kept Mum shuffling through shifts, coming home to cook and clean. Numbness kept me sleepwalking to school, nodding off with chin propped on a fist, flunking finals. Deciding I was stupid.

I sip tea with Mum in her studio apartment that looks out on Burrard Inlet. I'm pushing fifty, enrolled in art school. Dad's been dead and buried two decades. Mum's face is still severe. I catch a hint of Pears soap. Nobody wanted me born. I still carry that story.

"Your dad didn't like rubbers," she says, her lips thin as a pencil line. "After your brother, there were times I'd tell your dad I was expecting, and he'd peel off a couple of bills, hand them over, tell me to deal with it. There was a woman in lower Capilano who'd help. I lost a lot of blood."

Her hooked nose tips downwards. Her eyes, too. Mentions of procreation usually spark a frown. Bad taste.

"When you came along, I decided I wouldn't say a word," she says. "I was sick and tired of him telling me what to do. He always got what he wanted. I wanted something. All day, every day, I wore a pinny, and he didn't notice until it was too late. He was furious. Said he'd be an old man by the time you grew up and left home."

She hid me? Behind her apron? She strung me out and into life? She wanted me.

59.

Went West

Cynthia Woodman Kerkham

I came home from high school that day, ready for a glass of milk and a plate of French Crème cookies. My mother, then in her mid-forties, was sitting in the kitchen nook nursing a cup of tea. I slid in beside her on the U-shaped bench, and she told me what she'd discovered. I wasn't shocked. Mostly I was curious at how angry she was on learning this lie.

But first, a bit of history.

My mother grew up in Kerrisdale, Vancouver, in the poorest family on the block. Her parents both came from rural Nova Scotia, and a photograph of my grandfather's farmhouse, which my aunt framed and gave to each family member for Christmas in 1991, memorializes the family home atop our pianos and mantlepieces. That year, the farm was photographed for the back of the Maritime Tel & Tel telephone book—a cream clapboard farmhouse bathed in sunset light, with a narrow, red chimney. My great-uncle lived there when the photograph was taken. The two-hundred-year-old home nestles amongst flaming maples, the Stewiacke River, a cobalt blue band ribboning like a life story through its front yard.

That next summer, my husband, our two children, and I piled into a rusty red Ford truck with a camper on the bed and drove across the country. We visited my Great-Uncle Rob, and each evening of our stay, we adults would sip a finger of Schenley Golden Wedding Whiskey from cut-glass tumblers. Our chairs snugged up against the warm wood siding, we'd watch the sun dip in the west. He spoke little, my great uncle, and answered my questions about family monosyllabically.

"Is this where Grandpa Harry slept?" I'd asked when we first arrived and climbed the narrow stairs on a house tour.

"Yup."

In the snapshot I have from this visit, Uncle Rob and I look alike—both long drinks of water with our slim, tanned faces in thin-lipped smiles.

When Grandpa Harry left Nova Scotia, Uncle Rob, his younger brother, inherited the farm, which stretched down to the river and off into acres of hay fields and sellable timber. Down the road lived my grandmother's family in a gracious old home on a large parcel of fertile land. Many of my mother's cousins were still there, and they dropped by Uncle Rob's kitchen through the week of our stay, inviting us into their homes for meals. Cousin Keith took us to the well-tended family graveyard, stretching back nine generations. He wowed our children with his water-divining techniques and took us on long rambles. His war bride, Jessie, offered home-baked scones and bent patiently with me over fat family albums.

"This must be my grandmother, Jennie," I said one day, recognizing a portrait my mother had and pointing to an oval-faced woman with dark hair pulled smoothly back to cover her ears, her eyes lit by a soft smile. Not a great beauty, her nose a little large for her face, but sweet-looking as she gazes from the sepia headshot. Her flawless skin. Her shoulders rounded under a pale V-necked blouse. Her torso disappearing into an ivory ground. This grandmother I'd only ever seen in black and white. What colour were her eyes? I forgot to ask.

"Eggaaah, aye, tha'd be her," Jessie replied in her thick, Scottish accent, "and haire she is on a picnic."

On those warm afternoons in that comfortable living room, we never discussed why my branch of the family went west.

You might have guessed what the secret is, but I'm not going to tell you yet.

My mother, then, was born in Vancouver, the first of the two girls that her parents, Harry and Jennie, would have, her sister, Claire, coming two years later. My grandfather, separated from farming, the only work he knew, bounced from labouring job to labouring job. My mother told of her gentle, former-school-teacher mother, who polished the wood floors of their rented home and let the girls scoot their bums in old bloomers across the boards to give an extra shine. They grew a big garden, and the girls learned to work hard. They would need these skills because Jennie died when my mother was eighteen. What she died of is not clear. The story is that she went in for an operation and never came back from the hospital. A neighbour lady went in at the same time for the same operation and came home. Harry was angry. He blamed the doctor, yet he walked to the doctor's office and paid the fee just the same.

My mother, Phyllis, and her sister, Claire, took over the running of their home, both trying to live up to their father's standards of diligence and make up for the loss of undemanding Jennie, who'd always wanted a china dinner set, the kind you'd get as a wedding gift, but who'd never gotten one, as Harry could never afford one while she lived. Years after her death, Harry walked into the family home and presented a box to his daughters—a full set of fine china, white with gold rims.

Grandpa Harry lived with us for six months in Toronto, where my parents had moved. He was a slim, taciturn man, like his brother, and although my sister and I tried, we learned he was not a cuddler. In all the photographs, he is unsmiling. We also visited him when he was back in Vancouver, renting a large home with dark wood panelling, along with a widower friend, tending a garden of vegetables and fruits that surrounded the house. I remember, as a child, picking the long loganberries with him, popping their firmness into my mouth—a deep, old sweetness and slightly tart.

When we returned from seven years overseas back to Canada, the secret burst to the surface, accidentally untethered from the weights holding it down all those years. Grandpa Harry had died by then, so my mother and her sister were orphans. Before a vacation to Mexico, my mother had to reapply for a renewed passport. And—surprise—it came back with a different birthdate. The records were better in the early seventies than they were in the early sixties when we'd left the country, and she'd had to show a driver's licence the second time. At first, my mother thought they'd got it wrong. But no. She'd been born four months earlier than her parents had always told her. September 17, 1924, not the January 17, 1925, that she'd believed and had on all her other records. Not two years older than her sister but three. Not two years younger than her husband but one. Not a Capricorn, then, but a Virgo.

I tucked into the kitchen nook beside my mother that late afternoon and gazed at the steam rising from her cup, the secret drifting in the air between us.

"Both my parents are dead," she said, her voice shaking, "and they lied to me."

Her pale blue eyes watered behind her cats-eye glasses. She bent her head, and her fine, brown hair with frosted tips sparked in the late afternoon sun.

She couldn't challenge them; she couldn't forgive them. The pain my mother felt on discovering the secret of her birth—the sense of betrayal, of, perhaps, being unwanted—was hers to bear alone. My grandmother Jennie's secret allowed Jennie a freedom, allowed her to live the moral life in her daughters' eyes, and the perfection she and Harry preached to them. The perfection that they had tried to live up to. With that passport, my mother was unmoored, betrayed, and stranded. As the anger ebbed, she crumpled, as if her legs had been kicked out from beneath her. The two people who were the centre of her life colluded in a lie, calling into question her every truth. Could she ever trust her ability to know when she was being lied to? What else had they lied about? She would never know.

Meanwhile, it was the 1970s. Sex, thanks to the pill, had taken on a radically different tone. We tiptoed around our mother for a while, letting her grieve. Then we tried to make light of her double birth, giving her two birthday cards for a few years, saying she deserved to be celebrated twice. Time did what time does, though, and we all settled back into habit, into celebrating the January birth only. Somehow, we couldn't quite accept the true date. The truth, in fact, felt false. Was it habit? Or was it because it still caused my mother pain that caused us to drop September? The unspoken message was she'd rather forget it.

Only now does the magnitude of the secret strike me: It radically altered our family's map. My grandfather's life was severed from his calling and from his expected place of inheritance. Both Harry and Jennie were pitched into a life of financial struggle and banishment from family and friends. Jennie never got her wedding china because, perhaps, she never got her formal wedding and then could never afford such treasures. They never went back, even to visit. I knew of the lie when we went to Nova Scotia. Everyone must have known. But no one mentioned it. Without the secret, my father, born and raised in Vancouver, would not have met my mother; I would not have existed in this form, and on and on the conditionals go. I've come to love this secret and the changes it wrought. Their lie turned out to be my life.

I'm also struck by how a secret that was so cataclysmic for my grandparents has, for many, lost much of its punch in a mere two generations. The power of social convention gives a secret its strength or dissipates it: I, like my grandmother, conceived out of wedlock, but intentionally. I didn't see the point of marriage unless we were successful at the baby-making part; otherwise, why not just live together? Such were the hippie values that infused my youth. Even so, when, at age twenty-five, I announced my unwed pregnancy to my parents, their faces fell. Seventies values were not theirs. I'd made a special trip from an island to their Vancouver living room to announce what I thought was happy news. Silence. Until my sister, who'd driven from Ladner at my request jumped off the couch and shouted her congratulations, my stunned parents stumbling in her wake. They'd been such liberal parents, and I'd been gallivanting around the world since I was seventeen, so I was surprised at their reactions. But not surprised at how they generously rallied. My mother took me to a tailor in Gastown to have a peach-coloured wedding dress made, empire line, to allow for my swelling belly. And my father rose at 5:00 a.m. with my new husband on the day of our celebration at a family cabin to set the whole pig roasting over the pit they'd dug the day before. According to one friend at the party, though, my father slipped in sotto voce to a few guests that he'd "wished we'd done this in the right order." Nonetheless, and despite my pregnancy flying in the face of all they'd been taught, its echo of the secret of my mother's birth, my parents accepted and then offered only love to our family: There was no tearing apart, no running across the continent, no loss of roots. We were married in September, by the way, and our daughter was born in January.

Both my mother and her sister have died, so I feel I can tell what was for them a shameful family secret. Despite our trying to make light of it, my sister and I saw that my mother's hidden birth was always a tender topic for her. She never told her morally strict and quick-to-judge sister, who'd had no children and, perhaps for this reason, had not been nudged into adapting with the times. My mother, Phyllis, had gotten into the habit of taking care of her younger sister since their mother's death, and, no doubt, she did not wish to tarnish the golden image of Daddy and Mummy her sister held to the end. I wonder what the grandparents gave as their reason for moving west to their two curious daughters—something sensible like looking for work opportunities, I suppose, although that story has never come down to me.

Time has cleansed the secret of my mother's birth. My grandparents went to their graves thinking it would never surface. Every secret holds a lie, and every lie is a theft of power for good or ill. It might be power over how money is spent or time or personal freedom; it might be the power to tell one's own version of a story. Often, the secret is painful for the one from whom the truth is kept. Forgiveness may come in accepting our shared flaws and in understanding the circumstances beneath the secret. My mother had to carry the burden of its surfacing, but she was also able to witness its sea change. She recovered and lived according to her bedrock value of kindness, another thing she learned from her parents.

The night my grandmother Jennie Levetta died, she visited her eighteen-year-old daughter, my mother Phyllis, lying stricken in the dark. She shimmered at the foot of the bed and rested her hand on her daughter's feet beneath the blanket. Then she disappeared. Decades later, her family secret, too, arrived from the dark, slowly lost its earthly weight and dissolved into the light.

60.

Kingdom Hall

Leesa Hanna

The past couple of Fridays, Lana and I stopped by Gary's house after school to see what was happening for the weekend. Gary hung out at Cleary's Store with the rest of the high school kids; he was a stoner, kinda goofy, but friendly. His house was across the street from the store at the well-known five-corners stop in Brownville.

Centred between the local high school and elementary school, Mr. Cleary's store got a lot of afterschool business. He would sell us cigarettes without questions about our age or intentions. He was far more interested in his army of rusty lawnmowers that circled the shop's perimeter. He'd be down on his knees tinkering away, covered in today's and yesterday's oily machine soot, as we entered the store. A brass bell attached to the door's hinge rang, and he stood with a sigh, tucked his metal-wrench into his back pocket, and followed us into the store.

Standing behind the raised cash counter, Mr. Cleary watched us through his thick, black-rimmed glasses, making sure we didn't steal anything. Nestled into a four-by-four-foot, wood-framed glass case was an impressive candy selection. Once we were ready to choose our treats, Mr. Cleary lifted the hinged top flap, verbally calculating the cost as we filled our small, paper bags. For a couple of bucks, we'd fill our pockets and then sit at the picnic table around the side of the store smoking and gobbling Mo-jo's.

Mostly high school kids hung out at Gary's house, a hotel built in 1887, which had been converted into a house. But Lana liked to go there, and I usually followed her lead. The dark-wood wainscoting and built-in cabinetry reminded me of old saloon sets in the Clint Eastwood westerns I watched on late night TV.

Gary's house was warm, and going there was better than sitting outside in the cold, but being outside made me feel less committed to the bad things I did, the things I knew I shouldn't be doing. It was like the wide-open space diluted the booze, nicotine, and hallucinogens I put in my body. I wasn't even sure if I liked all the drugs or being drunk, but I didn't want to say no to my friends. They loved being high, and somehow, although I felt alone in many ways, I felt like I fit in here.

Today, after school Gary's house was rocking with tunes. The gang was all there, laughing and chatting under a cloud of tobacco and pot smoke. Putting my seventh-grade mathematics textbook and binder down by the door, I looked for a place to sit where I could fade into the backdrop. Scanning the room, I reached into my coat pockets, jiggling a few candy wrappers between my fingers, trying to avert my awkwardness.

Except for a couple of dropouts, everyone else there was in high school. Lana and I were more than a few years younger; I had just turned twelve. I think the only reason they let us in was that Lana's brother was friends with Gary. No one messed with us because they didn't want to mess with Lana's older brother, whose reputation preceded him. He handed out blackeyes and bruises to anyone within arm shot, including Lana if she fell from his graces.

The furniture in Gary's house looked like it had been there longer than the house itself. Off the front foyer, the dining room was to the right. An oval red-wood dining table held many elbows, ashtrays, and drinks. Today, all the tall-back chairs surrounding the table were full. Gary sat beside Johnny who had just turned nineteen; he bootlegged for us when we had money to buy beer. They flipped through issues of *Heavy-Metal* magazine, comparing cartoon boobs on comic-book vixens.

Sad-Billie was there. She had run away from home, dropped out of high school, and was working at the local chicken farm with a few of the other boys. Freckle-Face, a ginger with a frizzy, orange mop of hair, argued over something with Blake, half laughing and half shouting—each one trying to be heard over the other. Bubbly gurgles came from a foot-tall, purple bong being passed around the table. Lana elbowed Freckle-Face, suggesting he pass the bong to her next.

Blake was in eleventh grade. We weren't friends, but I'd seen him outside Cleary's Store lots of times. I don't think he knew who I was; he never said hello. He sat behind a mountain of thinly rolled joints. It was Gary's weed, or maybe it belonged to Gary's dad. Blake was focused, snipping buds and rolling joints, like he was the entire assembly line of the widget factory himself. He moved his head to the bassy drumbeats coming from a set of three-foot-high speaker boxes set in the corners of the room.

"Keep 'em thin, Blake. That shit is death," said Gary, punctuating with an uneasy giggle.

Blake was Mr. Cool. A black and red, plaid lumber jacket hung off his broad shoulders, and his white, Nike tennis shoes were always buffed. He laughed a lot, but not in a funny way, more like the way your dad laughs when you tell him about something that happened at school—something that seemed a lot funnier before you told him.

Jenny, Blake's ex-girlfriend, was at the table. They had been inseparable all year, and you rarely saw one without the other. Something had happened between them, and now they acted like they didn't know each other was there.

Jenny sat cross-legged on her chair. Dark denim tears framed her bumpy knee skin. Jenny's pencil case sat opened on the table, a mathematics set splayed. She clutched a metal protractor between her thumb and index finger. Her pinky finger curled in, resting on her upper arm as she scratched into her pale skin with its sharp point. A bloody, teddy-bear outline was taking shape.

"You want some of this?" said Blake.

He was looking at me, offering a freshly lit joint. Stunned, I nodded, walking around the table toward him.

Me? Why me? I thought. I instinctively looked back at Jenny for approval. But Jenny didn't flinch when Blake spoke, seeming not to care, her attention firmly on her Bic-ink tattoo.

I stood in front of Blake and reached for the joint. He pulled it back. "Come here," he nodded his head up, gesturing for me to come closer. He guided me to kneel in front of him. Once I was crouched at his side, he passed me the joint. Feeling everyone's eyes on me, I inhaled a hefty river of smoke. My heart pumped heavy and quick. I held the weed smoke in as long as I could until I started to cough. Uncontrollably. Tears gathered in my eyes, spilling out as I gasped for air. Heat flushed my body amid a crowd of laughter.

"She's a little lamb," said Jenny, grinning. I looked towards Lana. She was having fun. Not even my choking could get her attention.

Embarrassed, I stood, hiding my gasps for air as laughter. I kept walking around the table, back to the entry way. *I should leave*, I thought. But I was too high to go home. I turned back towards the stairs, looking up at the second-floor landing. Double-wide stairs covered in red, floral carpet that was heavily worn up the middle resembled a mouth. Open. Shouting at me, "Run!" or crooning, "Come." Maybe they were just screams, like the ones I'd let go into my pillow at night.

Denying the raging staircase, I moved into the living room and sat on the couch, sinking deeply into the back of its cushions. My feet came up off the wide-plank floors and dangled like bricks on a clothesline. The shabby, Victorian sofa with its carved wood arms and frame held my body in place like the chair-bucket of a roller coaster. Crimson, woven fabric had dulled to pink in spots, and you could see remnants of intricate cross-stitched roses that must have looked beautiful once.

Resting my wrist on the sofa-arm, I watched a ribbon of smoke dance off the tip of my freshly lit cigarette, floating up, winding, and then disappearing like my thoughts: *I shouldn't have inhaled the weed so deeply.* I was afraid to move. It felt like my legs were independent of my mind, and they threatened to take me away, maybe leading me to the top of the angry stairs to throw me into her screams. I didn't dare move.

This pot wasn't like the stuff Gary usually got. He bragged about snagging a bag from his dad. He said it was the "best fucking weed on the planet." I'd smoked enough pot to know just how much I could take, in and out, quick—maybe one or two tokes. Tops. But today I held it in. *Fucking idiot.* It was too late now. I just had to wait.

"Your smoke," said Gary.

"Hmm?" I looked up with weighty eyes.

"Your smoke," Gary pointed towards my hand. A two-inch-long ash arched off my cigarette. Leaning forwards, I tapped it into an ashtray on the table already heaping with ash and butts.

"Sorry," I said, sitting back.

"You look green. You okay?" Gary said.

"Yeah. I just need to stay here," I said.

I felt green, and other worldly. *Green. Green.* That word felt wrong. Was it even a word? *Green.*

"Want to lie down in my room?" Gary snickered.

"No, I'm good," I said, looking down, hopefully avoiding more conversation.

"Gary," said Blake, who stood against the door jamb, "my work is done." Blake held up a large baggie filled with rolled joints. He reached into it and pulled out a handful. "I'll take these, on the house," he said.

"Yeah, sure, man," said Gary, nervously scuffing out of the living room, grabbing the joint baggie on his way.

Over the voices and laughter coming from the dining room, rock band April Wine threw vivid, long guitar runs into the room, carrying my thoughts on the vibrato of wickedly plucked guitar strings. I bumped up and down on every octave with the guitarists quick picking, filling my lonesome place on the sofa. They sang of the gypsy queen. She knew about fear. She was a ghost, there with me, warning me. Maybe she was the one who summoned the screaming stairs, urging me to run.

Blake stood in the doorway. I could feel his eyes on me, but I kept mine on the deep welts in the floorboards, finding faces and shapes that weren't there.

"Hey," said Blake.

"Hey," I said, trying to act like a human as I manoeuvred the wicked high.

"You good? Want a drink?" Blake passed me his beer. I took a long swig. It was warm and felt like I was drinking cotton balls.

"Thanks. I'm good." I said, passing the stubby bottle back to him.

"I've seen you around," said Blake.

"Yeah. I'm just here with Lana. Her brother is..."

"I know who her brother is." Blake lit a cigarette and passed it to me. "Pretty heavy weed, eh?"

"Yeah." I said, taking the cigarette from him.

"Want more?" Blake held out one of his joints.

"I don't think I can."

"You'll be okay." Blake sat down at my side and put his arm around me, giving a snug pull in. He was warm. His embrace secured me; maybe I wasn't going to float off into the abyss like a parade balloon gone astray. My head fell into the soft, felt plaid of his jacket, and he wrapped his other arm around me. Holding me, he pulled back and looked over my sore, bloodshot eyes. "You're not like the other girls," he said.

His gaze drilled through me, leaving me dizzy. "I'm not?" I said, looking down into the comforting shadows of the room.

"Yeah," said Blake.

"I'm wasted," I said, adding a small laugh.

"Want to lie down?"

"No. I gotta go," I said. It was mid-November, and window light revealed dull clouds under dark skies. Bracing myself on the sofa's edge, I stood. I felt queasy, but I was alright. This was my chance to leave without looking stupid. *Keep it together, Leesa.*

"See ya, Blake." It felt nice saying his name. Blake. I walked out of the room, trying to be cool, catching his smile as I passed by.

I stopped in the dining room doorway, steadying myself before bargaining my way through the thick laughter and chatter to where Lana sat.

Kneeling to her ear, I said, "I gotta go. I'm too high."

Lana spoke softly, "Oh no. Stay. Why don't you lie down?"

"Here?" I said, "No. I can't. Just call me later."

"Okay. I'll call. I promise," said Lana. I nodded.

I didn't care if she called or not. I just had to be outside, in the cool, wide open space. Turning to leave, I saw Blake standing by the front door with my schoolbooks under his arm.

"I'm leaving, too. I'll walk you."

The corners of my mouth curled up. "Sure," I said.

Surprised and excited that Blake had taken an interest in me, we walked in the damp drizzle. He had told me I was different from the others. I felt that way about myself—always wondering why everyone else seemed so comfortable in their skin while mine trembled and wilted upon me. Why did he suddenly see me? Did he understand me? Was he like me?

Blake carried my books in one arm and reached for my hand with the other. It felt good to hold his warmth in my hand. It was only a few blocks to my house. I wanted to walk all night, holding his hand.

We had reached the end of my cul-de-sac. "Thanks for holding my books," I said. "I can take them." I didn't want to walk down my street with Blake. It felt too weird, being with a boy.

"I don't want you to go," said Blake. He squeezed my hand, raising our joined palms towards the Kingdom Hall on the corner. "Wanna go sit?" Blake motioned towards the covered stoop at the entrance. The Hall was closed, and the top of the stairs was dry.

"Sure," I said, feeling warm and squishy. Fluttering butterflies that I had heard about in books and on TV shows were churning inside me, circling my quivering guts. Blake liked me, and I think I liked him, too.

I had walked by this single level, dreary church hundreds, maybe thousands of times. It was a dingy shade of green without any windows and without a second glance, faded into the earthy background. On Sundays, the parking lot was hopping with eager, Jehovah's Witness churchgoers dressed in their finest threads. But tonight, besides the steady slap of drips from flooded eavestroughs, it was bleak and still.

We walked up a few stairs. Dim, amber-fluorescent light from a small, caged lamp flickered and buzzed overhead. Light rain turned to a heavy pour. I thought about how close we were to my parents' driving route home and worried they might see me.

Standing there, I was unsure of what to do next—sit, lean, keep standing? Blake sat down first, deep into the back of the alcove onto the cement pad in front of the door with his back against the chipped wall paint. He patted his hand to the spot at his side. "Sit?" he said.

My back to the wall, I slid down beside him, sitting with my knees bent. The air was chilled, and I wrapped my arms around my shins, holding them tight. I felt a twinge of discomfort, never having been so alone with a boy. "I have to go soon," I said.

"I know. Relax. You must be cold," said Blake. He tucked his left arm in behind me and pulled me in. Then, he reached over with his right hand and turned my head towards him, and he kissed me. I'd been kissed before, during truth or dare on the school ground, but I hadn't been kissed like this. Blake's tongue shot into my mouth, hard and deep. I didn't like it and instinctively moved my head away.

"It's okay," said Blake.

"I know," I said. But I didn't know anything about this. I searched, to do something, say something, but couldn't find words.

His hand slipped inside my jacket and into the deep v of my favorite baby-blue t-shirt. *Why had I worn a low-cut t-shirt?* I pulled back, pushing his arm off me. "I don't ...," I murmured, my incomplete sentence lacking authority.

Blake pulled back, out of my shirt for a moment, long enough to grab my wrist as he straddled me, pushing me further down the wall. With my body crumpled, half up the wall, and half on the slab, I struggled to get control of my arms. I found myself flat on my back. Neck crooked and my head pushed against the wall, he held both my wrists down against the cold, concrete floor.

"No, I don't..." I wrestled to push him off me. "Can we...," I said, bargaining.

"Shhhhh, it's okay," Blake soothed with his voice. His weighted thighs clamped my pelvis like a vice grip, and his hold on my wrists cinched. "Shhhh, I won't hurt you," he said. He sat on my hips, put one arm up to my throat, and leaned in with his forearm—pushing harder when I tried to get up. My airway closed, and I froze, panic consuming me. Was I going to die here?

Fear fueling my fight I attempted to break free. His forearm pushed in harder, blocking my airway again. Breathless for an instant, I gave up the fight. "I won't hurt you," he whispered.

But he *was* hurting me. Why lie? Maybe his whispers weren't meant for me. Maybe this chant was all his own. His hope for control, not of me, but of himself. Something told me to stop fighting. A voice? A feeling? It was there. He knew he'd won, and his forearm eased off my windpipe, moving onto my collarbone.

Threatening control of my breath, he worked on undoing the top button of my jeans. I lay, unmoving. Fear of harm coursing through me, controlling my mind. Raindrops got louder, and the earthy smell of dampness flooded my senses. I narrowed in on the faint, yellow flicker of the light-fixture above me. A moth fluttered, tapping at the lens, trying to get closer to the small bit of light.

I closed my eyes, and the amber light stayed with me. A spot under my lids.

He finished.

He got off.

He stood.

Fastening his pants and adjusting his clothing to hang straight, he slicked back his shoulder length shag. At his feet, I lifted my hips off the ground to pull my jeans up and button them. I fumbled to find the two halves of my ski jacket, securing it, zipping it high before I sat up.

Blake lit a smoke. "Want one?" he asked, passing it to me.

I shook my head, no.

He passed me my schoolbooks. "Want me to walk you?"

"No, I'm just down there," I pointed towards the end of my un-lit street.

"Cool. I'll see ya then."

"Yeah," I said. Over the loose gravel parking lot, Blake walked away, onto the road, disappearing into the dark. On the top step of the Jehovah's Hall, I wondered what had just happened. What had I done to invite Blake's violation? Was it something I said? Was it something about me, my makeup, my clothes, my solitude?

I walked the familiar, dark road home. The porch light was on. I opened the creaky, screen door, and then the front one.

"Hi, Leesa," Mom yelled from the kitchen. "Perogies for dinner."

"Okay, Mom."

I went into my room, grabbed some clothes, and took them into the bathroom, locking the door behind me.

"Are you having a shower now? Dinner's ready." Mom spoke through the door.

"Yeah, I got my period. I'll be quick." Water poured into the tub. I turned the shower lever to full and stepped into the downpour. Steam filled the room, and I began to sob. What do I do now?

Tears poured, blending with the water that needled my scalp. It stung. I reached up to feel a bump on the back of my head. Lathering a second and third shampoo onto my scalp, I pushed hard onto the bump, feeling intense pain with each prod. I liked it.

You're a fucking asshole. I pounded my fists against my thighs until they throbbed. Sitting on the tub floor, I sunk my head between my knees, hiding, breathing in the hot, wet air. *I won't tell anyone.*

The solution was clear. I wouldn't tell. I could hide from judgment if no one knew. Maybe it didn't happen—if no one ever knew.

61.

The Curse of Sin City

Sarah Williams

When I was a young child, my family moved to Prince Edward County, Ontario. We drove from the thick darkness of rural Nova Scotia, fog lifting out of the spruce trees, to the busy middle of the country. I sat on my mother's lap, as I strained to look out the window. This was the 1990s, after all, long before the sanitation of childhood. Our car was a rusty 1977 Mercury Zephyr, which was almost as long and yellow as a school bus, save for the large red spots it had acquired in my parents' care.

I fell asleep in Montreal's Lafontaine Tunnel. The St. Lawrence rushed above us as we shot like bullets through the sleek dark. When I woke up, we had arrived at the island county. The air was heavy off Lake Ontario, and the locust trees lining Main Street swayed like algae in the warm summer breeze.

We'd moved halfway across the country, and in all the packing and sorting and moving of boxes, we didn't realize our move was instinctual, like salmon going home to spawn, a pointless race to the end of our shared agony. We didn't realize it was something so deeply ingrained within us, this place, the stitching that holds the deteriorating quilt of our patchwork family together.

We had no choice.

We'd come to live on Ontario Street in the largest town on the island. The house was the same one my father had been sent to as an orphan in 1938. It had belonged to Myrtle, his adoptive mother. Solid wood and finely crafted trim adorned every inch of the structure that had been lived in by Myrtle's family since 1882.

She had broad shoulders and big hands. In the early 1940s, she could produce envy-worthy victory curls as easily as she could build a shed. She did both while living with her mother and the rotating brood of youngsters the pair of women took in. The children were wards of the crown and the house a primitive foster home. They were given pencils and erasers for birthdays. The girls learned how to darn their own socks at an early age.

Decades later, the floorboards, sturdy pine from the past century, still held the secrets of the little feet tiptoeing through the house at night and the whispered conversations about who had come there and why.

"If she comes back in a body bag, I'm blaming you," my father said to my mother one evening, beneath the noise of the television, shortly after we'd moved. His voice, one that would normally be characterized by rounded consonants, as though he had a mouth full of marbles, had became hardened. His words struck the air with staccato precision.

She was my sister, and she had just run away from home at the age of sixteen. This was not the first time. But it was the farthest she had gone. Several days earlier, my mother had gone to pick her up from school, not knowing her daughter was halfway to Los Angeles drinking coolers in the back of some pickup truck.

The last time, my sister disappeared before she had even rounded the corner of puberty. She was just twelve years old. Baby fat dimples still padded her cheeks. Pink was still her favourite colour, and her room was still lit up at night by the plastic glow of a strawberry shortcake night light, the Fisher Price label having begun to wear off as the 1990s took hold and her hair grew longer.

I remember the helicopter reverberating above our house like an aquatic butterfly, cutting through the sound waves high above. We lived at the edge of the forest, the forest where she had gone missing during a weekend camping trip with the local cadet squadron. Our father was the squadron captain, and she was a new recruit.

He hadn't thought his daughter would just disappear, much less survive for several days and nights in the thick brush of rural Nova Scotia, with legends of roaming bobcats—not even the savviest hunter dare tread without an exit plan.

Search and rescue were still scouring the province while the news station reported updates on her case when she waltzed out from behind the boulders and the spruce trees. When my sister walked out of the woods, it was not because she'd been found.

Several months later, we had moved.

About fifteen minutes down the road from Ontario Street is the small village of Demorestville. The woods surrounding the village are now largely scrub cedar and maple, but in the middle of the nineteenth century, the area was rich with white pine. At that time, Demorestville was the second largest city in Ontario. It was larger, even, than Toronto. Sitting on the Bay of Quinte, on an island full of fields and forests, the former city attracted loggers and other itinerant folk who would sail up the St. Lawrence from far-flung places. They brought the white pine to their knees until there were no more.

Some would find themselves moored there, perhaps distracted for a while in one of the many brothels or bars that lined the streets, now mostly barren, save for the town hall and the Methodist church. Party ships docked in the nearby bay, ferrying locals, loggers, and even the odd disgraced politician up and down the bay on a booze-soaked joyride. This was the town once known as Sin City, the only vestige of its former ill-repute being two street names: Sodom and Gomorrah.

There, it was not uncommon to find farmers parked outside a distillery midday, no doubt cicadas keeping rhythm with their thirst in the summer sun. Similarly, the women of Demorestville were well known for imbibing whisky in fine bone china at their quilting bees, although temperance had taken hold in many other places in Canada.

My father's family came from New York State during the American Revolution and landed there. In over two hundred years, they had barely moved more than ten miles away. Even in death, the street names they bestowed upon the place refuse to vacate.

This is where my father was from, a place that had been reaching for him, pulling him like a tightly wound umbilical cord around his neck. A place that is now considered a ghost town, fitting, in more ways than one.

I was five years old when I first saw my mother cry. This was before the move, before we realized the problems weren't temporary. I remember the carpet in the office was green shag, the walls brown, weathered wallpaper that boasted several degrees. But mostly, I remember wanting to cry with her. How strange it was to see an adult break down in an office while a man in a white coat and thick, black-rimmed glasses sat nonchalantly on the other side of the room staring at us and saying little but offering up a box of Kleenex. Years later, I would realize this was a psychiatrist, but at the time, I saw this man as an offending cardboard cut-out. Silent and dense with hard edges.

We were there to talk about my sister. The psychiatrist described her mental state as being like a tangled ball of yarn with too many mental ailments to unravel. Many people would eventually get caught in the tangled web of my sister's yarns, least of which was my father.

Soon after this visit, my mother and I went to live with my grandmother. I loved the routine, the calm, the unapologetic "Scottishness" of my grandmother's house. There, every morning started the same way, with toast, tea, and the chatter of CBC Radio in the background. Similarly, the end of the night would be signalled when Peter Mansbridge came on the television to deliver his nightly newscast.

The three of us would go out often to cafes, to restaurants, or to my favourite children's bookstore. We would take drives through the valley and spend the odd afternoon by the shore. Vague sensations of this three-month period cling to my adult memory like a faded photograph, almost escaping definition. The way butter would melt on my favourite muffin at my favourite cafe or the smell of the ocean mixing with salt and vinegar chips are so much more than the sum of their parts, but maybe that is merely because they were a prelude. They were order and logic before chaos.

Everything happens in spring in Prince Edward County. The land slowly opens up like a blossom, letting the dormant streams run freely through greening fields while the bitter Great Lake wind still harbours the sting of winter.

In the spring of 1922, Alton was a robust nineteen years of age when he set sail for the states. In a suit that was too big for him, he was heading for Chicago and all the speakeasies filled with Americans desperate for a drink. The work in Demorestville had long since dried up, although the town was far from dry. But this didn't matter to Alton. He was a labourer, and his work was the drink.

Although he had stood with the others, watching in anticipation as the last batch of moonshine had been bottled, their wet and muddy shoes unable to deter their own desire, Alton's job was not to pour his own sweat into that particular work. Instead, he was sent southwards, armed with an arsenal of samples and his unerring ability to disarm even the savviest of buyers with the mere and unintentional arch of his right eyebrow.

It was not long after my mother and I returned home that my father announced his plan to leave his position of principal at the nearby Shelburne Youth Centre. Known colloquially as the "Boys School," the centre was a government-run institution for adolescent boys who would, otherwise, end up in the prison system. Like a cross between juvenile detention centres and high school, it included a ball field, gymnasium, housing quarters, and, of course, classrooms.

My father had studied science and trained as a teacher. Later, he'd earned a certificate in guidance counselling. He was the kind of man who would listen, intently and profoundly, no matter who was speaking. He would listen through coarse words and harsh tones. Understanding subtext was his rare gift, and intuiting what someone needed when they spoke was his gift to those around him. His talent for disarming people with kindness made him an ideal candidate for working with even the most prickly people.

Much like a prison complex, the school was fortified with guards. And much like a prison, these guards had a reputation for being rough around the edges.

Perhaps because of this, the allegations of abuse that surfaced in the early 1990s seemed plausible. No doubt, some were. Eventually, thousands of students, past and present, came forwards detailing physical and sexual abuse. This was after the Nova Scotia government began implementing a compensation program, encouraging victims to come forwards without any form of cross-examination. While the government was doling out compensation to students based on a so-called meat chart, dictated by the type and duration of abuse, staff had no avenue for recourse or opportunity to refute allegations.

Having no allegations against himself, my father thought he could leave the centre relatively unscathed. He took early retirement, hoping to find peace back in Ontario.

In a few short years, there would be moss growing inside on the walls and ceilings. The nearby employee rentals, where my family lived, would be derelict. It is astounding how quickly a community can become a ghost town.

"You didn't know," my brother said to me one day when we were out for a walk. "Well, I guess they'd want to keep it hidden."

The silence between his words settled between us like a no trespassing sign.

But this was not the kind of thing you gloss over. In the silence were the lies my sister had told about my family. There were the lies she had told to police, to reporters, to anyone who would listen. In the silence, there was a gap between what was said and what wasn't. Perhaps she was inspired by recent events at the Boys School, perhaps not. My grandmother had pushed her down the stairs, and my father had abused her, she said. Although the allegations would be proven to be false, the violence of her words became like a cancer for my family. A malignant inertia had set in.

Trauma can make throwing things away difficult. Not necessarily things that were always destined to be tossed, an empty salad container and an old newspaper or chicken bones from last night's dinner. No, trauma makes it difficult to throw away big things like sofas, chairs, or beds. These are the objects that had been lived in, the kind of items that might still harbour a whiff of the past or the outline of someone's bottom, now long gone. When we arrived in Ontario, moving trucks in tow, there was already a furnished house waiting for us. Myrtle's furniture, though dusty, still sat where she had placed it, decades ago. For the first few months, or perhaps years, we lived among boxes. There was a collective silence, a holding of breath, as we scurried the well-worn, cardboard studded paths between the important rooms. As a child, it could be fun to feel like we were camping all the time.

When the boxes were unpacked, we just kept holding our breath. There was no room to exhale with the furnishings of two houses in one. Antiques, such as a sword from the Crimean War or Victorian baby clothes, crossed paths frequently with the mess of a young family. Meanwhile, we were all gathering dust.

It was 1928 when Alton returned from Chicago for another summer of farm work. Normally, when the fields started to turn golden, and the crickets started to move indoors, he knew it was time to pack a trunk full of swill and head state side. That year was different. He'd fallen in love. Her name was Kathleen, and her family had money. So much, in fact, they'd sent her to school to train as a stenographer. It was the ease with which they enjoyed each other's company, sometimes silently, sometimes in deep discussion, that kept his mind filled with thoughts of her. He felt as though she'd always been walking beside him.

This time, when autumn came, Alton followed her to Toronto, where she now worked. His heart beat faster than the rhythm of the train on its way to the city. They were married, eloped, with no family members willing or able to be present. Throughout Demorestville, Alton had garnered a reputation as a good-time Charlie and her family was against the union. Meanwhile, his could not afford a train ticket to see them.

Years later, but only hours after she had died, Kathleen's father would sign her death certificate. With Alton nowhere to be found, her father was the next of kin. Her father scowled as he scrawled his name, thinking back to how he had not signed their marriage certificate.

The baby would be sent to the nearest orphanage.

Trauma can take years to accumulate, growing in toxicity with each passing generation. Sometimes it begins as something small and seemingly surmountable, only to grow into flames that are all consuming like the flames that brought down Sin City. Barely a trace remains of the bustling place that was or the fire that tore it down. Though many must have been killed, more still fled. Few families remained. Those who did, seemed to bear an unusual amount of bad luck, ill fate of biblical proportions.

Like his father, my father had one particularly arched eyebrow. And, like his father, mine seemed to be outrunning some misfortune. The wolves were always at the door.

As an adult, after moving to Vancouver and subsequently returning home, I found my parents still living in service of their stuff. Chairs, coffee tables, books, and multiple china cabinets were among a litany of things that littered their living and dining rooms. To get from their upstairs to their kitchen, my parents now had to toddle down the stairs, out the heavy front door for all their neighbours to see and past the ancient Norway Maple to go through the door at the back, the one somehow always missing a pane of glass.

They had also found themselves guardians of a menagerie of cats. My sister, who blew in and out of their lives like an unpredictable, dusty spring wind, had left the cats there. Unbeknownst to my parents these cats were not fixed. The cats multiplied until there were so many they moved like a school of fish, obscuring the floor beneath them. For my parents, it became easier to put up with the cats than to do anything about it. From the outside, it appeared as though my parents were collecting cats, but it was something that just happened. There was a stillness to their situation and, as always, the possibility of better days. A cleaner house. A happy family.

Litters of kittens were born and died in the messiness of life that was that house. Feces were ground into the hardwood, entrenched so that only a sharp knife could chisel them out. Acrid air spilled from the windows and doors assailing the nostrils of any and all passersby.

Like the house, my father's health began to deteriorate. What started as diabetes progressed to kidney failure. Eventually, his legs would give out, and in his last days, he would need to be pulled up the stairs, socks slipping down off his bony ankles. Still, he refused to leave the house that was falling down around him.

My father had been cleaning litter boxes two days before he died when he called, his voice shaking like a stringed instrument. He was not feeling well and never would be again. I was home, pregnant and in the habit of having pandemic style visits with my parents in their yard. My father would be in his walker while I leaned with the full heft of pregnancy against their maple tree. But there would be no visit that day.

During the call, I could hear my mother in the background, berating my father as if he were right next to her. She breathing nothing but fire. While he spoke, I couldn't help but envision his walker, standing vacant in their yard.

By August, he was gone. Still, parts of him remain. His shoes sit unused by the leather couch beside the grandfather clock, home to a revolving number of sleeping cats. The jars of strawberry jam, made only a month previously, now sit on the kitchen floor collecting cat hair, dander, and urine. And he can even be found in the locust trees or limestone ledges in the cursed place he called home.

Notes on Contributors

Anonymous is a retired English literature lecturer and teacher trainer, the mother of four adult children, and the happy grandmother of five. She has researched, lectured, and published on mothering images in literary and sociological contexts and is well aware that her choice to write anonymously here is ironic. Old habits die hard.

Christine K. Anzur (PhD, West Virginia University) is an assistant professor of relational and family communication at East Tennessee State University. Her program of research is inspired largely by her own adoption and is focused on giving voice to adoptees, whose perspectives, experiences, and grievances are often overlooked.

Barbara Barry was born and grew up near Montreal as one of the first of the baby boomers. After graduating from McGill, she worked as a computer programmer. With her husband and two children, she has lived in many Canadian cities and has retired happily to Victoria BC, where she enjoys reading, writing, and walking by the ocean.

John Barton's books include *Polari, For the Boy with the Eyes of the Virgin: Selected Poems, Seminal: The Anthology of Canada's Gay-Male Poets, We Are Not Avatars: Essays, Memoirs, Manifestos*, and, most recently, *Lost Family: A Memoir*, which was shortlisted for the 2021 Derek Walcott Prize, and *The Essential Derk Wynand*. He lives in Victoria, BC, where he is the city's first male and first queer poet laureate.

Susan Braley lives in Victoria, BC. Her poetry has appeared in literary journals, such as *The Antigonish Review, Arc Poetry Magazine, CV2, Literary Review of Canada, Prairie Fire,* and *The New Quarterly*, as well as in several anthologies. Her poems have been recognized in numerous writing contests, including *Arc*'s Poem of the Year.

Linda Briskin is a writer and fine art photographer. She is drawn to writing about the small secrets of interior lives. Her creative nonfiction bends genres and highlights social justice themes—quietly. As a photographer, she is intrigued by the permeability between the remembered and the imagined and the ambiguities in what we choose to see. www.lindabriskinphotography.com/

Michelle Poirier Brown is a Cree Métis writer living in Victoria. Her prose has appeared in *The Malahat Review, Release Any Words Stuck Inside of You II* and *III, The Fieldstone Review, The Sun,* and *Dis(s)ent.* Recordings of her *Flame* performances can be found on her website: www.skyblanket.ca.

Pat Buckna is a graduate of the Writers Studio at Simon Fraser University. In addition to his writing, he has enjoyed a long career as a singer-songwriter and concert promoter. He resides in Powell River, where he published his family memoir *Only Children* in 2019.

Jessie Carson is a professional writer, facilitator, and yoga teacher. She is the mother of two boys and lives with her family in Almonte, ON. This story is the reason why she started writing and is currently working on a longer piece on this event in her family's past.

Joan Conway is a poet and arts facilitator who lives on a small acreage in northern British Columbia. She is the associate representative for the League of Canadian Poets and coedits the ongoing publication *Fresh Voices* on the league website: greenblossomstudio.wordpress.com.

Sharon Anne Cook is distinguished university professor emerita at the University of Ottawa. She has authored or coedited thirteen books. The recipient of a number of teaching awards at the university and provincial levels, she continues to teach Canadian educational history in the Faculty of Education's graduate studies program.

Jean Crozier's perspective has been shaped through her experiences as a too-young wife and mother, a woman who reentered the work force, earned a science degree, and became a successful entrepreneur. She studies history and genealogy, seeking understanding and compassion, the essence of narrative and the beauty of family intricacy.

Liana Cusmano (Luca/BiCurious George) is a writer, poet, and filmmaker. They were the 2018 and 2019 Montreal Slam Champion and runner up in the 2019 Canadian Individual Poetry Slam Championship. They are a 2022 QWF Spoken Word Prize nominee and their first novel, *Catch & Release* (2022), was published with Guernica Editions.

Yaana Dancer acquired a bachelor's as well as a master's degree in fine art before studying creative writing with mentors Jen Currin and Betsy Warland. She has published short works and given many public readings in Western Canada. A collection of short stories based on ancestors is in progress.

Ann Davis is a retired director of The Nickle Arts Museum at the University of Calgary, where she also initiated and taught museum and heritage studies. Her publications include eight books, most recently *Museum & Place*, numerous exhibition catalogues, and articles.

Wendy Donawa lives in Victoria on the traditional unceded lands of the Songhees and Esquimalt People. Her poems have appeared in numerous Canadian magazines and anthologies. Her début collection, *Thin Air of the Knowable*, was a Gerald Lampert finalist; her second collection, *Our Bodies' Unanswered Questions*, appeared in fall, 2021.

Renee Duddridge writes about ancestors of Canada and from France circa 1500–1700 and Scandinavia as well as Ireland and Scotland since the 1800s. She pursued women's issues in "Saskatchewan Décor Data" in *Décormag* and *Art Education and Aging: Views of Four Older Women in Saskatoon*, her master's thesis. Renee and husband live in Saskatoon where they operate BackDoor Gallery SK, and New York.

Kate Eckland is a writer, storyteller, and a chronic oversharer. Her upcoming memoir *What Parents?* is about the experience of losing both of her parents to cancer before her twenty-fourth birthday. Kate writes with a wry sense of humour and unapologetic honesty about caregiving, grief, and so-called resilience.

Ralph Friesen is a retired therapist and writer living in Nelson, BC. He believes there is such a thing as truth, even if there are varying versions of every story. He is the author of *Between Earth & Sky: Steinbach, the First 50 Years*, numerous historical articles, and a biography/memoir, *Dad, God, and Me*.

Helen Gowans is an emerging writer who writes poetry and prose. *There and Here*, a chapbook of poems arising from travels since 1967, was published in January 2021. *And Back Again*, a second chapbook, was published in fall 2021. She has contributed to two upcoming anthologies. In 2020, she won Pandora's Collective Poetry Contest for the poem "Mackenzie Stone," and her poem, "Crete," was shortlisted for the Magpie Award.

Adrienne Gruber is the author of three books of poetry, *Q & A* (Book*hug), *Buoyancy Control* (Book*hug), and *This is the Nightmare* (Thistledown Press), and five chapbooks. She lives on Nexwlélexm (Bowen Island), the traditional territory of the Squamish people, with her partner and their three daughters, and is currently working on a collection of linked essays on motherhood and mental illness.

Amanda Hale began her writing career as an immigrant in 1970s Montreal. She won the Prism International prize for creative nonfiction and has twice been a finalist for the Relit Fiction award. She wrote the libretto for *Pomegranate*, an opera to be premiered by the Canadian Opera Company in 2023. www.amandahale.com

Leesa Hanna is a writer. After the 2019 release of her children's chapter book, *The BIG Adventures of Little O*, Leesa continued her literary path, writing a memoir. Delving into the shadows of her youth, her current manuscript, a YA/fantasy novel, explores the challenges of adolescence and a longing for peace through deeper discovery of the natural world.

Maureen Scott Harris, a Toronto poet and essayist, has published three collections of poetry: *A Possible Landscape*, *Drowning Lessons* (awarded the 2005 Trillium Book Award for Poetry), and *Slow Curve Out*. In 2019, she won the Great Blue Heron Poetry Contest and was runner up in the Edna Staebler Personal Essay Contest.

Cornelia Hoogland's recent publications include *Dressed in Only a Cardigan, She Picks Up Her Tracks in the Snow*, (Baseline) and *Cosmic Bowling* (Guernica). *Trailer Park Elegy* and *Woods Wolf Girl* were finalists for Canadian national awards. Hoogland was the 2019 writer-in-residence for the Al Purdy A-Frame and the Whistler Festival. www.corneliahoogland.com

NOTES ON CONTRIBUTORS

Carole Harmon is a poet and memoirist and writes about nature, family, and history. She writes after a career in theatre, publishing, and photography, based in and inspired by the Canadian Rockies. She is coproducer, with Ingrid Rose and Gary Sill, of Writers Radio, an independent online radio program, which broadcasts internationally.

Maureen Hynes, a Toronto poet, has published five books of poetry. Her first collection, *Rough Skin,* won the League of Canadian Poet's Gerald Lampert Award, and her most recent collection, *Sotto Voce,* was a finalist for the League's Pat Lowther Award and the Golden Crown Literary Award (US). www.maureenhynes.ca

George K. Ilsley is the award-winning author of three books, and his work has been selected for Best Canadian Poetry. *Bingo and Black Ice* is reprinted with permission from *The Home Stretch: A Father, a Son, and All the Things They Never Talk About* (Arsenal Pulp Press, 2020).

Nancy Issenman has retirement to thank for reenergizing her love of reading and writing. She has published a chapbook, *The Name of Yes,* and her poems appear in various other publications. Nancy is grateful to Arleen and Donna for providing the opportunity to "out" her family secret.

Cynthia Woodman Kerkham has worked as a journalist, poet, teacher and editor. Her writing has appeared in journals and anthologies, and her poems have won awards, including finalist for the CBC poetry prize. She is the author of *Good Holding Ground* (Palimpsest Press) and co-editor of the anthology *Poems from Planet Earth* (Leaf Press).

Myrna Kostash's recent books are *Prodigal Daughter: A Journey to Byzantium* and *The Seven Oaks Reader*. Her essays and creative nonfiction have been widely anthologized. She is a recipient of the Writers' Trust Matt Cohen Award for a Life of Writing. *Ghosts in a Photograph: A Chronicle* was published fall 2022.

Judy LeBlanc's story collection *The Promise of Water* was published by Oolichan Books in 2017, and her writing has appeared in several literary journals, most recently in *Geist*, Summer, 2022. She's working on a collection of personal essays in which she explores her mixed Coast Salish/European heritage.

Shelley A. Leedahl is a multi-genre writer in Ladysmith, BC. Her most recent books are *Go* (Poetry, Radiant Press), *The Moon Watched It All* (Children's illustrated, Red Deer Press) and *I Wasn't Always Like This* (Essays, Signature Editions). Leedahl's an avid hiker, kayaker, runner and cyclist. See www.writersunion.ca/member/shelleya-leedahl

Joy Thierry Llewellyn is happiest living out of a backpack. She writes travel adventure novels and is working on a memoir about living in international communities. Her scriptwriter and story editor career let her combine her love of writing, travel, and mentoring by teaching screenwriting in Canada, India, and China.

Blaine Marchand's seventh book of poetry, *Becoming History*, was published by Aeolus House Press in 2021. Active in the Ottawa literary scene for fifty years, he was president of the League of Canadian Poets from 1991 to 1993 and a monthly columnist for Capital XTRA, the LGTBQ2+ paper, for nine years.

Lenore D. Maybaum is an associate professor of English and Writing Center Director at Kirkwood Community College in Iowa City, IA, home of the Iowa Writer's Workshop. Her PhD is in language, literacy, and culture, and she's currently completing an MFA in creative nonfiction that will culminate in a collection of lyric essays on mothers and daughters.

JoAnn McCaig is the author of *The Textbook of the Rose* and *An Honest Woman*. She is currently at work on a new novel called *The Vigo Reaction*. Since 2010, she has been the proud owner of Shelf Life Books, an independent bookstore located in her hometown of Calgary.

Jane Munro is an award-winning Canadian poet, writer, and educator. Her newest poetry book is *False Creek* (Harbour Publishing, 2022). *Open Every Window* (Douglas & McIntyre, 2021) is a genre-bending memoir. Her previous books include *Blue Sonoma* (Brick Books, 2014), which won the 2015 Griffin Poetry Prize, and *Glass Float* (Brick Books, 2020).

Jim Nason is the author of six volumes of poetry, a short story collection, and three novels. His poetry book *Rooster, Dog, Crow* was shortlisted for the 2019 Raymond Souster Award. His new book, *Blue Suitcase: Documentary Poetics* was published with Mansfield Press.

NOTES ON CONTRIBUTORS

Arleen Paré (co-editor) is a Victoria writer with nine collections of poetry, inclu-ding a recent chapbook. She has been shortlisted for the BC Dorothy Livesay BC Award for Poetry and has won the American Golden Crown Award for Poetry, the Victoria Butler Book Prize, a CBC Bookie Award, and a Governor Generals' Award for Poetry.

David Pimm lives in Vancouver and has just retired (for the second time). He writes poetry and prose, and sings choral music whenever possible (in Vancouver and Victoria). Growing up in London, England, subsequently shaped a great deal of his life. While his memory begins to fade, secrets still surface.

Patricia Preston is a former journalist whose career also included: journalism instructor, media advisor to a federal cabinet minister, public affairs vice-president for an international pharmaceutical company, and features writer for a US city magazine. Currently, she curates art exhibitions in local cafes while writing a memoir.

Caroline Purchase is a graduate of the Writer's Studio at Simon Fraser University and holds degrees from the University of Toronto (MA) and Antioch University (MFA). An art therapist and educator, Caroline writes both fiction and nonfiction. She lives on the West Coast with her husband and their Groenendael.

Heather Ramsay writes some things that are true and some that are not and lives in unceded Ts'elxwéyeqw territory (Chilliwack, BC). Her fiction, nonfiction, and poetry have appeared in *The Fiddlehead, The Malahat Review, carte blanche, The Antigonish Review, Numero Cinq, Maisonneuve, Canadian Geographic*, and more. She has also cowritten two books for the *Haida Gwaii Museum: Gina 'Waadluxan Tluu: The Everything Canoe* and *gyaaGang.ngaay—The Monumental Poles of Skidegate*.

Frances Rooney's books include *Working Light: The Wandering Life of Photographer Edith S. Watson*; *Working the Rock: Newfoundland and Labrador photographs of Edith S. Watson*; *Extraordinary Women Explorers*; and *Our Lives*. After 22 years beside a wondrous ravine in Toronto she and her partner now live by the sea in Victoria.

Ingrid Rose's contribution to this anthology was written after the completion of her memoir *The Walk*. She now lives on Coast Salish unceded lands, far from her homeland of London, England. Graduate of SFU's the Writers Studio and Vancouver Manuscript Intensive, she teaches writing from the body and coproduces and cohosts writersradio.ca

Laurel Ross lives in Chicago, where she is a writer, birder, prairie restoration volunteer, chorister (alto), photographer, and Soto Zen practitioner. A retired conservation ecologist, she is currently working on a memoir that celebrates her youthful excesses.

Susan Scruton is a writer who lives in Ottawa, Canada, with her partner, parrots, and bunnies. She's a civil servant by day and a serial obsessionist by night. Her most recent obsessions include indoor farming, worm composting, genealogy, and searching for urban bird nests.

Donna McCart Sharkey grew up in Montreal and now lives in Ottawa. Her most recent books are *Falling Together: A Family's Memoir of Mental Illness and Grief* and *Always With Me: Parents Talk About the Death of a Child*. She has also contributed to various creative nonfiction anthologies. She is a former professor at the State University of New York. Her research has been published in numerous academic journals.

Phyllis A. Shuell was born and raised on a farm in central Alberta. She is a poet/writer and teacher and resides in Edmonton and performs her poetry at the reading series sponsored by the Edmonton Stroll of Poet. She has held executive positions with the Canadian Authors Association (Alberta Branch) and the Writer's Guild of Alberta. Recent publishing credits include *New Forum* and the *Stroll of Poets* anthologies.

Claire Sicherman is the author of *Imprint: A Memoir of Trauma in the Third Generation* (Caitlin Press, 2017). Claire speaks and writes about her experience as a granddaughter of Holocaust survivors and facilitates workshops supporting writers in bringing the stories they hold in their bodies out onto the page.

Leslee Silverman, MFA, is a Canadian director, recognized internationally as a leader in theatre for young audiences. Her collaborative work, dedicated to social change, has played on four continents and across Canada. Leslee has been honoured by the Human Rights Commitment Award and a Governor General's Laureate for Lifetime Achievement.

Kae Solomon's publications include "Hands on the Piano," with Barren Magazine, and stories in the upcoming anthologies *Don't Tell: Family Secrets* and TWS's *emerge 21*. She writes memoir, personal essays, and has completed a teen novel. She works as a teacher librarian near Vancouver with her family.

Christine Smart's poem "Hummingbird" won the 2020 FBCW Literary Writes contest. Her book, *Decked and Dancing*, won the Acorn-Plantos Award in 2007. Hedgerow Press also published *The White Crow* (poetry). She has worked as a nurse and a writer while living on Salt Spring Island since 1989.

Laurel Sproule hails from Winnipeg, Manitoba, lived in Pierrefonds, Quebec, and Buckinghamshire, England, before attending the University of Alberta. After a career in education, she now writes poetry, fiction, and nonfiction. She is currently working on a novella *No Way Out but Through*, a nonfiction narrative, *Invisible Ink*, and short story collection, *In the Neighbourhood*.

Ruby Remenda Swanson is the author of *A Family Outing*, the story of how Ruby moved past her initial shock, fear, and denial of having a gay son to become a public advocate for equality and the acceptance of the LGBT community. *A Family Outing* is dedicated to her uncle, Fred Sopotyk, who had to hide.

Elizabeth Templeman lives, writes, and works in the central interior of British Columbia. She has two books of essays, *Notes from the Interior* (2003) and *Out and Back, Family in Motion* (2021). You can find more about her at elizabethtempleman.trubox.ca.

Soriya Turner practices writing from the body. She has edited and published journalism, poetry, horticultural memoir, procedures manuals, teaching handbooks, and recipes. A long-time artist in schools, she works to integrate arts and traditional curriculum. She champions creativity in all ages.

Kathleen Vance is a lover, friend, mother, grandmother, sister, writer, and dancer. She obtained her PhD from the University of British Columbia and taught at the British Columbia Institute of Technology. She has published journal articles, trained teachers in Taipei, Beijing, Hunan. She coauthored with Dale Fitzpatrick *Writing for Success* (Pearson ERPI, 1998) and was a contributing author to *Hard Jobbin'* (Ceridwen Collins-West, ed., Ride the Wind, 2001).

Betsy Warland has authored fourteen books of poetry and creative nonfiction. In the fall of 2021, a second edition of her 2000 memoir, *Bloodroot—Tracing the Untelling of Motherloss*, was published and includes a new essay by Warland reflecting on her memoir twenty years later as well as a new foreword by Susan Olding. This second edition launched Inanna Publications' Feminist Signature Edition. In 2022, the premiere of a street opera by composed by Lloyd Burritt based on Warland's 2014 memoir, *Oscar of Between—A Memoir of Identity and Ideas*, will be performed in Vancouver.

Sarah Williams is a writer, reporter, and mother who is fascinated by the geography of home and the personal stories that resonate through place. Sarah studied English at Acadia University before returning to Prince Edward County, Ontario, where she lives with her partner, Aussie Shepherd, and baby.

Deborah Yaffe was led to Victoria, BC, through a circuitous geographical and political route, and has retired from teaching. During the recent pandemic, she refined her pottering-about skills and now can do almost nothing quite happily. She loves her family and friends, making music, and being outside.

Deepest appreciation to
Demeter's monthly Donors

DEMETER

Daughters
Rebecca Bromwich
Summer Cunningham
Tatjana Takseva
Debbie Byrd
Fiona Green
Tanya Cassidy
Vicki Noble
Naomi McPherson
Myrel Chernick

Sisters
Amber Kinser
Nicole Willey
Christine Peets